KS-179-895

An Introduction to Children's Literature

PETER HUNT

Oxford   New York

OXFORD UNIVERSITY PRESS

OXFORD
UNIVERSITY PRESS

Great Clarendon Street, Oxford OX2 6DP

Oxford University Press is a department of the University of Oxford.
It furthers the University's objective of excellence in research, scholarship,
and education by publishing worldwide in

Oxford New York

Auckland Cape Town Dar es Salaam Hong Kong Karachi Kuala Lumpur
Madrid Melbourne Mexico City Nairobi New Delhi Shanghai
Taipei Toronto

With offices in

Argentina Austria Brazil Chile Czech Republic France Greece
Guatemala Hungary Italy Japan South Korea Poland Portugal
Singapore Switzerland Thailand Turkey Ukraine Vietnam

Oxford is a registered trade mark of Oxford University Press
in the UK and in certain other countries

© Peter Hunt 1994

First published as an Oxford University Press Paperback 1994

All rights reserved. No part of this publication may be reproduced,
stored in a retrieval system, or transmitted, in any form or by any means,
without the prior permission in writing of Oxford University Press,
or as expressly permitted by law, or under terms agreed with the appropriate
reprographics rights organizations. Enquiries concerning reproduction
outside the scope of the above should be sent to the Rights Department,
Oxford University Press, at the address above

You must not circulate this book in any other binding or cover
and you must impose this same condition on any acquirer

British Library Cataloguing in Publication Data

Data available

Library of Congress Cataloging in Publication Data

Hunt, Peter, 1945- .
An introduction to children's literature / Peter Hunt.
p.   cm.l / "An OPUS book"—P. i.
Includes bibliographical references (p.) and index.
1. Children's literature, English—History and criticism.
2. Children—Great Britain—Books and reading.   I. Title.
820.999282—dc20   PR990.H86   1994   93-29619

ISBN 0-19-289243-6 (pbk.)

13 15 16 14 12

Printed in Great Britain by
Clays Ltd, St Ives plc

00198873

Tower Hamlets Schools Library Service
Tower Hamlets Professional Development Centre
English Street, London E3 4TA
Tel: 0171 364 6428

To

Ethel, Margaret, Dennis, Tony, Michael,

and, of course, Sarah;

all of whom could have done it better

Preface

As this book developed, I found myself wishing for the more commodious title-pages of the eighteenth century.

It is 'an introduction to children's literature' in the sense that it provides a map of what has been written for, and read primarily by, children. But it also discusses the 'subject' of 'children's literature': what it is, how it is used, how we can approach it, how the study of it has developed. That title-page might also have mentioned that the book is British-centred; North American and other children's literature is mentioned when it has influenced British children and books. This is a reflection of the parameters of this book, and not of the value or importance of other cultures.

Both beginners and any stray experts may notice some distinctive features of the history presented here. The first is that while it is largely chronological, I found that some thematic and generic groupings—notably in the period after 1945—have forced themselves upon me, while writers who span many genres (such as Kipling) or many years (such as Blyton) have been treated most conveniently in one place.

Secondly, this book is, unashamedly, a work of synthesis; children's literature has long since passed the stage where it is possible for one mind (with a very few outstanding exceptions) to encompass all its facets. Consequently, I have tried to make the history reasonably comprehensive, but I have as far as possible allowed the books and authors to speak for themselves. I have also quoted extensively from expert and specialist writers, so that new readers can use the references as a basis for pursuing their interests.

And the third feature, which I hope is not too obvious, is that every page could have been expanded to a chapter; children's literature has so many ramifications and so many areas of interest that making shorthand judgements has been both necessary and frustrating. Readers may take comfort from the thought that, if I have missed out some of their favourites (where, for example, is Ted Hughes's *The Iron Man*?), I have also been forced to miss out a good many of mine (such as Gabrielle Vincent's 'Ernest and Celestine' series).

The history thus constructed can only bear a faint resemblance to what actually happened, especially in terms of influence. Survival and influence are not the same thing, and it is probably true that books that are forgotten are the keys to how the literature developed, passed lovingly from childhood to childhood until they disintegrated.

This book, then, is the public face of an intensely private literature.

Contents

1

Approaching Children's Literature

> It is probable that many people who would consider
> themselves extremely sophisticated and 'advanced' are
> actually carrying through life an imaginative background
> which they acquired in childhood.
>
> (George Orwell)

1. Children's Literature and Adults

Children's literature is a remarkable area of writing: it is one
of the roots of western culture, it is enjoyed passionately by
adults as well as by children, and it has exercised huge talents
over hundreds of years. It involves and integrates words and
pictures, it overlaps into other modes—video, oral story-
telling—and other art forms. For both adults and children it
serves the purpose that 'literature' is frequently claimed to
serve: it absorbs, it possesses, and is possessed; its demands
are very immediate, involving, and powerful.

Its characters—Cinderella, Pooh bear, the Wizard of Oz,
Mowgli, Biggles, the Famous Five, Peter Rabbit—are part of
most people's psyche, and they link us not simply to childhood
and storying, but to basic myths and archetypes. Children's
books are important educationally, socially, and commercially.
And yet, talking about them—even defining their borders—is
a much more complex business than might be supposed.

As A. A. Milne observed:

Children's books . . . are books chosen for us by others; either because they pleased us when we were young; or because we have
reason for thinking that they please children today; or because we
have read them lately, and believe that our adult enjoyment of them
is one which younger people can share. Unfortunately, none of these
reasons is in itself a sure guide.[1]

Milne pinpoints the key problem: the writers and manipulators of children's books are adults; books are makers of meaning for their readers, and the readers are children. Thus, while I would like to begin by exploring just what children's literature is, and how we, as adults, can fruitfully talk about it, we have to consider first the curious relationship that many of us have with it.

It is common to find that adults are wary about approaching children's books critically (approaching them emotionally is another matter). This may be because they fear the loss of a valued part of childhood—that the spell will be broken; or, as Ursula Le Guin suggested, because the modern adult has been taught to downgrade the imagination;[2] or because, in the critical hierarchy, children's books are so trivial that to study them is not a legitimate activity. The critic J. M. S. Tompkins, writing about Kipling's children's books, was, until quite recently, typical:

It is not easy to take a dispassionate view of a book to which we have been much indebted in youth . . . If this study were aimed at critical evaluation, I think I should not have dared to write this chapter . . . [However] there should be some value in the testimony of a reader who was a child of the generation for which they were written.[3]

In short, with the exception of those of us who can hide, as it were, behind 'working with children', we suspect that children's literature is a kind of private vice; we do not have the confidence of C. S. Lewis (a man whose attitude to children and children's books was nothing if not ambiguous), who wrote: 'When I was ten, I read fairy tales in secret and would have been ashamed if I had been found doing so. Now that I am fifty I read them openly. When I became a man I put away childish things, including the fear of childishness . . .'[4] Even for the confident, there is a danger that, as Perry Nodelman put it, 'people who take literature seriously [think that] children's literature can only be important if it isn't really for children at all, but actually secret pop-Zen for fuzzyminded grownups'.[5]

Yet, surely, however we view it, children's literature is *for children*, and cannot thus be worthy of, let alone sustain, the interest of the adult. After all, that quotation from Orwell in the epigraph to this chapter actually begins: 'the worst books are often the most important because they are usually the ones that are read earliest in life.' However sentimental we may feel about, say, Pooh, he is, after all, only an imaginary creature, based on a toy; there is nothing serious about him. Surely the whole business is trivial?

If this argument were pursued to its logical conclusion, then all fiction could be discounted, but what needs to be emphasized is that children's literature is a powerful literature, and that such power cannot be neutral or innocent, or trivial. This is especially true because the books are written by, and made available to children by, adults. (Even the most famous of the rare exceptions—*The Far-Distant Oxus* (1937), published when Katherine Hull was 16 and Pamela Whitlock 17, *The Swish of the Curtain* (1941) by Pamela Brown (16), and *The Outsiders* (1967) by S. E. Hinton (16)—were heavily influenced by specific writers or genres.) Equally obviously, the primary audience is children, who are less experienced and less educated into their culture than adults. This does not mean that the texts are 'less experienced' as well; on the contrary, it means that they are part of a complex power-relationship.

It is arguably impossible for a children's book (especially one being read by a child) not to be educational or influential in some way; it cannot help but reflect an ideology and, by extension, didacticism. All books must teach something, and because the checks and balances available to the mature reader are missing in the child reader, the children's writer often feels obliged to supply them. Thus it may seem that children's books are more likely to be directive, to predigest experience, to 'tell' rather than to 'show', and to be more prone to manipulation than others; but, in fact, it is only the mode of manipulation that is different. The relationship in the book between writer and reader is complex and ambivalent.

Children's writers, therefore, are in a position of singular responsibility in transmitting cultural values, rather than 'simply' telling a story. And if that were not enough, children's books are an important tool in reading education, and are thus prey to a whole area of educational and psychological influences that other literatures escape. Far from being exploratory and mind-expanding—as they are very frequently seen by idealists to be—children's books often become a debased form of adult text, rather than being either genuinely of childhood or a bridge to adulthood. Because they are, in the main, marginalized by the arbiters of literary taste, children's books are thought to have certain appropriate characteristics (such as simplicity of language, limited viewpoint, or perfunctory characterization) and, consequently, many books are produced which have these characteristics.

But there is a cheering paradox here: children's books, whether 'inspired' or 'manufactured', seem very often to produce an incommunicable 'literary' experience when children read them; in fact, they tend to absorb their readers so thoroughly that some observers have seen them as a site of considerable danger.[6]

In short, this is a rich and paradoxical area, and this richness is reflected in the diversity (not to say chaos) of the thinking that permeates it and surrounds it. In this book, I would like to identify the main areas of dispute over what the literature is and what it is used for. But, to begin with: just what is it that we are talking about?

2. *Marking the Boundaries*

Children's literature seems at first sight to be a simple idea: books written for children, books read by children. But in theory and in practice it is vastly more complicated than that. Just to unpack that definition: what does *written for* mean? Surely the intention of the author is not a very reliable guide, not to mention the intention of the publisher—or even the format of the book? For example, Jill Murphy's highly successful series of picture-books about the domestic affairs of a family of elephants—*Five Minutes' Peace* (1986), *All in One Piece* (1987), and *A Piece of Cake* (1989)—are jokes almost entirely from the point of view of (and largely understandable only by) parents. Then again, *read by*: surely sometime, somewhere, all books have been read by one child or another? And some much-vaunted books for children are either not read by them, or much more appreciated by adults (like *Alice's Adventures in Wonderland*), or probably not children's books at all (like *The Wind in the Willows*), or seem to serve adults and children in different—and perhaps opposing—ways (like *Winnie-the-Pooh*). And do we mean *read by* voluntarily or, as it were, under duress in the classroom? And can we say that a child can really read, in the sense of realizing the same spectrum of meanings as the adult can?

Which brings us to 'children'. To define that concept is to chase another chimera: concepts of childhood differ not only culturally but in units as small as the family, and they differ, often inscrutably, over time. Fred Inglis, in a brilliant brief discussion, points out that 'the history of childhood is, necessarily, an intercalation in the history of the family',[7] and that we know surprisingly little about pre-Romantic concepts of the child.

Perhaps the most satisfactory generalization is that childhood is the period of life which the immediate culture thinks of as being free of responsibility and susceptible to education. Equally, the most useful definition would be Piagetian in pattern at least: that children are people whose minds and bodies have not yet matured in various definable ways. Yet again, from the literary point of view we need to distinguish children as *developing* readers—that is, in terms of experience of life and books they have not reached the theoretical plateau upon which mature readers can be said to operate in mutual understanding.

This is important because what a culture thinks of as childhood is reflected very closely in the books produced for its citizens. Despite the fact that what adults intend is not directly related to what children perceive, children's books very often contain what adults think children can understand, and what they should be allowed to understand; and this applies to 'literariness' as well as to vocabulary or content.

Finally, 'literature'. Interestingly, the concept of literature is popular neither with enthusiasts for, nor with antagonists of, children's books. For both camps, and for totally opposing reasons, the idea is irrelevant. For those within the traditional literary establishment, 'children's literature' is a straightforward contradiction in terms. A few books—*Alice's Adventures in Wonderland*, certainly, *The Wind in the Willows* or *Treasure Island* possibly—might be admitted as minor canonical works. The rest, designed as they are for an unsophisticated audience, must, necessarily, be beyond the pale—at best, footnotes to literary history, at worst 'popular culture'. To claim anything else is merely self-defeating: as E. M. Forster observed, 'too many little mansions in English fiction have been acclaimed to their own detriment as important edifices'.[8]

Many children's book practitioners feel the same, but their suspicion of 'literature' implies a strong suspicion of the dominant cultural system. The characteristics of literature— seen as exclusive and intellectual—are not merely inappropriate, they are positively undesirable.[9] For example, on the death of Roald Dahl, one of the two or three most successful children's book writers ever, in 1991, the editor of *Books for Keeps* (a journal aimed at parents, teachers, and librarians (and emphatically not at academics)) found it appropriate to gibe at the idea that 'big sale must equal bad books', observing that this 'implies a massive dim-wittedness on the part of Dahl's young readers—the sort of dim-wittedness normally to be found only amongst persons who are too clever by half, such as adult critics'.[10]

This stance is further justified by the observable fact that those books that have been accepted (however marginally) into the scheme of 'literature', or have been awarded the highest prizes, are most likely to remain unread by children; the others, like Enid Blyton or Roald Dahl or Judy Blume, are the most popular and, for practical purposes, the most useful. The uncanonical works are the more likely to be of and for childhood, and less likely to conform to adult social and literary norms.

Consequently, children's books do not fit easily into the patriarchal world of literary/cultural values. They are (despite the dominant reading of history) primarily the domain of women writers (and, latterly, women educators), just as children are: in that literary hierarchy they are necessarily at the bottom of the heap. It hardly comes as a surprise to find that among specialist children's literature teachers at colleges in the USA, for example, 'about 92% are women; about 50% are assistant professors; about 40% are associate professors and only 5[%] are professors'.[11]

Children's books, then, are rarely acknowledged by the literary establishment. Few people know that Thackeray, Woolf, Plath, Hardy, Joyce, and many other major authors wrote for children. Children's books are invisible in the literary world, in much the same way as women writers have been—and still are—invisible in the eighteenth-century novel.

All of this has some radical implications for the study of children's books/literature. The first is that children's books should be removed from the literary hierarchy, and that they should be treated as a separate group of texts, without reference (at least in principle) to 'literature' as it is known and misunderstood. That is, I want to look at it as an important 'system' of its own, not as a lesser or peripheral part of 'high' culture. Of course, it does not exist separately, nor, even with the best deconstructive will in the world, can I write about it without using at least some of the tools and implicit values which the dominant literary culture imposes.

But this is an important move because, as we shall see, much of the confused thinking about children's books stems from including them in—or reacting against their inclusion in—the standard hierarchy. Barbara Wall, in her stylistic study of the history of children's books, quarrelled with the common approach 'which partly denies the existence of a genre *writing for children* by insisting that a good children's book is a good book "in its own right", and partly demands that good writing for children, such as it is, should not too obviously appear to be *for* children'.[12] Thus C. S. Lewis's famous dictum, so often quoted in support of children's books ('I am almost inclined to set it up as a canon that a children's story which is enjoyed only by children is a bad children's story'[13]), is not as benign as it seems, and could well be called 'adultist'. It denies to children's books an individuality, a difference from their dominating adult counterparts. If we can shake free from the unsupportable suspicion that what we are dealing with is intrinsically inferior, we can see fascinating areas of achievement and debate.

This also allows us to widen the field of children's literature to include those vital texts which are read by and which influence and have influenced most people, those commonly relegated to the sidelines of literary study: the comics, the 'penny dreadfuls', the 'commercial series'. The schizophrenia which elevates, say, Arthur Ransome or Philippa Pearce over W. E. Johns or Enid Blyton is unproductive and alienating to the vast mass of adult people who use children's books.

It also, perhaps just as contentiously, allows us to narrow the field—or, better, to divide it. Children's literature is defined by its audience in a way that other literatures tend not to be: I have yet to see books recommended for 40–50-year-olds, for example, although, of course, the books recommended by, say, *Woman and Home* may differ from those recommended by *Cosmopolitan* or the *London Review of Books*. Consequently, for most children and most practitioners, there is a dividing line between books that *are* for children, and books that *were* for children. The dividing line is, of course, a blurred one, and it is impossible to say where some of the 'classics' actually lie. Children's books have a commercial shelf-life that can be much longer than adult equivalents; they are sustained by being passed down through families; children seem to be less sensitive than adults to 'dated' content. However, it is clear that interest in the two groups is very different, from the academic to the practical, and some of the pain in the development of the study of children's literature has come from the mismatch of the two sets of interests. (It could be argued that in consigning books which were for children to the historians and bibliographers, we are missing the chance to follow important clues about how children's texts operate—how they relate to childhood. But, paradoxically, some of the best evidence that we have about childhood derives from its literature; solid clues about past childhoods are quite rare.)

I would suggest, then, that rather than seeing the 'epicentre' of children's literature as about 1850, the point at which books began to move from the didactic to the recreational, we should move it on about a hundred years. By 1950 children's literature was established as a distinctive area, with hundreds of distinguished titles: since then it has developed and expanded considerably.

There are four other subjects that are closely bound up with books for children and which must also be considered: poetry, illustration, 'educational' books, and fairy-tales. What is their status? In conventional literary thinking, poetry for children is another contradiction in terms, but, as Brian Morse has pointed out, 'neat categorization doesn't suit poetry'. However, as he says, in the face of the popularity of *When We Were Very Young*, 'lit. crit. falters—is this poetry? Is this verse?'[14] This is a very interesting area where, on the one hand, the weaknesses of value-centred criticism are exposed, and on the other hand a genre has become public property: children can write poetry too.

Illustrated books and picture-books pose another problem: that of developing a vocabulary, a mode of attack, on a tremendously varied and complex form which scarcely exists in other literary areas. Here there is the central paradox of children's books: that pictures are accessible to children, but that the meanings derived from them are not; that the picture 'closes' the text—that is, limits and cuts off the possibilities of interpretation—as well as stimulating the imagination; that a picture may complement or contradict the words, but it is not read in a linear way.[15]

Conventional literary studies have, until recently, operated on the curious principle that readers' responses to texts are unaffected by other media, or that literature exits in a vacuum. Children's literature has never been afforded this privilege; because it is popular, a version of a text in one medium has not necessarily been privileged over a version in another. Therefore, just as I shall make no distinction between literature and non-literature or literature and 'reading matter', so I shall ignore the prejudice against books 'manufactured' for the popular market, or for educational purposes. The assumption that texts written 'purely' from artistic or personal impulses are necessarily better, or more worthy of attention, than those produced, for example, to a template for a reading scheme is false on two counts. The first is that the merest glance at the way in which all books—not especially children's books—are produced should dispel any romantic concept of authors as uninfluenced by society and the market-place. Second, it is not how books are produced, but how they are read, that is important; the most basic school reading book can be given a literary reading; the reading of the most literary text can be transformed into an analytic task. (And, ironically, it is educational and tractarian materials that form the heart of 'respectable' children's literature before 1800.)

Books produced specifically to teach reading or in series aimed at a specific reading age have an influence which has been generally ignored by critics and literary historians. The kind of middle-class social, racial, and sexual stereotyping of the classroom texts such as the 'Janet and John' series (1949 on), which is only slowly being eroded, is an important part of literary conditioning.[16] And it should be noted that a 'series' book, Kevin Crossley-Holland's *Storm* published as one of Heinemann's 'Banana Books', won the Carnegie Medal for 1985, as the best children's book of the year.

Fourthly, folk- and fairy-tales. No one has put it better than Tolkien when he wrote that 'the association of children and fairy-stories is an accident of our domestic history . . . Children . . . neither like fairy-stories more, nor understand them better than adults do.'[17] Indeed, virtually from their appearance in print there have been doubts expressed about their suitability. As the redoubtable Sarah Trimmer wrote in 1802 of the *Histories and Tales of Past Times, Told by Mother Goose*: 'the terrific images, which tales of this nature present to the imagination, usually make deep impressions, and injure the tender minds of children, by exciting unreasonable and groundless fears.'[18]

In the late twentieth century criticism has tended to centre on the political and sexual implications of the tales, and one of the most fascinating socio-literary excursions is to trace the various versions through the centuries: from the folk-tales which evolved when flesh-eating werewolves were assumed to roam the woods of a feudal society to apparently cosy de-sexed late-Victorian pastel versions or to the realigned sexism of today. However, as Alison Lurie pointed out:

The traditional tale . . . is exactly the sort of subversive literature of which a feminist should approve. For one thing, these stories are in a literal sense women's literature . . . For hundreds of years, while written literature was almost exclusively in the hands of men, these tales were being invented and passed down by women . . . In content too . . . In the Grimms' original *Children's and Household Tales* (1812), there are sixty-one women and girl characters who have magic powers as against only twenty-one men and boys: and these men are usually dwarfs and not humans.[19]

The fairy- and folk-tale is, then, an interesting demonstration of the kinds of confusion that surround children's literature in general—and a potent indicator of the strengths and dangers of that literature.

The boundaries of children's literature, as a body of work and as a subject of study, are, then, ambiguous, although this ambiguity is a very positive and stimulating one. And, as we explore the territory of children's literature, we shall find that it has its own characteristics, and its own influences and internal logics. It is not inferior to other types of writing, it is different.

For all that, children's literature is obviously what people think it is, and in this book I shall attempt to balance the traditional view with the radical; the epicentre may not shift as far as 1950, but the emphasis will be very much on the modern, the practical, the alive.

3. Inside Children's Books

Defining children's books is not simply a matter of staking out academic territories: a satisfactory definition would be useful educationally and commercially. And, as it is quite obvious to most people when a book *is* a children's book, it seems equally obvious that there must be some textual characteristics that the books all share.

The difficulty is that the spectrum of books is so huge that it is virtually impossible to discriminate through form or content. Certainly, pictures and large print are more common in children's books, explicit sex, violence, or soul-searching more common in adults'. Children's books may lay more stress upon action than reflection, have more central characters who are children, or be generally shorter.[20] There is a certain language set which tends to recur. But this will not do. We are on firmer ground if we look at the 'implied reader': in any text, the tone or features of the narrative voice imply what kind of reader—in terms of knowledge or attitude—is addressed, what kind of attention the book is requesting, and what the relationship of the narrator and the reader is assumed to be. (There will naturally be all kinds of mismatches between what the narrative voice implies and how the reader reads, especially if the reader is not, or is unprepared or unable to adopt the role of, the implied reader. This is one of the things that makes reading children's books rather more difficult than we might assume.)

This approach to criticism through the 'implied reader' was formulated (for children's books) by Aidan Chambers[21] and has been refined by Barbara Wall, who identifies three modes of address within children's books: *single address, double address*, and *dual address*—with the rather disconcerting corollary that there are far fewer 'pure' children's books than one might suppose. As she observes:

First, [authors] may write . . . for a single audience, using single address; their narrators will address child narratees . . . showing no consciousness that adults too may read the work. . . . Secondly, they may write for a double audience, using double address . . .; their narrators will address child narratees . . . and will also address adults, either overtly . . . or covertly, as the narrator deliberately exploits the ignorance of the implied child reader and attempts to entertain an implied adult reader by making jokes which are funny primarily because children will not understand them. Thirdly, they may write for a dual audience ... More usually ... writers who command a dual audience do so because of the nature and strength of their performance ... confidentially sharing a story in a way that allows adult narrator and child narratee a conjunction of interests.[22]

As books are usually written by adults, one might question whether the first type of book is anything more than a theoretical possibility. If it exists at all, it is most likely to exist in the picture-book, where the reader is at once obliged to register a certain image, but not bound by knowledge of the mechanics of text. (However, we must not overlook the fact that even the reading of pictures has to be learned, and, as John Stephens puts it, 'It is merely sentimental to assert that children see with unspoiled perceptions and therefore see everything in a scene, whereas corrupted adult perceptions see only in part because they ignore minor details.'[23]

Pat Hutchins's *Rosie's Walk* (1968), Hoban and Blake's *How Tom Beat Captain Najork and his Hired Sportsmen* (1974), or Rosemary Wells's *Stanley and Rhoda* (USA 1978, UK 1980) might be offered as examples of books that can be read as being tacitly 'on the side' of the child and against that adult domain, the Word. Others might include (as we shall see later) Carroll's *Alice's Adventures in Wonderland* or many of Beatrix Potter's sardonic series—not necessarily books that adults take to.

Far more common, and more famous and lasting, are books that use 'double address', where the author writes for two separate audiences, such as A. A. Milne's 'Pooh' books. Many of the jokes—Pooh living 'under the name of Sanders', Milne's use of Significant Capital Letters, and probably the whole of the character of Eeyore—are aimed at an adult audience. In the books of poems, there is no doubt that, as Milne said himself of *When We Were Very Young*: 'They are a curious collection; some *for* children, some *about* children, some by, with or from children.'[24] A poem from *Now We Are Six*, 'Buttercup Days', shows how delicate the balancing act is between observation and patronization, between the child's view of the child and the adult's view.

> Where is Anne? . . .
>   Walking with her man,
> Lost in a dream,
>   Lost among the buttercups.
> What has she got in that little brown head?
> Wonderful thoughts which can never be said . . .
>   Brown head, gold head,
>   In and out the buttercups.[25]

Because of this uncertainty of focus Milne's books can be seen as uneven, although by comparison, as we shall see, other famous classic cultural monuments, such as *The Water Babies*, *The Wind in the Willows*, and *Peter Pan*, are positively unstable. Perhaps surprisingly, there are many contemporary examples of this uncertainty of focus. For example, in Robert N. Munsch's well-known quasi-feminist *The Paper Bag Princess*, it is Prince Ronald who is carried off by the dragon, and the wily Princess Elizabeth who rescues him by playing on the dragon's (male) vanity. Ronald is not impressed, and the book has a memorable ending, whose meaning is perhaps slanted a little too strongly to the adult side for the comfort of the child:

He looked at her and said, 'Elizabeth, you are a mess! You smell like ashes, your hair is all tangled and you are wearing a dirty old paper bag. Come back when you are dressed like a real princess.'

'Ronald,' said Elizabeth, 'your clothes are really pretty and your hair is very neat. You look like a real prince, but you are a toad.'

They didn't get married after all.[26]

How far we find books which are covertly aimed at adults a betrayal of the concept of writing for children or a natural concomitant is an ideological decision. It is easy to see that the real interaction (the 'narrative contract') in J. M. Barrie's and C. S. Lewis's children's books is between adult and adult, not adult and child, and that this is manipulative and not quite healthy (perhaps because one might suspect that children's books often take on a therapeutic role for their authors). But the core of children's literature rests on those books that are primarily for children, but which satisfy adults, either when they are reading as quasi-children (taking on the implied role) or when they are responding as adults. Perhaps the greatest classic

examples are Beatrix Potter, Frances Hodgson Burnett, Rudyard Kipling, and Robert Louis Stevenson; in recent times,
Jan Mark, Alan Garner, Philippa Pearce, and William Mayne.

The picture-book presents a problem here, because of the
mismatch between what the book appears to be, and what it
might actually be. An outstanding example of an artist who
ranges across the types is John Burningham; he has produced
books which speak 'purely' to children (and which are much
misunderstood by adults), such as *Granpa* (1984), ones which
address adults and children separately, such as *Come away
from the Water, Shirley* (1977), and ones which speak to both,
such as *Where's Julius?* (1986). In *Where's Julius?* the parents
and the child collude: Julius cannot come to meals because he
is elsewhere—in his fantasies, an adult might assume—and so
the parents, trudging across deserts or through jungles, take
the mundane meals to him.

Other books suffer from the problem of generic expectation:
some books look like children's books but are actually adult
books (obvious examples are Raymond Briggs's *Fungus the
Bogeyman* (1977) and *When the Wind Blows* (1982), and
Quentin Blake's *The Story of the Dancing Frog* (1984)); others
look like adult books but are actually for a developing
audience. 'Teenage fiction' (which forms this latter category)
is a comparatively recent phenomenon. In 1971 Frank Eyre
was still pondering on the difficulties of this genre: at the end
of a chapter in which he had considered K. M. Peyton's
'Flambards' trilogy (1967–9), Alan Garner's *The Owl Service*
(1967), and John Rowe Townsend's *Goodnight, Prof. Love*
(1970) he wrote: 'Are we witnessing the birth of a new kind of
book, that is neither a children's book nor an adult novel, but
something in between? ... If [we] are, there will be some
interesting problems for publishers, editors, and designers.'[27]

These problems have been thoroughly solved since then,
and publishers actively market 'teenage' novels of two kinds. At
one extreme are the 'quality' novels, such as Garner's *Red
Shift* (1973) or Aidan Chambers's *Now I Know* (1987) and *The
Toll Bridge* (1992), which are distinguishable from adult
novels, if at all, by being focused through teenage eyes, or

centred on teenage characters. At the other are the 'manufactured' series novels, which often have the subject-matter of the adult novel and the plot-shape (that is, resolved, or circular) of the children's novel. These are usually now, in a term which originated in the USA, described as 'young adult' (or 'new adult') literature. The books are, however, frequently classified in terms of adult-perceived content. There are certain topics which are generally agreed to be irrelevant to children who have not reached certain developmental stages, but beyond that there is little guide as to what is appropriate, attractive, or even comprehensible—and there is a considerable tension between adults' and children's expectations.[28]

However, there is a good deal of disagreement over such matters, and the water is likely to be muddied by taboos, notably of sex and death. For example, the illustrator Edward Ardizzone was forced, by what he called 'silly women librarians', to make changes to the plot of his second picture-book, *Lucy and Mr Grimes* (1937; revised edition 1970). (The old man whom Lucy befriends in the park was changed from stranger to family friend, and he does not die at the end of the book.) Ardizzone dismissed the reasoning behind this as 'absolute nonsense', and put a case for realism in fiction that I shall look at in Chapter 7:

I think we are possibly inclined, in a child's reading, to shelter him [sic] too much from the harder facts of life. Sorrow, failure, poverty, and possibly even death, if handled poetically, can surely all be introduced without hurt . . . If no hint of the hard world comes into these books, I am not sure that we are playing fair.[29]

Hence the innocence of childhood—or, at least, the adult concept of innocence—is preserved by the 'even-handedness' imposed upon writers; the tones and styles in which this is expressed are very strong 'markers' of the children's book.

4. Children's Literature and Literary Criticism

If children's literature is worth reading, it is worth writing about, but the contrast between emotional involvement and intellectual distance causes certain problems. In an entertaining defence of one of childhood's more durable heroes, Biggles, Don Aitkin produced a pastiche of Captain W. E. Johns's prose, in which Biggles is told by Air Commodore Raymond 'that a new deadly menace has arisen'.

Biggles whistled slowly. 'Has von Stalhein joined the Americans?'
  'No, it's not that.' The Air Commodore passed his hand wearily across his brow. 'It's something bigger, and stranger, too. Tell me, Bigglesworth, have you ever heard of academics?'[30]

A good many people who work with children's books might echo this sentiment; the academic study of children's literature (together with the dialect in which it is couched) seems to be at once remote from and irrelevant to 'books-and-children', while being a parasite on a living activity.

There are two distinct, if shifting, categories of people who write about children's books, categories that have almost become traditional since they were named by John Rowe Townsend in 1968: 'book people' and 'child people'.[31] These groups are almost conterminous with the distinction between critics and parents, or theorists and teachers, or between the literary establishment and non-professional ('real') readers.

Any discussion tends, therefore, to be polarized: only a few critics (often working in education) manage to cross the gulf between the academics and the 'practitioners'. It takes an optimist to reconcile, for example, the extremes of the British journal *Books for Keeps* and the Yale annual *Children's Literature*. *Books for Keeps* is, as we have seen, resolutely untheoretical and appeals to a 'neutral' common sense and an enthusiastic view of the child, which a postmodernist critic might well interpret as being deeply conservative. (For example, a writer in its pages attacked the experimental metafictive *Dance on my Grave* by one of the foremost advocates of intelligent writing for and about children's books, Aidan Chambers, as an example of the 'Arty-farty self-regarding stuff that has plagued British teenage fiction for years'.[32] This is a very suggestive example of what appears to be a radical defender of the child reader actually proving to be the opposite.)

In comparison, *Children's Literature* is aimed at academics (not necessarily children's literature specialists) and, conservative in its own way, has tended to avoid any reference to children. The books are seen as fodder for the academic mill; texts that can be examined with reference to the academic system. As an academic exercise, this exploitation of the children's book is something of a dinosaur in the final stages before extinction, but it is clear that these two journals represent totally different attitudes.

The positive view of all this is that children's literature is a truly democratic phenomenon: everyone feels that they have a voice; the negative one is that the criticism and management of the texts is pulled and influenced in many directions, in a way that no other literature is.[33]

There is also a sentimentality about childhood that pervades adult commentaries on children's books; and it should be pointed out that sentimentality is not a notable characteristic of childhood itself. A typical example is Hugh Walpole, writing an introduction to Hugh Lofting's *The Story of Dr Dolittle*. He observed that 'Writing for children . . . can only be done, I am convinced, by somebody having a great deal of the child in his own outlook and sensibilities . . . The imagination of the author must be a child's imagination and yet maturely consistent,' although, with a characteristic refusal to analyse, he goes on: 'I don't know how Mr Lofting has done it; I don't suppose he knows himself.'[34] Pronouncements such as this (which can be multiplied) tend to undermine the quality of comments on the texts—and, ultimately, texts themselves. Similarly the many pious remarks from authors that books for children should be better than those for adults seems to me to be misplaced positive discrimination.

The argument for using the tools of literary criticism and theory to discuss children's literature is in fact a tribute to the value of the subject. As Geoffrey Williams put it: 'To attempt to find a more reasoned theoretical ground to discuss books for children is not to betray the field . . . but genuinely to respect children, their reading capacities and the efforts of those who write and illustrate for them.'[35] Literary criticism may seem arcane to many, but it does provide ways of talking about texts, and without some vocabulary, there is a considerable danger that those who want to talk about children's books will not understand each other—or not seem worthy of anyone else's attention.

If that is a somewhat ingenuous defence of what is rapidly becoming an academic industry, it is certainly true that children's books studies have emulated other academic disciplines for tactical reasons.[36] English Literature departments have been more powerful than Education or Popular Culture departments, and so writers on children's literature have taken on a certain style and approach that has alienated many interested readers.

This situation is changing. The status of the literary canon has been weakened politically and socially; works of popular culture and women's writing are, in a close parallel with children's literature, seen as the voice of the previously voiceless. The tone of criticism is becoming less formal, less élitist, and children's books will increasingly be studied across the old disciplinary divides, without the confusions of status.

The academic study of texts is at a crossroads, and in children's books the involvement of the reader, and many different specialist disciplines, gives us the opportunity to develop an intelligent, accessible, useful discourse. Literary and cultural studies can meet over many children's books, although there are certain areas, notably books for younger children and picture-books, where a new synthesis is needed.

In 1970 Wallace Hildick observed that 'We need closely pursued investigations and closely argued conclusions. We need, in fact, studies of children's fiction of the same calibre as such classics in the adult field as *Seven Types of Ambiguity* ... and ... *Theory of Literature*.'[37] Mr Hildick's wishes have come true, with something of a vengeance: in the 1980s there were twenty-seven specialist journals on children's literature active in Britain alone.[38] The advantage of the increased output of writing about children's books is that almost anyone coming to the area can find something sympathetic; the disadvantage is that it is all too easy to rerun futile academic territorial disputes.

Children's literature is not so much suffering from neglect, as from a cacophony of approaches; but, if specialists have a place in children's literature, they need to be able to communicate outside a specialist world. As Elaine Moss has said, 'Our specialist task is to know more—much more—than the public, but to wear our knowledge so lightly, and present books to people . . . in so easy a manner, that no-one would guess we are specialists.'[39]

5. *Two Case-Studies: Roald Dahl and* Pollyanna

Before we look at the history, I would like to take two case-studies to demonstrate the questions that come into play when we talk about children's books.

To begin, let us consider the rhetoric surrounding the most successful British children's writer in terms of sales and overall 'exposure' (after Enid Blyton), Roald Dahl. Dahl was a very intelligent, highly professional, self-aware writer, with a sharp eye for the less attractive sides of the human condition, and an edgy sense of humour. Some of his books, such as his autobiographical *Boy* (1984) and *Going Solo* (1986) and the later books for children, notably *Matilda* (1988), have crossed the adult–child divide (in opposite directions—*Boy* has been published for children, *Matilda* is popular with adults).

Dahl's work is summed up neatly by Elizabeth Hammill:

The most widely-read contemporary children's author whose popularity stems, in part, from his ability to realise in fiction children's innermost dreams, and to offer subversive, gruesomely satisfying, sometimes comic solutions to their nightmares. His . . . heroes tend to be underdogs—the poor, the bullied, the hunted, the orphans—whose lives are transformed by the fantastic, sometimes disconcerting events of the stories.[40]

His books are energetic, vulgar, violent, and often blackly farcical. Dahl appears to be wholly on the side of anarchy;

and he is equally popular with many adults who are just as delighted as children to see, for example, farting referred to—and thus, in a sense, legitimized—in text. His prejudices are well out in the open; his most successful book, *Charlie and the Chocolate Factory* (USA 1964, UK 1967), is a robust moral tale, a direct descendant of a genre well established in the eighteenth and nineteenth centuries (and well parodied by Hoffmann's *Struwwelpeter*—of which more later), with the fat and the greedy and the stupid being dealt with summarily. The Oompa-Loompas (the pygmy workers whose colour was changed from the early editions) break into songs which are positively reactionary. For example, against television:

> The most important thing we've learned,
> So far as children are concerned,
> Is never, NEVER, NEVER let
> Them near your television set
> Or better still, just don't install
> The idiotic thing at all . . .
> *IT ROTS THE SENSES IN THE HEAD!*
> *IT KILLS IMAGINATION DEAD . . .*

or against chewing-gum:

> Dear friends, we surely all agree
> There's almost nothing worse to see
> Than some repulsive little bum
> Who's always chewing chewing-gum.[41]

In the later books, a rather brutal brand of pantomime justice is wreaked upon, generally, the adult world, and Dahl's macabre sense of humour has greater play. The majority of reviewers have been enthusiastic, on the lines of 'children adore . . .'. Some, however, have not been charmed, and the alternative point of view was summed up by Michele Landsberg, who accused Dahl of racism, sexism, sadism, and a generally unhealthy attitude. Her particular target in this passage is *The Witches*, a book that verges on the horrific:

Children's literature is so rich in humour of the genuine, humane, affirmative kind. There are so many well-written stories, for every age group, that do not reek of dog excrement or 'red-hot sizzling hatred'. No parent, teacher or librarian needs to be intimidated by the sheer commercial success of an author whose works may trouble them; they need not become advocates and promoters of a comic style, however popular, which they find destructive. Humour can sputter with indignation and rage, and often does, but hatred is not funny.[42]

One of the earliest attacks was by the veteran American critic Eleanor Cameron, in a discussion of *Charlie and the Chocolate Factory*. She objected to 'the book's tastelessness, expressed through its phoniness, its hypocrisy, its getting laughs through violent punishment . . . Dahl caters for the streak of sadism in children which they don't realise is there because they are not fully self-aware and are not experienced enough to know what sadism is.'[43] Dahl's reply, to the effect that he had written the book for his disabled son, and that such accusations were therefore personally insulting, was characteristic: his defence moved the focus away from the books. Similarly, when it was put to him that there had been complaints about the Oompa-Loompas on the grounds of racism, he replied that he had had 'No complaints at all from children or teachers, only from those slightly kinky groups who I don't think are doing any good at all.'[44]

It has been pointed out that Dahl's readers are 'jerked along through the story by . . . wonderment at what new outrage can be perpetrated next and certainly not out of any sense of development'.[45] But although there is considerable evidence of a slackening of his powers in later books, there is no question that he is a writer of considerable range and subtlety.

Chris Powling, writing in *Books for Keeps*, pointed out 'the sheer daftness' of moralizing about the fate of figures of farce and melodrama, but his dismissive tone, which legitimizes the 'innocent' over the 'clever', reflects a common anti-intellectualism. However, he makes a very astute point when he questions the names of authors whom Eleanor Cameron put forward as being 'better' reading matter than Dahl. They are almost all prizewinners, 'quality' books; they are deserving prizewinners, yes, but aren't they all just a little bit . . . *respectable*? Aren't these the very names you'd expect to conjure with if you wanted to win friends and influence people amongst those who like books a lot but aren't necessarily so keen on kids. Dahl, needless to say, hasn't won a Top Prize in his life. His situation reminds me of certain superstars in bygone Hollywood—the ones who could pack cinemas year after year but who watched the Oscars being handed out to classier performers thought to bring 'tone' to the movie business, to help it upgrade its desperately insecure image of itself.[46]

It is clear that, whatever Dahl's merits or demerits, they are only being discussed here as part of a battle. Thus, to suggest that there is an undercurrent of sadism and sexuality in Dahl's books cannot be a neutral statement: it is, paradoxically, taken as a repressive, anti-popularist stance. Balanced, firmly grounded opinions, such as Fred Inglis's (on *Charlie and the Chocolate Factory*), are quite difficult to find:

Dahl has a vigorous feel for the raucous, crude vengefulness of children: he catches and endorses this nicely. But his book is stuck forever in the second and third stages—the legalistic, retributive stages—of Piaget's and Kohlberg's moral development. There is no way . . . of balancing the claims of one's childishness, one's morality, and the mysteries of the natural world.[47]

All of which is merely to say that, when entering the world of children's books, we need at least to be aware of the range of skills appropriate to the subject. Books and readers are inevitably intertwined.

Historical examples are equally illuminating. Take, for example, a book whose eponymous heroine has given a word to the English language, Eleanor H. Porter's *Pollyanna*. First published in 1912, this is a fairly late example of a genre which flourished in the USA—and which was very influential in Britain and elsewhere—from the mid-nineteenth century onwards: the domestic tale centring on a strong, often displaced, female hero. A good early example is Elizabeth Wetherell's *The Wide, Wide World* (1850); better known, perhaps, are *What Katy Did* (1872), *Little Women* (1868), *Rebecca of Sunnybrook Farm* (1903), *Heidi* (1880, translated 1884), *The*

Secret Garden (1911), and, in Australia, Ethel Turner's *Seven Little Australians* (1894) and Mary Grant Bruce's *Mates at Billabong* (1911). (This genre has continued, again notably in the USA: more modern examples are Laura Ingalls Wilder's *Little House in the Big Woods* (1932) and its sequels.) *Pollyanna* was probably popular with British children because, as with many nineteenth-century American books, its central character was (comparatively) more robust and certainly more liberated, and the family structure was often more egalitarian, than in Britain. Its continuing popularity may well depend more on a combination of wish-fulfilment and melodrama.

Pollyanna is an orphan, sent to stay, after the death of her mother and father (in a classic example of displacement), with her bitter spinster aunt, who is not enthusiastic about children. (Children's books are singularly unhealthy places for parents.) Pollyanna's power as a child lies in her somewhat obsessive cheerfulness; she is contrasted with the embittered and narrow adults around her. In a series of confrontations, Pollyanna breaks down the adult ways of thinking, and finally survives a serious accident.

We might speculate that her appeal to children could be both sympathetic and empathetic: she is lonely, isolated, and yet is superior to every adult she encounters, defeating them by a simple (and apparently self-evident) formula. What is not clear is how far children who can respond to the book on this level would be able to understand the ramifications of the adult world, which suggests that Mrs Porter had at least one eye on the adult audience. Indeed, as in the work of Frances Hodgson Burnett, there are chapters of very obvious didacticism.

For adults, and perhaps for children, the simplicity of the relationships and the ease with which Pollyanna makes her conquests act at the level of fairy-tale. The skill of the author is undeniable; there is a satisfying conquest of evil by good on virtually every page; but it could be said that such skill is more or less mechanical, and that *Pollyanna* is really nothing more than a 'three hanky weepie'. Yet its simple answers to life's *Angst* have not stopped it acquiring a reputation as a children's classic, and but for that reputation it might well have disappeared along with its many pulp and dime-novel sisters. Indeed, we could argue that books such as *Pollyanna*, Jean Webster's *Daddy-Long-Legs* (1912), and Eleanor Farjeon's romantic *Martin Pippin in the Apple Orchard* (1921) survive in the same way as the majority of Disney's feature-length animated films survive. His films are, after all, about adolescence and marriage and the fulfilment of a particular cultural stereotype; they are the secret daydreams of the adolescent (and of certain adults) rather than being for their ostensible audience, the younger child.

From the point of view of the literary establishment, *Pollyanna* might merely confirm the suspicion that we are dealing with inferior materials which appear on children's lists precisely because they are simplistic and bathetic. But, like the folk- and fairy-tale, there is no denying the potency and accessibility of such books. To deal with them with an open mind, indeed, to find an idiom in which to address them, is one of the challenges of children's literature studies.

To make children's literature the site of wrangles over ideology or critical stances invites ridicule from some, and honest doubts from others. Ann Thwaite, for example, in her biography of A. A. Milne (1990) felt that 'There is often so little to say about [children's literature] without sounding pretentious or absurd.'[48] Certainly, all critics of *Winnie-the-Pooh* have had to work in the shadow of Frederick C. Crews's *The Pooh Perplex*,[49] a spoof 'student case-book' whose satire has been overtaken by the development of criticism; but *pace* Ann Thwaite, there is a lot to be said about books that sell millions of copies and are known world-wide.

The study of children's literature, then, encompasses everything from board-books to fairy-tales, from exercises in bibliotherapy for teenage *Angst* to scarcely disguised political tracts on feminism; from novels dealing with the complete range of human activity to primers for learning to read. They exist, are sustained by, and are accessible to the vast majority of the population. In a world of experts, non-specialists are confident that they can make judgements about them, and it can be argued that children's classics are true, living classics in that they are passed down from generation to generation: they become cultural reference points.

As such, while they survive changes in fashion for far longer than adult texts, they are not sacrosanct, as witness revisions to books by Enid Blyton or Beatrix Potter or Hugh Lofting; books can be updated and sanitized, rewritten and adapted: they are part of living culture. In a sense, 'revisionism' demonstrates the importance of the books in the culture, rather than implying that they can be violated with impunity because they are trivial. The 'classics' are evidence of the way in which a culture wishes to form itself, of the relations of adults and children, of power-structures.

For specialists, children's books provide a focus for basic questions: how is meaning made? Does what an adult reads bear any relation to what a child reads? How do we assess quality or effect? Just what place does the printed text have in relation to other cultural influences? If children's books cannot be ideologically innocent, then what is implied by their guilt? How do we deal with texts that are not, or are no longer, intended for us? What are the most valid ways of talking about texts?

This book outlines these issues by looking at the texts that have been, and are, considered to be 'for' children, and then by examining any useful generalizations that can be made. But all this is done with the recognition that I am an adult reader writing to adults about an experience that is concerned with children and childhoods: there will be an inevitable mismatch between the adult-generated text and the child-perceived text.

And, regardless of whether we are interested in children's books as literary artefacts, educational tools, or sociological phenomena, we are entering a world where the core of the texts is concerned with *play*, and where 'the pleasure of the text' is foremost.

2

History and Histories

Children used books long before books were produced specifically for children—a fact that has given rise to the not very
helpful argument that, as childhood was scarcely recognized
or recognizable before the eighteenth century, all pre-1700
texts can be considered as (also) children's texts. It would
undoubtedly be interesting to discover what children made
of Shakespeare or *Reynard the Fox*, but only if we could discover with any certainty what adults made of them. Because
the twentieth-century reader sees a repressive, dry, crude, or
simple text which would not appeal to the modern, liberated,
multi-media child, we cannot assume that such texts would
not appeal to the child of the time. None the less, historical
evidence about childhood is lacking, and territorial lines have
to be drawn somewhere, and so I propose to give only the
briefest mention to texts produced before 1700 and, more
radically, relatively little space to texts produced before about
1860.

This may seem somewhat cavalier, especially as the two most
important histories (by F. J. Harvey Darton and John Rowe
Townsend)[1] both devote a lot of space to them: Darton over
two-thirds, Townsend approaching a quarter. But, as Darton
wrote in the introduction to the first edition of his book: 'There
is really only one "text" in these pages, and that is, that
children's books were always the scene of a battle between
instruction and amusement, between restraint and freedom,
between hesitant morality and spontaneous happiness.'[2]

Of course, nothing has changed in general principle: what
has changed is the coinage of the debate. Reading a text 'for
children' from the eighteenth century is roughly equivalent to
reading Middle English poetry in the original: it may be
rewarding for the specialist, but unless it is translated and

modernized, it has little to offer the general reader. All children, I would submit, are in the position of being 'general readers'. The division between books that *were* for children and which *are* for children is, as I have suggested, a very useful one.

It is true that the fairy-tales and the oral tales and the rhymes that form a part of childhood and children's literature originate in these early days, and we should take note of them. But it is only of interest to the specialist scholar that there are variants or different editions of the tales, or that an ur-text might be established. Alan Garner's collections of traditional tales *A Bag of Moonshine* (1986) and *Jack and the Beanstalk* (1992) may have been produced because Garner 'fears a prettifying of them so that they have lost the special unique features of the storytellers',[3] but to the child, to the real reader, what is important is what has been passed down. Consequently, I would like to emphasize what the fairy-tale, for example, is actually about—what it really does—and how society has altered it, rather than the minutiae of its origins.

The 'landmark' texts in the history of children's books, such as Carroll's *Alice's Adventures in Wonderland* or Stevenson's *Treasure Island* or Nesbit's *The Treasure Seekers*, did not spring fully armed from their authors' minds. If their historical prominence is at least partly a matter of chance and the influence of a predominantly male critical establishment, equally they were produced in the context of what had been written in the previous century. (A good parallel elsewhere is the supposedly revolutionary *Lyrical Ballads* of 1792 (Wordsworth and Coleridge); almost every element in it had already appeared in the eighteenth century.) And so it is useful to consider the books in their context, while bearing in mind that it is just as important to consider the history of the mode of address used: 'That most of the early [books] now seem dated and *Alice* perennially fresh is in no small degree a matter of narrative address.'[4] We react as much to the attitude as to the content.

A conventional history of children's books might begin with the period before 1744, when most of the books used by children—educational texts, chap-books, tracts, and folk-tales—were used by adults as well. But, as the reading population increased, and the adult novel became established, those early texts were relegated to the nursery and formed the basis (either in spirit or in the solid fact that their woodcuts were reused) of eighteenth-century books for children. They can, however, only be described as children's books in any modern sense by a species of courtesy. As Percy Muir points out in his *English Children's Books*,

the early authors were most frequently Calvinists of an unrelenting severity . . . Bunyan was the best of them by a very long way . . . But when [he] addressed himself expressly to a juvenile audience he failed almost as miserably as any of his contemporaries. The title of his book is the best thing about it: *A Book for Boys and Girls: or, Country Rhymes for Children* [1686].[5]

Little has survived, although some of Isaac Watts's verses have lingered (if only in hymnals).

In 1744 one of the most influential of London booksellers, John Newbery, brought out one of the first commercial books for children: *A Little Pretty Pocket Book*. For the rest of the century there was a battle between the religious/educational and commercial interests for the market in children's books, with a considerable interchange of styles and techniques. 'Commercial' publishers used materials from folk traditions, with a strong strain of fantasy.

Change was slow in the nineteenth century; its utilitarianism gradually forced fantasy out of the mainstream (it became the backbone of the popular market-place), and the religious tractarians placed their stamp on the developing genres of the domestic tale for girls and the empire-building adventure stories for boys.

Generally, the form and content of children's books lags behind the form and content of the adult book, and the adventure story provides a good example. The 'page turner' was the staple of the eighteenth-century adult novel (notably in Defoe, Fielding, and Smollett), but was gradually displaced by more reflective books (with a corresponding downgrading of Defoe, Fielding, and Smollett in the literary hierarchy). And yet, the adventure story was the staple of *nineteenth-*century children's books. As Margery Fisher observes:

Stevenson's romantic adventures were put in their place by a reviewer in the London *Daily Chronicle* [24 April 1897] who remarked that 'great literature cannot be composed from narratives of perilous adventures'. In the increasing number of critical surveys of the English novel . . . Conrad is the sole writer ever to be included in the safe, accepted progression from Fielding to Henry James and beyond who could, to some degree, be considered to write of adventure in the traditional sense; and it is always made perfectly clear that Conrad's moral and philosophical probings constitute his true value, his story-telling expertise being, by implication, no more than a means to an end.[6]

But there was a gradual move away from heavy moralizing, and some notable individualistic sparks, such as Edward Lear's *A Book of Nonsense* (1846) (limericks had been printed at least as early as the 1820s), John Ruskin's *The King of the Golden River* (1851), and Heinrich Hoffmann's *The English Struwwelpeter* (1848). These are generally regarded as being interesting oddities rather than turning-points or touchstones. One such, nominated by historians as a book much imitated (assuming historical development to be as unsubtle as this), is Catherine Sinclair's *Holiday House* (1839), which allowed at least some light of naturalistic behaviour into the moralistic gloom of its tractarian predecessors (although it does have a meaty pious death at the end).

The real change in writing for children, perhaps the point at which we can see an empathetic, rather than directive narrative relationship with children, comes with Lewis Carroll, George Macdonald, and Charles Kingsley, whose work began the 'first golden age' of children's literature. This period (whose development was, ironically, rather hampered by childhood itself being seen as a golden age) has recently received a good deal of critical attention.[7] Certainly it is here that we find many of the earliest survivors into 1990s print, some, like Macdonald, perhaps little read, others, like Beatrix Potter and Kenneth Grahame, selling in huge numbers; others like Frances

Hodgson Burnett and E. Nesbit enjoying periodic revivals through television and film. As we shall see, the end of the century brought a new approach to childhood, based on smaller families, which were in turn based on fashionable attitudes as well as better sanitation and medicine. Both the ways in which children were valued and the relationships between parents and children were altering a good deal.

The status and impact of children's literature was also changing, and with the work of Kipling we can see the turning-points of several genres, despite the fact that some of the books—notably *Rewards and Fairies* (1910)—'had to be read by children, before people realized that they were meant for grown-ups'.[8]

The golden age was generally remarkable for synthesizing what went before. Richard Jefferies's *Bevis* (1882), a good example of a borderline text (at the time of writing it is still in print in an abridged edition for children and a scholarly edition for adults), introduced a new freedom of action and amorality into a book quickly adopted by children, while still being a product of the empire-building mode. *Treasure Island* (1881; book form 1883) is another book which is on the very edge of the mainstream canon of literature, but this time dominantly for children. (Stevenson read each morning's work out to his stepson: 'I had counted on one boy, I found I had two in my audience. My father caught fire at once with all the romance and childishness of his original nature.'[9]) It drew on (and, as Stevenson admitted, plagiarized) a line of sea stories that goes back to the eighteenth century, but added the kind of moral ambiguity that is now much more commonly a feature of children's literature. The book looks both backward and forward.

The inter-war years of the twentieth century have been described variously as an 'age of brass' between two golden ages (Leeson) or 'one of the most important [periods] in the history of the children's book' (Crouch).[10] If the bulk of the output was in the popular (not to say opportunist and transitory) end of the market, an impressive list of writers remain in print: Milne, de la Mare, Farjeon, Lofting, Masefield,

Ardizzone, Tolkien, Travers, Trease, Streatfeild, and Ransome.
It might be said that this period saw the development of the
'acceptable face' of children's books: literate, stable, middle-
class, with an uncomplicated author–reader contract.

Since the Second World War, children's literature has become
a powerful separate force in publishing and bookselling, with
its trends closely following the sociological features of the
period. In the mid-1950s fantasy began to dominate the field
in Britain, and continued to do so in the drug-culture of the
next decade—for once, children's books led the adult book. In
the more materialistic 1970s and 1980s, children's books have
returned to various kinds of realism. Also, the adoption of
children's literature as an educational tool, together with the
development of 'young adult' literature, has brought about a
change in content, a self-consciousness in the field that has
meant a swing back, if anything, to the earliest didacticism.
As publishing houses have merged and consolidated, so hard-
back production has declined, backlists have been pruned,
and prudence has won over experimentalism.

That is one, conventional, reading of history; it is a neat and
convenient one, but is not, of course, the only one. It does not
make clear, for example, that women have dominated children's
books from the beginning. The starting-point of children's literature is generally held to be 1744, as we have seen, because
of Newbery's *A Little Pretty Pocket Book*; less celebrated is
the publication in that year of the oldest known collection of
nursery rhymes, *Tommy Thumb's Pretty Song Book*, published
by Mary Cooper, who had produced a novelty *ABC* two years
before. Both of these events could easily be claimed as more
important than Newbery's contribution. Similarly, the first
book that might be described as a novel for children was
Sarah Fielding's *The Governess; or, The Little Female Academy* of 1749 (the title-page reads 'By the Author of David
Simple')—a book which has survived into the twentieth century in both a scholarly edition and a popular edition (albeit
one for adults).[11]

For the next hundred years, the vast output of religious
tracts and pamphlets (the dominant mode of children's

reading) was largely produced by women, and there is no evidence that—by any yardstick—these works were inferior to those by men. Of the writers in verse, Ann and Jane Taylor's work ('Twinkle Twinkle Little Star' amongst it) was at least as worthy of parody by Carroll as the work of Isaac Watts.

Outstanding among the moralists for the glimmering of naturalism at the turn of the century was Maria Edgeworth, while Charles and Mary Lamb's *Tales from Shakespeare* (1807) was largely the work of Mary. And if the most notorious of the Calvinistic books for children, *The History of the Fairchild Family* (1818), was by a woman, Mary Martha Sherwood, so was the first landmark of freedom, *Holiday House*. If Henty and the empire-builders were popular and influential, no less were the many women, some of them prodigiously prolific, who, although writing within a sexist strait-jacket, produced domestic tales (and some fantasies) which moved the children's story slowly towards the domain of the child. Some of their work still survives, if only in reputation, such as *Froggy's Little Brother* (1875) by 'Brenda', *Jackanapes* (1884) by Juliana Horatia Ewing, and some of Charlotte Yonge's output—Charlotte Yonge of whom Robert Liddell wrote in 1947: 'she had a real literary gift which anyone might envy, and which, if he possibly could, Hardy ought to have tried to cultivate, since he wished to be a novelist.'[12] Probably the most underrated is Mrs Molesworth, whose *The Cuckoo Clock* (1877 and still in print) was almost as popular, and quite easily can be seen as being as influential, if not as original, as *Alice*.

The most famous school story may well be *Tom Brown's Schooldays* (1857) by Thomas Hughes, but there is some claim for Harriet Martineau's *The Crofton Boys* (1841) to be the first—and no dispute that Anna Sewell's *Black Beauty* (1877) is the most famous animal story. Of illustrators of the same period, Randolph Caldecott has a medal named after him, and so has Kate Greenaway.

The golden age—already the age of Mrs Molesworth—can be seen as the period when a genuine change of tone was achieved by Edith Nesbit, when there was a truly transatlantic novelist (Frances Hodgson Burnett), and when irony came into books for small children with Beatrix Potter; and we have already noted the influence of the American domestic writers.

There is no doubt that A. A. Milne's has been the most lasting of children's verse from the 1920s, but it should not be forgotten that Rose Fyleman asked him to write it; Tolkien began his career as a children's author between the wars, and so did Enid Blyton; and while Arthur Ransome was the first recipient of the Carnegie Medal awarded by the Literary Association for the best Children's Book of the Year, in 1936, the next five medals were won by women, including one of the first social realists, Eve Garnett, and one of the first career-book writers, Noel Streatfeild.

Such a reading of history can be continued after the war. Certainly the importance of C. S. Lewis and Alan Garner in fantasy cannot be ignored, and they won the Carnegie Medals for *The Last Battle* and *The Owl Service* in 1955 and 1967. But six of the eight awards for fiction between those two dates went to women, and included four formidable works of fantasy: Philippa Pearce's *Tom's Midnight Garden*, Lucy Boston's *A Stranger at Green Knowe*, Pauline Clarke's *The Twelve and the Genii*, and Sheena Porter's *Nordy Bank*. In the USA women won the Newbery Medal (the American equivalent of the Carnegie) from 1973 to 1983, with writers such as Ellen Raskin and Susan Cooper contributing fantasy, and Fox, Paterson, Voigt, Hamilton, and Mildred Taylor contributing to the growth of realism.

The history could be written in other ways: paralleling these 'respectable' histories are the texts read by 'the people', texts that exploited and simplified and reinforced all the themes that we have mentioned. Through the eighteenth century Newbery and his successors and rivals provided cheap books that ruthlessly mixed religion and commercialism, education and folk-tale. In the later nineteenth century there was a major industry producing penny dreadfuls which had huge sales. There was some competition from such organizations as the Religious Tract Society, which began the *Boy's Own Paper* in 1879, while major publishing empires, such as the Amalgamated Press (founded by the Harmsworth brothers), laid their foundations with papers that exploited the juvenile market.

Sociologically, the history could explore the way in which national ideologies and institutions were reinforced by children's literature. Writers such as G. A. Henty and W. H. G. Kingston both reflected and 'invented' the Empire; the writers of school stories (culminating in the most prolific of all writers, Charles Hamilton (alias Frank Richards)) arguably invented and sustained the acceptable public face of the British public school; the writers for both girls and boys inculcated strong sexual stereotypes. The importance of these texts for social and political stability can scarcely be underestimated—a fact that has not escaped those manipulators of contemporary texts who are concerned with sexism, racism, and other attitudes.

The greater range of reference in children's books, and the toppling of taboos of all kinds, has been paralleled by a decline in the influence of religion. The history of religion in children's books has been one of great influence in the eighteenth and early nineteenth centuries (especially through the Sunday School movement), and then of a steady decline, to the point where, as mainstream publishing for children flourished in the 1950s and 1960s, it became a very small and eccentric corner of the industry. Few 'religious' writers have had any impact on mainstream thinking, and even C. S. Lewis's reputation is not secure. However, in recent years history has repeated itself, and religious publishing companies are imitating the quality and tactics of popular publishers of children's books, just as they did a hundred years ago.

Again, a similar history can be written for illustration, where the landmarks might be the introduction of woodblocks, of lithography, of colour-lithography, and photolithography, with milestone texts being produced by the Dalziel brothers, Caldecott, Ardizzone, Frank Hampson (in the *Eagle*), John Burningham, and Raymond Briggs. Other

versions might chart the fluctuations between realism and
fantasy, or the design of books, or their use in education, or
the treatment of race, charting the interaction between children's literature and society.

The following chapters will attempt a balancing act between
presenting the broad picture and discussing in some detail
books which are significant and/or popular, regardless of their
canonical status.[13] The only difficulty is an embarrassment of
riches.

3

The Early History of Children's Literature

It is often overlooked that children's literature is in fact
not a natural phenomenon—any more than the notion of
'childhood' which bore it—but instead a social construct,
born of the European Enlightenment of the 18th century.

(Birgit Dankert)

1. Children's Literature before 1800

When F. J. Harvey Darton wrote the 'first assault' on the
history of children's books, he began with a definition: 'By
"children's books" I mean printed works produced ostensibly
to give children pleasure, and not primarily to teach them, nor
solely to make them good, nor to keep them *profitably* quiet,'
and so he intended only to mention didactic works that 'gave
much latitude to amusement' [1] That Darton had anything to
write about at all demonstrates how liberal he was in interpret-
ing amusement in terms of pre-eighteenth-century childhood.

In the Middle Ages ' "children's literature" . . . was simply
the literature of the entire culture';[2] Chaucer, famously, addressed his *Tretis of the Astrolabie* to 'little Lewis my son', in
English because 'Latin ne canst thou yet but small, my little
son.' The fact that fables and folk-tales were amongst the
earliest printed books seems to have confused the issue.
Caxton printed a version of Aesop's *Fables* in 1484, and
Reynard the Fox in 1481, while his successor Wynkyn de
Worde produced the *Geste of Robin Hood* around 1510, but
these were texts shared by, rather than produced for, children,
whatever may have happened to later versions.

The way in which texts of this period were passed down
is illustrated by de Worde's printing of the *Gesta Romanorum*

(c.1510): 'Versions of this text, in abbreviated form and illustrated with crude little woodcuts, were read by children for their own amusement throughout the next four centuries.'[3] These were the chap-books, the wares of the 'Company of Walking Stationers', which included the hornbooks, and which, until well into the nineteenth century, 'preserved the old traditional tales and rhymes for the benefit of later generations of children [and] showed the way for the publication of cheap illustrated books for the less privileged reader'.[4]

Thus it seems that there was, as early as the sixteenth century, a division between cheap simplified texts sold by pedlars and chapmen which were used by adults and children alike, and the primarily instructive works directed at children, which may well have entertained incidentally, perhaps because of the novelty of the medium. Bibliographically important candidates for 'the earliest' of these include two illustrated books, Jost Amman's *Book of Art and Instruction for Young People from Which they may Learn Sketching and Painting* (*Kunst und Lehrbuchlein*), published to 'confer particular benefits upon the young' (1580), and Comenius's *Orbis sensualium pictus* (Nuremburg (German-Latin), 1658), published in English as *Visible World; or, A Nomenclature, and Pictures of All the Chief Things that are in the World, and of Man's Employment therein* (1659). The latter reached its twelfth edition by 1777 and, in assuming that the child was a damned soul from birth, who needed to be saved, it was the precursor of many books of the seventeenth century 'zealously depicting for children the holy lives and joyous deaths of their little contemporaries'.[5]

Other books generally assumed to have special appeal to children have shown remarkable powers of survival; the medieval bestiaries linger on in Hilaire Belloc's *A Bad Child's Book of Beasts* (1896 and current editions) and Roger McGough's *An Imaginary Menagerie* (1988); Robin Hood has survived both in children's books (including Geoffrey Trease's politically revisionist *Bows against the Barons* (1934; revised 1966)) and in contemporary film, which restores the legend to its original adult audience.

But the legends and folk-tales met with the Church's disapproval (just as they did in the more utilitarian eighteenth century) and probably the greatest contrast between contemporary and early views of childhood can be seen in the Puritan texts that dominated the century. 'The books produced for children in the 17th century offered them no entertainment, since the very idea of reading for pleasure was an abhorrence—a prostitution of the God-given ability to read.'[6]

The history that follows is formidable—perhaps even more so in the USA, which at first imported the English Calvinist texts, and then produced its own—and the evangelistic attitudes dominated children's books until the end of the eighteenth century, and influenced, directly or in reaction, attitudes almost to the end of the nineteenth.

A few samples will suffice. The title of James Janeway's most famous tract speaks for itself: *A Token for Children: Being an Exact Account of the Conversion, Holy and Exemplary Lives and Joyful Deaths of Several Young Children* (1692). In one of the stories, he describes the death

Of one eminently converted between Eight and Nine years old, with an account of her Life and Death.

Upon the Lords Day she scarce spoke any thing, but much desired that Bills of Thanksgiving be sent to those who had formerly been praying for her . . . and seemed to be much swallowed up with the thoughts of Gods free love to her soul. She oft commended her spirit into the Lords hands, and the last words which she was heard to speak were these, Lord Help, Lord Jesus help, Dear Jesus, Blessed Jesus—And Thus upon the Lords Day, between Nine and Ten of the Clock in the Forenoon, she slept sweetly in Jesus, and began an everlasting Sabbath.

Such books as John Bunyan's *The Pilgrim's Progress* are, of course, more cultural symbols than live texts, but the audience for his *A Book for Boys and Girls; or, Country Rhymes for Children* (1686) is clear enough. He begins:

> The title-page will show, if there thou look,
> Who are the proper Subjects of this book.
> They're Boys and Girls of all Sorts and Degrees,
> From those of Age, to Children on the Knees.

By 1724 this book had been transmogrified into *Divine Emblems; or, Temporal Things Spiritualised*. Demers and Moyles sum up these writers: 'Relying on a dour pedagogy . . . they brought to their task of exhorting the young an impassioned solemnity and the threat of imminent doom—forceful ingredients that were not to be reserved for adults. We are uncertain of children's response . . . The books tell us little about them and their tastes, though much about the Puritan view of the young.'[7]

John Locke, with his *Some Thoughts Concerning Education* (1693), is commonly credited with influencing children's educational/religious publishing towards entertainment as a means to an end, although to the modern ear such an influence seems rather subtle. Isaac Watts was certainly a little more persuasive in his *Divine Songs Attempted in Easy Language for the Use of Children* (1715) than some of his contemporaries. Watts, whose hymns—such as 'When I survey the wondrous cross', 'Jesus shall reign where'er the sun', and 'Oh God our help in ages past'—are still well known, has for some critics, such as Darton, the combination of tolerance and verse-technique that 'made up a real children's book, even if they had a didactic aim'.[8] Watts himself wrote that 'There is great delight in the very learning of truths and duties this way. There is something so amusing and entertaining in rhythms and metre, that will incline children to make this part of their business a diversion.' That such material was deeply embedded in the child-consciousness for more than a century is shown by the fact that among Isaac Watts's *Divine Songs* was one that surfaced in parody in *Alice's Adventures in Wonderland*, and is still in use.

> How doth the little busy bee
> Improve each shining hour,
> And gather honey all the day
> From every opening flower . . .

In the 1740 edition seven 'Moral Songs' were added, including

> 'Tis the voice of the sluggard; I heard him complain,
> 'You have waked me too soon, I must slumber again.'

>As the door on its hinges, so he on his bed,
>Turns his sides, and his shoulders, and his heavy head.

This became, of course, Carroll's "Tis the voice of the lobster . . .'

The beginning of the eighteenth century saw the importing of fairy-tales from France (just as they were imported from Germany in the nineteenth century). 'Literary' folk-tales were fashionable at the court of Louis XIV, such as the Countess d'Aulnoy's collection *Diverting Works* (1707). This included versions of 'The Yellow Dwarf' and 'Goldilocks'. Collections by Charles Perrault were also popular; a version of his *Histoires ou contes du temps passé; avec des moralitez* (Paris, 1697) came into English as *Histories, or Tales of Past Times, Told by Mother Goose* in 1729. This included 'Red Riding Hood', 'Puss in Boots', and 'Cinderella'. The *Arabian Nights* joined the fairy-tale, again via the French, in 1705-9, and these tales found their way into the chap-books, the contents of which were reprinted into the nineteenth century.

Indeed, a glance at late twentieth-century children's books shows that these tales are still current, although parody is increasing—regardless of whether children can now be assumed to be familiar with the original tales or not. Examples are Roald Dahl's *Revolting Rhymes* (1982), Tony Ross's ironic versions of folk-tales, such as *The Three Pigs* (1983), which begins, 'Pig and his two friends, Pig and Pig . . .',[9] and Fiona French's *Snow White in New York* (1986). The tales' continued potency, and the way in which they are changed for each generation, is demonstrated in, for example, Jack Zipes's survey *The Trials and Tribulations of Little Red Riding Hood* (1983) and his collection of feminist fairy-tales *Don't Bet on the Prince* (1986).[10]

But if there is a gap between the popular and the Puritan, there is an even greater one between what was going on in adult literature and in children's literature. When it is considered that the eighteenth century saw the rise of the novel— in a very robust and subversive form—and of sophisticated satire and political and periodical journalism, it is difficult to recognize any connection. *Robinson Crusoe* and *Gulliver's*

Travels are interesting examples of the way in which 'adult' texts—the one a mercantilist-Dissenting tract, the other a political (and wider) satire—had appeal across the age ranges because of their fundamental themes and devices. Both of them soon found their way into chap-book form: a shortened version of *Gulliver* was issued as early as 1727, and it was sufficiently well known for Newbery to be able to issue the *Lilliputian Magazine* in 1751. A variation on its devices was T. H. White's *Mistress Masham's Repose* (1947). *Crusoe* increased its popularity in the nursery after it was singled out by Rousseau in *Émile*, and the *Robinsonnade* became a genre of its own; over 200 years after its first publication, it was carried by Titty Walker to the rather more domesticated desert island of *Swallows and Amazons*.

There was a cross-over between children's and adults' books even in such an unlikely person as Samuel Richardson, who produced a version of Aesop in 1740, the title-page declaring that it was 'abstracted of all Party considerations' (unlike *Gulliver*). Also, the first edition of that concupiscent work *Pamela* (whose status as the 'first novel' is as ambiguous as that of *A Little Pretty Pocket Book*) declared that it was 'published in order to cultivate the principles of virtue and religion in the minds of the young of both sexes'. In 1756 a spectacular feat of abridgement of *Pamela*, *Clarissa*, and *Sir Charles Grandison* appeared for the young, with the predictable title *The Paths of Virtue Delineated*.

Commercial publishing for children seems to have got under way in the 1740s with Thomas Boreman's *Gigantick Histories* in ten volumes (1740–3), Thomas Warren's *Little Master's Miscellany* (Birmingham, *c.*1742), and Mary Cooper's nursery rhymes, perhaps the first genuine literature *of childhood*; they included such rhymes as 'Sing a song of sixpence | A bag full of rye | Four and twenty | Naughty boys | Bak'd in a Pye.'[11]

Newbery's *A Little Pretty Pocket Book* (of which the earliest extant edition seems to be the seventh, published in 1763) is most notable not for its combination of 'instruction and delight' but because it was a commercial, mixed-media text. Geoffrey Summerfield has dismissed its moralizing verses and crude woodcuts as part of 'a sneaky piece of work [which] serves only to show how calamitous the didactic book for children could be . . . [I]t is the work of a thoroughly trivial, commercial, and disinherited mind, and its continuing *succès d'estime* is something of a mystery.'[12] That well may be, and it is certainly indistinguishable in both layout and content from its contemporaries. But we should note that the original advertisement for it states that the book includes 'an agreeable Letter to read from *Jack the Giant-Killer*, as also a Ball and Pincushion, the use of which will infallibly make Tommy a good Boy and Polly a good Girl'. Almost from the beginning, it seems, we find both intertextuality and the need to bribe children (suitably sexually stereotyped) to read—or parents to buy. The devices seem to be very familiar when we look at contemporary texts which are both toys and books, let alone the most distinguished and most praised of contemporary picture-books, such as Janet and Allan Ahlberg's *The Jolly Christmas Postman*.[13]

Sarah Fielding is perhaps more famous for her children's book than her adults' books. What is curious about *The Governess* (1749) is that, in an age of narrative, it harks back to the earlier tradition of emblem books; it is a series of moral tales and morals hung loosely on the framework of daily sessions at Mrs Teachum's school. As Jill E. Grey notes:

Sarah became the first author for children to establish a distinct contemporary social environment with a definite set of characters taken from ordinary life and using ordinary everyday speech . . . and, more important for young readers, characters who were supposed to be real children like themselves . . . Sarah was the first writer for the young to try to give life to her characters by . . . making the ordinary happenings of their daily lives a subject for literature.[14]

Fielding was influenced by Fénelon's *Instructions for the Education of a Daughter* (Paris, 1687, trans. 1707) and by Locke, adapting his theories on the upbringing of boys to girls. The 'dedication' is characteristic:

The design of these Sheets is to endeavour to cultivate an early Inclination to Benevolence, and a Love of Virtue, in the Minds of young Women, by trying to shew them, that their True Interest is concerned in cherishing and improving those amiable Dispositions into Habits; and in keeping down all rough and boisterous Passions; and that from this alone they can propose to themselves to arrive at true Happiness, in any of the stations of Life allotted to the Female Character.[15]

On the whole, this is a restrained and liberal regime of education, and, as a school story, as Mary Cadogan has pointed out, it 'preceded the first school story for *boys* by over 60 years'.[16]

Fielding's book had an interesting history; it was 'revised' by the redoubtable Mrs Sherwood, a latter-day Puritan, eighty years later. 'Raising its low-keyed and reasonable tone to one of high-pitched religious exhortation, and altering the tales accordingly, she put the book out in 1820 under her own name, thereby squeezing the original out of the educational picture until it was resurrected by Charlotte Yonge in 1870.'[17] *The Governess* was reprinted by Charlotte Yonge in her anthology *A Storehouse of Stories* in 1870.

The trade in children's books grew steadily; Rousseau had some influence, but the shift towards (or reaction against) Deism ('natural religion', which rejected revelation and other Christian doctrine), or the way in which 'the growing sensibility to the beauty of nature began to affect writings for children',[18] are hard to discern with a modern eye.

The rational moralists and tractarians, largely women of considerable literary stamina, included Anna Laetitia Barbauld (*Lessons for Children* (1778, 1794, 1803) and *Evenings at Home* (1792–6)), whose influence was such that she was mentioned in Nesbit's *Wet Magic* as late as 1913 as one of the 'bad authors'. A sample of her attitude may be seen from her preface to *Hymns in Prose for Children* (1781): 'It may well be doubted whether poetry ought to be lowered to the capacities of children, or whether they should rather be kept from reading verse till they are able to relish good verse;'[19] although such a view is not uncommon in today's classrooms.

Equally formidable was Sarah, Mrs Trimmer, who started her own Sunday Schools from 1782, following Robert Raikes, who began the Sunday School movement in 1780. The title-page of her *The Guardian of Education* (1802–6) can speak for itself:

The Guardian of education: containing memoirs of modern philosophers both Christian and infidel, and extracts from their respective writings. Also Abstracts of Sermons on some of the most important points of Christian Doctrine; together with extracts from other works of established reputation, religious and Moral, and a copious review of Modern Books for Children and Young Persons.

As might be expected, she condemned the fairy-tale, although she did produce *Fabulous Histories: Designed for the Instruction of Children, Respecting their Treatment of Animals* (1786), perhaps better known as *[The History of] The Robins*. However, she prefaced it with the warning that children should think of the story 'not as containing the real conversation of Birds (for that it is impossible we should ever understand) but as a series of Fables, intended to convey moral instruction'. Despite such fearsome literal-mindedness, she remained in currency, at least in Sunday School circles, until the First World War.

Other long-lasting 'rational moralists' included Hannah More, with her *Sacred Dramas: Chiefly Intended for Young Persons* (1782); she is mainly noted for starting the 'Cheap Repository Tracts' in 1795, which had a massive influence and led to the founding of the Religious Tract Society in 1799. We might also note in passing Lady Eleanor Fenn's popular (and significantly titled) *Cobwebs to Catch Flies* (1783); Dorothy Kilner with *The Life and Perambulations of a Mouse* (1783), one of the earliest to employ a first-person animal narrative; and her sister-in-law Mary Ann (Maze) Kilner, who used a similar device in *The Adventures of a Pincushion* (1780).

Although their declared intention was religious, many of these books are striking for their social engineering: children, women, and the poor were to be kept in their places, and this at least was a constant undercurrent for the next hundred years. But there were gradual changes. In the eighteenth century, 'the implied objective of children's reading passed from religious education in the early decades to social education in the later ones. By the 19th century the objective had changed again, to that of social advancement through practical knowledge.'[20]

2. The Early Nineteenth Century

In revolutionary times, children's books were a bastion of conservatism. There was, as Mary Thwaite notes, 'no intention of educating poor people beyond their station';[21] indeed, it is interesting that the 'Romantics', who had a elevated conception of childhood, had so little to say *to* childhood. The position of Blake, sometimes included in anthologies and histories as a children's poet on the strength of *Songs of Innocence*, is neatly put by Mary V. Jackson, who describes his poetry as 'accessible to, if not precisely for, children'.[22]

Even among the revolutionary writers stories were not liberal by modern standards. Mary Wollstonecraft, who had written *Thoughts on the Education of Daughters* in 1787, produced a book for children, *Original Stories from Real Life* (1788). It was intended to 'cure those faults by reason which ought never to have taken root in the infant mind': the result was very much the same as the cold, adult-centred tracts.

William Godwin, among his many ventures, went into publishing for children, and he and his second wife promoted both the Lambs' *Tales from Shakespeare* (1807) and other books by the Lambs, although Darton dismisses them as no more than 'common objects by the wayside of social history'.[23] Godwin's own translation of the first part of Johann Wyss's *Der Schweizerische Robinson*, *The Family Robinson Crusoe; or, Journal of a Father Shipwrecked with his Wife and Children on an Uninhabited Island*, was published in 1814. *The Swiss Family Robinson* is an interesting example of an 'unstable' text (like *Peter Pan*). The book had been originally printed in German in 1812–13, having been prepared for the press from a 'family manuscript' by the author's son; a French translation of 1814 expanded the text, and William Godwin used some of this new material in his translation into English 'from the German' in the same year. This process of adding to and altering the story continued through the century.

Perhaps the most readable of the writers from this period is Maria Edgeworth, whose story 'The Purple Jar', from *Early Lessons* (1801), has often been reprinted. Edgeworth was, as her novel *Castle Rackrent* (also 1801) showed, an excellent narrator, and this story has a pleasantly ambiguous ending that suggests the presence of a real child. Rosamond, who chooses to have a pretty jar (which turns out only to contain purple liquid, and not to be purple itself) rather than to have a pair of shoes, is treated coolly, as in the manner of the old moral tale, by both an unsympathetic mother and a scornful father. But, at the end, when her father refuses to take her on an outing because she is slipshod:

Rosamond coloured and retired. 'O mamma,' said she, as she took off her hat, 'how I wish that I had chosen the shoes! They would have been of so much more use to me than that jar: however, I am sure—no not quite sure, but I hope I shall be wiser another time.'

But if Edgeworth showed at least some understanding of children as they are rather than as they should be this was difficult to see in other writers. As Charles Lamb wrote in a famous letter to Coleridge in 1802:

Mrs Barbauld's stuff has banished all the old classics of the nursery, and the shopman at Newbery's hardly deigned to reached [*sic*] them off an old exploded corner of a shelf, when Mary asked for them. Mrs Barbauld's and Mrs Trimmer's nonsense lay in piles about . . . Think what you would have been now, if instead of being fed with tales and old wives' fables in childhood, you had been crammed with geography and history.[24]

And change was slow in coming. For example, the output of poetry increased towards the end of the eighteenth century. A typical volume was *Original Poems for Infant Minds, by Several Young Persons* (1804–5), largely by Jane Taylor and her sister Ann (Taylor) Gilbert, who were 21 and 22. The Taylors' *Rhymes for the Nursery* (1806) 'invented the "awful warning" school of poetry, which has led to a thousand cheerful parodies very remote from the authors' intentions'.[25] Other versifiers, rather more human, included Sara Coleridge, who wrote *Pretty Lessons in Verse, for Good Children* (1834).

Of course, one can hardly overlook Mary Martha Sherwood's immensely popular, and now rather notorious, *The History of the Fairchild Family* (1818). Her attitude can be summed up in her own words:

All children are by nature evil, and while they have none but the natural evil principle to guide them, pious and prudent parents must check their naughty passions in any way that they have in their power, and force them into decent and proper behaviour and into what are called good habits.[26]

The scene in which Mr Fairchild takes his naughty children to contemplate (at what seems immense length) the decomposing corpse on the gibbet is famous. Here is one of the less notorious moments, which can stand for a thousand others of the time:

Miss Augusta had a custom of playing with fire and carrying candles about, though Lady Noble had often warned her of the danger of this . . . And the night before last . . . Miss Augusta took a candle off the hall table, and carried it up stairs to the governess's room . . . Lady Noble's maid, who was in a room not far off, was frightened by dreadful screamings: she ran into the governess's room, and there found poor Augusta all in a blaze, from head to foot! The maid burnt herself very much in putting out the fire; and poor Miss Augusta was so dreadfully burnt, that she never spoke afterwards, but died in agonies last night—a warning to all children how they presume to disobey their parents.

As Mr Fairchild says to his children: 'I stand in place of God to you, whilst you are a child.'

The evangelical movement flourished in a context of social and religious unrest, the wars in France, an economic depression, and 'thanks to Mrs Sherwood and the tract publishers, the moral and religious code and the restraints of Evangelicalism were perpetuated . . . By the end of the century, the works of Mrs Sherwood might have been out of sight for six days a week in many nurseries, but their basic principles . . . had become part of the very foundation of middle-class family life.'[27]

Mrs Sherwood had many very popular compatriots, such as Barbara Hofland, who, typically, turned out moral tales, historical novels, and *The Young Crusoe* (1828), and Henry Sharpe Horsley, whose *The Affectionate Parent's Gift, and the Good Child's Reward* (1828) included such edifying verses as 'A Visit to Newgate', 'A Visit to the Lunatic Asylum', and 'The Death of a Mother'.

During the isolationist period after the Napoleonic wars, technology and the standard of book-production improved, and there were several bright moments, some of which are alive today. Among them are William Roscoe's rather grotesque *The Butterfly's Ball and the Grasshopper's Feast* (1807) and what seem to be the earliest printed limericks, *The History of Sixteen Wonderful Old Women* (1820), pre-dating the much more famous *Book of Nonsense* by Edward Lear (1846).

Amongst this mixture of seriousness and change, Catherine Sinclair's *Holiday House* (1839) is generally credited with being a landmark text, attacking the monotony and unreality of the Puritan texts and endeavouring 'to paint that species of noisy, frolicsome, mischievous children which is now almost extinct'. In the preface to her first book, *Charlie Seymour* (1832), Sinclair notes that she had looked at many books for children that had a death-bed frontispiece and 'the memoirs of the children *especially*, which I examined, were almost invariably terminated by an early death'. *Holiday House* does contain a death, and a sad ending, but the important point is that Uncle David, the guardian of the anarchic Harry and Laura, distinguishes between the children being 'thoughtless and forgetful' and deliberate wrongdoing. He sets the tone for many fictional uncles—for example, Uncle Jim of Ransome's 'Swallows and Amazons' series—in colluding with the children against adult authority (in this case, the Governess, Mrs Crabtree. He describes her as 'that old vixen'). And so Laura and Harry break most of the rules of child-conduct, and at one point Laura cuts off her hair, and Harry sets fire to the nursery. Uncle David's reaction would not have won approval from the moralists of the period: ' "Did any mortal ever hear of two such little torments!" exclaimed [Uncle David], hardly able to help laughing. "I wonder if anybody else in the world has such mischievous children!" ' (chapter 3). Sinclair is, however, still addressing two audiences; as Barbara Wall says, she is 'caught in two minds and unable to take up any one narrative stance ... Sinclair produced a work that is uneven in tone and uncomfortably episodic in structure, with an uneasily shifting narrative stance ... torn between entertaining and instructing, and between pleasing children and pleasing adults.'[28]

Fairy-tales slowly re-established themselves. The earliest printed collection, *Lo cunto de li cunti*, collected by Giovanni Battista Basile in Naples (1634-6), was not translated into English until 1848, as *The Pentamerone* (an edition specifically for children, 'omitting offensive words and expressions and adapting the stories to juvenile ears', came out in 1893).[29] Perrault's tales were published 'with morals' in the 1829 edition, and the *Kinder- und Hausmärchen* of the Grimm brothers appeared in translation as *German Popular Stories* (1823), illustrated by George Cruikshank. Some of the 'literary' tales, like 'Cinderella', appear in the Grimms' collections, along with 'Rapunzel', 'Hansel and Gretel', 'Snow White', the 'Frog King', and the 'Bremen Town Musicians'. It is commonly assumed that the 'literary' stories are further from their origins than those collected by the folklorists, but modern evidence is that the Grimms 'were not merely collectors ... their major accomplishment ... was to *create* an ideal type for the *literary* fairy tale', and they 'made major changes while editing the tales. They eliminated erotic and sexual elements that might be offensive to middle-class morality, added numerous Christian expressions and references, [and] emphasized specific role models for male and female protagonists according to the dominant patriarchal code of that time.'[30]

Such was the urge to moralize that the illustrator, Cruikshank, rewrote four of the tales in 1854—'Hop o' my Thumb', 'Jack and the Beanstalk', 'Cinderella', and 'Puss in Boots'—as the *Fairy Library*, turning them into teetotaller tracts. Dickens, who clearly understood the value of fantasy, offered a famous riposte, 'Frauds on the Fairies':

In a utilitarian age, of all other times, it is a matter of grave importance that Fairy tales should be respected ... To preserve them in their usefulness, they must be as much preserved in their simplicity and purity, and innocent extravagance, as if they were actual fact. Whosoever alters them to suit his own opinions, whatever they are, is guilty, to our thinking, of an act of presumption, and appropriates to himself what does not belong to him.[31]

Collections of fairy stories began to be quite common as the century progressed, and the tradition of 'authored' rather than collected stories begins with Hans Andersen, who had four collections (by different translators) published in 1846: *Wonderful Stories for Children* (Andersen's name was misspelt on the title-page), *Danish Fairy Legends and Tales, A Danish Story-Book*, and *The Nightingale and Other Tales*. (The last two were reissued in one volume in the same year as *Tales from Denmark*). Among the survivors in this new tradition are Ruskin's cheerful imitation of the Grimms, *The King of the Golden River* (1851), and Frances Browne's *Granny's Wonderful Chair* (1857). Thackeray's *The Rose and the Ring*, his Christmas book for 1855, introduced elements of burlesque, which implies an audience familiar with several conventions. (The closest twentieth-century equivalent, A. A. Milne's *Once on a Time* (1917), has a similar ambiguity about its audience.)

Another influence on British children's books around the mid-century was the USA, with the widespread pirating of the work of S. G. Goodrich, better known as Peter Parley, from 1827 (*Tales of Peter Parley about America*). In thirty years over seven million copies of 116 genuine 'Parley's' were sold in America alone. These utilitarian—and not always accurate—books were a kind of commercial reaction to Puritanism. 'Peter Parley', in the conclusion of *Make the Best of It*, wrote: 'it has been my chief object . . . to set forth the excellence of good temper and cheerfulness, united with energy and perseverance; to show that sources of proper enjoyment will be found all around us if we but look for them in a right spirit.'[32]

There was, in turn, a reaction to these unimaginative texts in England in the form of Sir Henry Cole under the pseudonym of 'Felix Summerley', who produced 'The Home Treasury of Books' (1843–7). This series raised the general standard of books for children, and, not insignificantly, began with Bible stories before it moved on to use folk materials, its aim

being to go beyond the simple 'cultivation of the understanding'.

Other influential items included Punch and Judy, who date
from 1662, although they did not appear in print form until
1828, and a book which satirized (if it were possible) the
cautionary tales, Heinrich Hoffmann's *Struwwelpeter* (translated 1848). Hoffmann's account is enlightening:

Towards Christmas in the year 1844, when my eldest son was three
years old, I went to town with the intention to buy as a present for
him a picture-book ... But what did I find? Long tales, stupid
collections of pictures, moralizing stories, beginning and ending with
admonitions like 'the good child must be truthful' ... The child does
not reason abstractedly, and the old tale ... will certainly impress
him more than hundreds of general warnings.[33]

Apart from Hilaire Belloc's *Cautionary Tales* (1907), which
have one eye on the adult reader, the most anthologized
examples are Harry Graham's *Ruthless Rhymes for Heartless
Homes* (1899).

From the mid-century, the popular literature industry expanded with a steady growth of literacy; the size and orna-
mentation of children's books increased, as well as the use of
colour printing. Books were now produced specifically for
girls, using domestic and religious themes, and for boys, where
school, games, and Empire were linked; both types are ideologically connected, both were stabilizing forces.

In 1886 Charlotte Yonge observed that as 'girls are indis-
criminate devourers of fiction ... the semi-religious novel or
novelette is to them moralising put into action, and the most
likely way of reaching them'.[34] Thus we can follow the progress of Victorian fiction for girls from the tractarians, by way
of *Holiday House*, into the work of Charlotte Yonge and Mrs
Molesworth, who gradually slackened the religious constraints.
But they also reinforced the domestic role of women, as pallid
mothers or dutiful daughters—often with a concern for the
noble poor. Many of these books remain readable, despite
what J. S. Bratton described as 'the balance between religious
concern for the soul to be saved and sympathy for the
suffering child [having] two artistically deleterious consequences

... sentimentality ... and the assumption that the reader is well-off, comfortable, completely insulated from the story'. It is also interesting that many of the writers derived the form of their stories from the popular press.[35]

A characteristic example, which sold in huge numbers and was translated widely, is *Jessica's First Prayer* by 'Hesba Stretton', in which the heroine is saved from drudgery and poverty by a clergyman; in the process she converts the bigoted chapel-keeper. In this scene, she is visited by the minister:

'My child,' he said. 'I'm come to ask your mother to let you go to school in a pleasant place down in the country. Will she let you go?'

'No,' answered Jessica; 'mother says she'll never let me learn to read or go to church; she says it would make me good for nothing ... She always gets very drunk of a Sunday.'

The child spoke very simply, and as if all she said was a matter of course; but the minister shuddered, and he looked through the broken window to the little patch of gloomy sky overhead.

'What can I do?' he cried mournfully, as though speaking to himself.

'Nothing, please, sir,' said Jessica; 'only let me come to hear you of a Sunday, and tell me about God.'[36]

Jessica—fortunate among waifs—survives a terrible illness, and reappears in a sequel—perhaps inevitably called *Jessica's Mother*.

Charlotte Yonge, who taught at the village school in Otterbourne, Hampshire, for seventy-one years (beginning when she was 7),[37] wrote over 150 books, including *The Little Rick-Burners* (1886) and a classic forerunner of the domestic stories, *The Daisy Chain* (1856). Her 'adult' books were also read by the young: *The Heir of Redclyffe* (1853), for example, was read by Jo March in *Little Women*. Quayle feels, reasonably enough, that 'Yonge was one of the last of the old guard of children's writers, and to today's readers most of the characters she portrays would be merely ghosts of a bygone age, old-fashioned wax-faced dolls bowing and scraping at the pull of a string.'[38]

Among the other writers, all with considerable output, were Maria Louisa Charlesworth, who had a best seller in *Ministering Children* (1854, sequel 1867), and A.L.O.E (A Lady of

England—Charlotte Maria Tucker), whose first children's book was in a tradition that still survives, *The Rambles of a Rat* (1857).

Two hugely popular American books stand out as links between sentimentality, evangelically based social reform, and, particularly, girls' reading. Harriet Beecher Stowe's *Uncle Tom's Cabin; or, Life among the Lowly* (serialized 1851–2, UK 1852) had twenty different pirated editions all dated 1852; within five years it had been translated into twenty-three languages, and had considerable political effect. *The Wide, Wide World* (1850) by Elizabeth Wetherell looks forward to the genre of displaced female heroes, although it is also firmly in the lachrymose tradition. When Alice Humphreys dies (after waiting for her brother to arrive at her bedside) her adopted sister Ellen sings five long hymns over her body.

As far as book design is concerned, it is only in the mid-century that contemporary artistic motifs begin to appear in children's books, such as rococo frames, neo-classical motifs, and romantic backgrounds. Children were originally shown as small adults, but around 1840 artists were using the child for other ends: 'We sometimes get the feeling that the artist was making a conscious comment on the child: "See how quaint—cute—amusing—pretty." '[39]

For boys, the evangelical tradition merged with imperialist thinking, *Robinsonnades*, the sea story (which had its origins at least as far back as Smollett), and the school story. All of these were generators of the British 'stiff upper lip' codes, and were as popular at the cheap and opportunist end of the market as in 'respectable' writing.

Although, as we have seen, school stories can be traced back as early as Harriet Martineau's *The Crofton Boys*, the most influential book was *Tom Brown's Schooldays* 'by An Old Boy' [Thomas Hughes] (1857). This book, like many others, had a clear—perhaps over-clear—moral purpose, and contributed to school reforms. Hughes himself was an adherent of the 'muscular Christianity' movement. Bristow suggests that

Representing a new variety of morally responsible and physically strong manliness, Hughes's novel was attempting to raise a long-standing tradition of disreputable tales of unruly schoolboys up to an acceptable level. Hughes was modifying, for political ends, one of the most notorious aspects of the public schools: namely, that these were places where boys had to learn to stand their own ground. Stories such as Maria Edgeworth's *Frank: A Sequel* (1822)—that depict public schools as places where innocent boys learn to be roughed up into experienced men—are in some respects prototypes for highly masculine young men who populate *Tom Brown*.[40]

One of the most notorious, and most mocked, of the genre was *Eric; or, Little by Little: A Tale of Roslyn School* (1858) by Frederick Farrar. 'Nearly everything that can be said against maudlin sentimentalism, against sincere and pious self-delusion, can be and has been said against this astonishing book',[41] and one of its less predictable astonishing features is its very strong story-telling as we follow the decline and fall of Eric from public school to brutal life at sea and repentant death. The more sadistic passages were suppressed in later editions, and Quayle calls it 'a vivid example of the *maladie d'anglais* style of sexual sadism that lay close to the surface in so many tales of school-life written by ex-schoolmasters and clerics'.[42] It was certainly well remembered. In Kipling's scurrilous school story *Stalky and Co.* (1899) a maiden aunt of Stalky's sends him two of Farrar's books, *Eric* and *St. Winifred's; or, The World of School*; they are both thoroughly ridiculed as being 'drugs' on the market, and *Eric* gets 'thrown into a corner'.[43] (Kipling was forced to apologize—after a fashion— to Farrar for the reference.) The ethos was one still very much connected (despite Hughes's disclaimers) to the moralists, and Talbot Baines Reed reacted against these writers with *The Fifth Form at St. Dominic's* (1887), *The Cock-House at Fellsgarth* (1893), and *The Adventures of a Three Guinea Watch* (1883). The books, all of which were published by the Religious Tract Society, and remained in print well into the twentieth century, are altogether more lively affairs; the morality is still there, but it is expressed in action. As the narrator observes in *The Fifth Form at St. Dominic's*: 'A pair of well-trained athletic schoolboys, with a plucky youngster to help them, are a match any day for twice the number of half-tipsy cads' (chapter 20). The school story has an obvious appeal to both readers and writers: it describes a closed world, dealing with initiation and hierarchies, rules and rituals, and a clear relationship to adult life, although it was, of course, limited by these very things.

Sea stories and desert island stories had a similar appeal, and similar themes—initiation, imperialism, the individual man in a strange world, surviving by skills.[44] The fanciful *The Swiss Family Robinson* provoked the writing of another important book, Captain Marryat's *Masterman Ready* (1841–2). Marryat 'put down Wyss's book with scorn when he read it, contemptuous of its errors in seamanship and geography, and holding, as he says in his Preface, that ... "Fiction, when written for young people, should, at all events, be *based* on truth." '[45] The religious, pious element was very strong; as Green points out, 'if Pastor Wyss's story can be called reactionary and partly evangelical, Captain Marryat's is Victorian and wholly evangelical'.[46]

Marryat's popularity and influence spread into other genres. The prospectus for *The Children of the New Forest* (1847) promised 'to elevate the moral feelings' and stylistically Marryat is a typical example of a writer 'weighed down by his feelings of responsibility'. At his most relaxed, in *Children of the New Forest*, 'Marryat had learned at last, as implied author, to efface himself as narrator, to talk easily to his young readers, and to allow the values he cared for to emerge naturally through his story.'[47] That may be so, but it is difficult to imagine many contemporary readers coping with the opening:

The circumstances which I am about to relate to my juvenile readers took place in the year 1647. By referring to the history of England of that date, they will find that King Charles the First, against whom the Commons of England had rebelled, after a civil war of nearly five years, had been defeated, and was confined as a prisoner at Hampton Court . . .[48]

Marryat insisted that the covers and title-pages should be designed to catch the child's eye, and in a sense this marks the beginnings of the 'teenage' market; he had a generation of

devoted followers, including one writer who did make it into
the adult canon, Joseph Conrad, who wrote of Marryat:

He is the enslaver of youth, not by the literary artifices of presentation, but by the natural glamour of his own temperament. To his
young heroes, the beginning of life is a splendid and warlike lark,
ending at last in inheritance and marriage . . . To the artist his work
is interesting as a completely successful expression of an unartistic
nature . . . There is an air of fable about it.[49]

Other books in the genre include Kingsley's *Westward Ho!*
(1855) and Ballantyne's *The Coral Island* (1858), which was
obviously aimed at boys (although girls did read their brothers' books). Ballantyne's first book *Hudson's Bay; or, Every-
Day Life in the Wilds of North America* (1848) had been
privately printed, but *The Young Fur Traders* (1856) and *The
Coral Island* confirmed his success (although not financially—
he had sold the copyright to Thomas Nelson, and received
only £90). That this movement was international is suggested
by the fact that much of the plot of *The Coral Island* was
taken from James F. Bowman's *The Island Home; or, The
Young Castaways* (Boston, 1851). Ballantyne minimized the
moralizing and moved rapidly towards the out-and-out adventure story, although the role of the Englishman, with his
Christian duty towards the Empire, could sit heavily on his
heroes' shoulders. From Ballantyne onwards 'the Victorian
fictional hero is a protean and complex projection of action
and introspection, straightforward brutality and conscience-
wracked philosophising'.[50]

Richards argues that imperialism was 'the dominant national ideology, transcending class and party divisions. Britain
was saturated in the ethos and attitudes of empire'. The literature exalted the 'warrior-explorer-engineer-administrator-
imperial paladin . . . Juvenile literature operates on the
lower slopes of this Parnassus of adventure, steeped in
every aspect of imperialism.'[51] This was linked to romantic
chivalric public school manliness—while the view that it is
'sexist, racist, chauvinist, thuggish and hedonistic' is submerged.

The earliest magazines such as the *Child's Companion, or Sunday Scholar's Reward* (1824–1932) and the *Children's Friend* (1824–1930)—again, moral tales—had been soundly based on religion. The first annual 'in the modern sense' was the *Excitement* (December 1829), whose editor Adam Keys had to defend himself for his lack of moralizing: 'It does not appear to us essential that *every* work put into the hands of the young should necessarily contain something of a religious nature.' (He was dismissed in 1838 but began the *New Excitement* in the same year.[52]) By 1860, as we shall see, the juvenile magazine was beginning to flourish.

Several verses that have become part of British and American culture date from across this period, including Clement Clarke Moore's 'A Visit from St. Nicholas', published anonymously in the *Troy Sentinel*, 23 December 1823, with its classic opening

> 'Twas the night before Christmas, when all through the
>   house
> Not a creature was stirring, not even a mouse . . .

Other universally known texts have obscure origins. For example, 'Mary Had a Little Lamb' and 'Three little kittens they lost their mittens, And they began to cry . . .' are the work of two American writers, the first being from Sarah Josepha Hale's *Poems for our Children Designed for Families, Sabbath Schools and Infant Schools* (1830), the second from Eliza Lee Follen's *New Nursery Songs for All Good Children* (1843). Mary Howett and her husband William represent the Quaker influence, which was generally more liberal than the Puritan. Mary translated Andersen, and her most famous verse, from *The New Year's Gift* (1829), was ' "Will you walk into my parlour?" said the Spider to the Fly'.

The scene, then, was set for what has been called the golden age of the children's book; from religious and educational beginnings, writers were responding to a redefined childhood, one that required a distinctive literature. In the following sixty years, that literature was to become firmly established.

4
Maturity, 1860–1920

> Fiction is a social product but it also 'produces' society . . .
> It plays a large part in the socialisation of infants.
>
> (Joan Rockwell)

1. Overview

Conventionally, the period between the publication of Kingsley's *The Water Babies* (1862), Carroll's *Alice's Adventures in Wonderland* (1864), and the First World War has been regarded, as we have seen, as the first golden age of children's books. Many authors whose works are still in print and who have had a large influence flourished; notable years were 1871, when Lewis Carroll's *Through the Looking Glass*, Susan Coolidge's *What Katy Did*, G. A. Henty's first children's book, *Out on the Pampas; or, The Young Settlers*, and George Macdonald's *The Princess and the Goblin* were published, and 1902, which saw Rudyard Kipling's *Just So Stories*, E. Nesbit's *Five Children and It*, Walter de la Mare's *Songs of Childhood*, and Beatrix Potter's *The Tale of Peter Rabbit*. Mrs Molesworth began her career; Charlotte Yonge continued hers; Alfred Harmsworth was building his Amalgamated Press. Distinctively, the books of this period are for a recognizable childhood, and begin to use a tone that is increasingly 'single address'; the books become more complex, and any didactic intent (which is, perhaps, inescapable) is a poor second to entertainment. In a sense, children's literature was growing up—growing away from adults.

The direct narrative contract with children was becoming more common, rather than stories being mediated through the controlling adult mind. The clearest example of this might be the contrast between the voices used by Grahame in

The Golden Age (1895) and *Dream Days* (1899), when he was writing *about* children in a period when childhood was idealized, and Nesbit's work in *The Story of the Treasure Seekers* (1899), where there is almost exactly the same situation, but seen from a child's viewpoint. The same thing can be seen within Nesbit's own work, where there is a war between control and complicity. Similarly, Carroll is virtually entirely on the child's side, while Kingsley and, especially, Macdonald cannot forget the adult–child relationship. By the time we have reached Potter and Kipling, the problem is, in a sense, solved.

In children's reading, there was a rapid expansion of both the middle-class 'respectable' market—in 1875, Routledge could print a catalogue of 1,000 children's books[1]—and the penny dreadfuls. Why did this happen? The period between 1860 and the outbreak of the First World War saw some dramatic social and political shifts. Families became smaller and more stable, major artistic movements such as the Pre-Raphaelites legitimized the vein of fantasy that parallels Victorian utilitarianism; the Empire, at its peak, began to seem a little less sure of itself; and women's position in society was changing subtly. Books became cheaper with the introduction of Hoe cylinder press in the 1860s, cardboard book covers in the 1870s, and inexpensive pulp paper in the 1880s. In the 1880s and 1890s photomechanical reproduction of pictures took over (the famous engravers the Dalziel brothers went bankrupt in 1893).

Although colour printing had been practicable since the 1840s, it was only in the golden age that individual illustrators rose to prominence. Illustrations were given by-lines, John Tenniel was knighted, and three major figures emerged, whose influence is still with us. Kate Greenaway, with *Under the Window* (1879), produced stylized, idealized children, dressed in her individualistic designs; Randolph Caldecott's much more robust work began with *The Diverting History of John Gilpin* (1878), and Walter Crane's work with the publisher Edmund Evans has links to the Arts and Crafts movement in the 1880s, inspired by Ruskin and Morris. Crane in turn influenced Arthur Rackham, whose first major success, an edition of Grimm, was published in 1900. There was also a trend towards naturalism, stemming perhaps from Sir John Millais's *Little Songs for Me to Sing* (1865) (Millais was a friend of the Potter family), which reached its apotheosis in the work of H. R. Millar and the Brock brothers. Other notables were Arthur Hughes, whose work 'sums up better than most those qualities of mystery and imagination which had now entered children's books';[2] his work is best seen in *Tom Brown's Schooldays* (1869 edition), Macdonald's *At the Back of the North Wind* (in *Good Words for the Young*, 1 (1868–9)), and also in Christina Rossetti's *Sing-Song: A Nursery Rhyme Book* (a collection of original verse).

Forster's Education Act of 1870, which legislated for free elementary education, had by 1880 created over one million new places at schools. Juvenile departments were established by publishers such as Macmillan, Routledge, and Nelson in the late 1860s. The number of periodicals for boys, for example, increased rapidly from one in 1855 (the *Boy's Own Magazine*) to twenty-three in 1900. The publishing houses of Cassell, Blackie, and Nelson dominated the market alongside the Society for the Propagation of Christian Knowledge (SPCK) and the Religious Tract Society (RTS).[3]

Although this seems to be a rich period in retrospect, it must be remembered that children's reading was, as ever, rather out of date; Arthur Ransome, born in 1884, listed his childhood reading as including Andersen, Carroll, Grimm, Ewing, Yonge, Scott, Blackmore, Ballantyne, Lang's Fairy Books, Kingsley, Lear, Marryat, *Holiday House*, and *The Rose and the Ring*.[4] And yet it was the period when the living 'classics' were established, and behind them, as it were, are others, such as Kingsley and Macdonald, who are traditionally accorded a place in history—and behind them, again, is the dense undergrowth of 'popular' literature.

2. *The Popular Press*

This was not just the era of *The Wind in the Willows*, it was the era of Spring-Heeled Jack, the terror of London, Sweeney

Todd, the demon barber (first seen in a mid-1840s serial by
T. P. Prest, *String of Pearls*, and who appeared in a version
aimed at boys in the 1860s), the *Magnet*, and the *Gem*. That
such material is undervalued is largely a matter of cultural
fashion: but its influence on the working classes for whom
much of it was designed, and the middle-class children who
delighted in it (illicitly), was immense. The social and educational reforms

attempted to make a distinction between the working-class's ability
to read and the familiarity with literature and literary language which
came about through the extended education received by their social
betters. The result of this effort was to designate children's literature
as pre-literary. It quickly came to be associated with popular culture
and uncanonised writing.[5]

Thus the cheap popular papers and the comic strips that
developed in this period 'are ephemera. But this is an age
when higher premiums are beginning to be placed on the
ephemeral arts. They more honestly represent their time than
the work that is deliberately created to last.'[6] It is perhaps a
pity that one of the staunchest defenders of popular literature
is an ambivalent, paradoxical figure himself, G. K. Chesterton. Chesterton observed that to suppress the 'dreadfuls'
because they were 'ignorant in a literary sense' was equivalent
to accusing a novel of being deficient in a chemical sense:
'The simple need for some kind of ideal world in which
fictitious persons play an unhampered part is infinitely deeper
and older than the rules of good art, and much more important. . . . [The literature of] the vast mass of humanity . . . will
always be a blood and thunder literature.'[7] As most books
were, as they always had been, priced out of reach of ordinary
families—for example *Alice's Adventures in Wonderland* sold
for six shillings or about one-third of the average worker's
weekly wage—the success of cheap, sensational texts was
hardly surprising.[8]

A dominant figure in Victorian cheap fiction was Edwin
John Brett, whose eight-page 'gallows' literature (with a lurid
illustration) had titles such as *Black Rollo, the Pirate* (1864–5).

The pressure from the 'mainstream' market led him to produce the *Boys of England* (1866–1906), which was a great success, sales rising to 150,000 copies; it contained the first comic strip, and this declaration: 'Our tales and articles do not contain "sermons in disguise" which are always distasteful to boys, but a moral and healthy tone may be maintained in conjunction with the boldest fiction.'[9] He also produced the first magazine to be printed in full colour (*Boys of the Empire* (1888–1901)).

Rivals in this 'literary abattoir' were the Emmett brothers, who went out of business in 1875. The way in which their writers used everything from the school story to folk legend is illustrated by the case of Dick Turpin:

The glorification of Dick Turpin (born 1705, hanged 1739) had begun in eighteenth-century broadsheets and chapbooks. The short, dumpy, balding butcher's assistant, horse-thief and robber, renowned for his brutal methods of torture, became a gay blade with magnificent moustachios, a bold and daring highwayman, a gentleman of the road, a protector of the weak and oppressed.[10]

The religious organizations tried to harness this huge market, notably the RTS with the *Boy's Own Paper* (1879). G. A. Hutchinson, the first editor (he continued until his death in 1912), had to fight with the RTS before they would allow spirited fiction into his pages. The RTS Annual Report for 1879 noted that the Committee, while 'fully admitting the terrible necessity of a publication which might to some extent supplant those of a mischievous tendency, yet hesitated . . . To have made it obtrusively or largely religious in its teaching would have been to defeat the object in view.'[11] The first edition included a school story by Talbot Baines Reed, and W. H. G. Kingston's *From Powder Monkey to Admiral* (the title of which sums up a great deal), and the mixture of the old and new writers was also typical: violence was acceptable in the imperialist context. *BOP* soon had a very large circulation: by 1889 it had a print run of well over 250,000 per week. It was supported financially by the RTS, but made a profit in the 1880s and claimed to have a wider circulation than all

other boys' journals put together. Other quality journals
were Cassell's rival *Chums* (1892), and the Sunday School
Union's *Young England* (1880), but it was a cut-throat
business; even Henty's involvement in the *Union Jack*
(1880–93) did not save it. (The *Union Jack*, along with *Pluck*
and the *Halfpenny Marvel*, feature in James Joyce's story
'An Encounter' in *Dubliners* (1914).) Girls had been partly
catered for since 1866 by the rather old-fashioned and piet-
istic Aunt Judy's Magazine, edited by Mrs Gatty (the mother
of Juliana Ewing); however, the first periodical devised especially for girls was *Every Girl's Magazine* (1878–88); by
1884 the *Girl's Own Paper* (founded in 1879) was reputed
to have the highest circulation of any English illustrated
magazine, and, after becoming a monthly in 1914, it survived
until 1967.

The evidence suggests that, on the whole, older girls read
their mothers' books, the younger, their brothers'. But, as
Reynolds observes, 'Girls have always read more, and read
more widely than boys' and sexual discrimination within the
educational system against girls 'helps to explain why the de-
valuation of girls' reading tends to be based more on gender
than on class'.[13] An indication of the size of the market is that
between 1880 and 1900 over 150 magazines of sufficient status
to appear in the *British Museum Catalogue* and the *Periodicals
Index* were published in Britain.[14]

Alfred Harmsworth's contribution to children's reading
may not have been quite so innocent. The first issue of *Boy's
Friend* (1895–1931) contained a somewhat meretricious article,
'The "Penny Dreadful" and the Scoundrels Who Write it',
which drew this picture: 'It is creeping not only into the houses
of the poor, neglected and untaught, but into the largest
mansions; penetrating into religious families and astounding
careful parents by its frightful issues.'[15]

The penny dreadful, then, was not only corrupting the
middle classes, but misleading the workers. As the *Edinburgh
Review*, no less, observed in 1887, the penny dreadfuls 'were
to be found anywhere and everywhere, throughout the whole
domain of poverty, hunger, and crime'. There was clearly a

political dimension: 'The anxious debates about the dreadfuls reveals [*sic*] one thing very clearly indeed—that literacy is a precarious instrument of power. While reading was designed to equip pupils to rise up in a meritocratic society, it simultaneously managed to drag down the standards demanded by the ideologues of culture writing in the periodical press.'[16] Other attempts to combat the 'dreadfuls' were the Revd Erskine J. Clarke's *Chatterbox* (1866, running until 1948), *Good Words for the Young* (1869), which included work by Kingsley, and which was edited in one of its manifestations by Macdonald, and *Little Folks* (1871–1933).

Any contemporary critic of the comic strip who suggests that comics contribute to poor reading standards, restrict children's fantasy lives, and inculcate and generate immorality may or may not be consoled by the thought that the same strictures were voiced by the Victorians. For some reason there is a prejudice against the convention of the speech balloon—although it requires a certain skill to read texts in this mode, and they go back to Rowlandson and Gillray 'and have even been traced in woodcuts as far back as the 14th century'.[17] In the twentieth century Edward Ardizzone was one of the first to rehabilitate them in 'respectable' literature, and Raymond Briggs may have completed the task. The immediate ancestor of the comic strip was the Swiss Rodolphe Töpffer, who had been encouraged to publish by no less a writer than Goethe. The first regular British 'comic' was *Ally Sloper's Half-Holiday* (1884–1923), published by the Dalziel brothers and aimed at what we would now call 'young adults'.

In 1890 Alfred Harmsworth started *Comic Cuts*, a mixture of what would today be called 'one-liners' and snippets of information. The first number sold 118,864 copies, and this went up to a steady 300,000. Its first full-page comic strip appeared in 1891. This magazine and its companion *Chips* (1890 on) were part of Harmsworth's declared intention to divert attention from the 'penny bloods'. A. A. Milne was rather scathing about this: Harmsworth, he wrote, 'killed the penny dreadful by the simple process of producing the ha'penny dreadfuller'.[18] But some of the characters had enviably long lives: Weary Willy and Tired Tim lasted until 1953.

There were also the American imports, both respectable and not so respectable. The most famous of the American magazines was *St Nicholas* (1873–1939), which was edited by Mary Mapes Dodge, author of *Hans Brinker; or, The Silver Skates* (1865), and which published material by Stevenson and Kipling. The USA had a similar tradition to the British penny dreadfuls in its 'dime novels', perhaps the most famous of which was Horatio Alger, Jr.'s *Ragged Dick* (1868). British entrepreneurs imported materials and adapted them in many different ways; the cowboy, already a myth created by these magazines, was a particularly popular figure. Another immortal, at the end of the period, was Edgar Rice Burroughs's *Tarzan of the Apes* (1914), whose status (for adults/for children?) remains ambiguous after eighty years.

And then there was the comic strip. As a form specifically for children it was unknown in the USA, the comic strips there being designed for the daily papers and aimed at adults and children equally. Speech balloons, usually supplemented with typeset text—a fashion that continued until well after the Second World War, and which survives in the 'Rupert' strip— began to be widely used in 1901; in Britain, the first true 'comic' for a younger age group was *Rainbow* (1914). In the USA the earliest strip cartoon began in 1896. As Perry and Aldridge conclude:

There is, in Britain, a great gulf between children's strips and those designed for adults. The absence of British-style comics in America has given the strips there a greater universality in readership. American parents, on the whole, are more familiar with their children's reading matter than British ones. British comics are at a disadvantage. They lack the incentives for improvement that an audience broader-based in age and intelligence could provide.[19]

This conclusion is similar to that so vilified by Barbara Wall: that the less like a product 'for children' the text is, the more likely it is to get approbation. There is, somewhat surprisingly, no appreciation here that comics for children and for adults may well be different creatures entirely.

3. Popular Writers

The golden age, then, did not consist merely of 'great' books, but had a remarkable backdrop of popular writers, and writers whom literary history, in its arbitrary fashion, has consigned to the second rank.

If we consider the use of texts by contemporary children, it is certainly true that no writer of poetry for children has weathered well. One anomalous survivor is Christina Rossetti's *Goblin Market*, a sensual indulgence which the most tolerant observer might be forgiven for thinking verges on the perverted. That Darton could say that it is 'the most magical and vivid of all poems put before children'[20] says a lot for his character. Robert Louis Stevenson in *A Child's Garden of Verses* (1885), despite his own view (to Edmund Gosse) that 'I have now published, on 101 small pages, *The Complete Proof of Mr R. L. Stevenson's Incapability to Write Verses*',[21]

laid the ground-rules for children's poetry with his clarity of expression, his directness, his use of common speech . . . However, he spawned a tradition of poetry for children—fixing the agenda of form, subject matter and tone for years to come—that must have put off as many children as it enticed and that thoroughly diverted it from the main stream of adult poetry.[22]

Their poetic diction and subject-matter mark them out as speaking to a particular period—as does much of A. A. Milne's verse. Some, though, have entered the language:

> The world is so full
> of a number of things,
> I'm sure we should all
> be as happy as kings.

Perhaps the most important genre in fiction was still the 'empire-building' novel, led by G. A. Henty and W. H. G. Kingston, and followed by the mass-market 'manly boy' cult in which Christianity and the rights of Empire (and the right to plunder the Empire) were more or less conterminous.

Henty was the out-and-out imperialist. In the preface to *St. George for England* (1885) he wrote: 'The courage of our forefathers has created the greatest Empire in the world around a small and in itself insignificant island; if this Empire is ever lost, it will be by the cowardice of their descendants.'[23] Henty produced around a hundred titles, often historical, and some indication of his popularity is that twelve years after his books came out of copyright in 1952, forty were back in print. He wrote quickly, doing some basic reading; as he wrote in 1902 in 'How Boys' Books are Written':

When I get to the purely historical part I have three or four [history] books open before me, as I insist particularly that all my history shall be absolutely unassailable. I dictate every word—in that way I think you obtain larger, finer sentences, and I smoke the whole time. My work is extremely rapidly done. On more than one occasion I have completed a book of one hundred and forty thousand words in twenty days.[24]

This process produced as many as four 100,000–150,000-word novels each year, for which he earned as little as £100 each. He was clearly not the most fastidious of craftsmen, but, at least at the outset, he sounded a note for freedom of thought: in the preface to *The Young Buglers* (1880), his third book, he wrote:

I remember that, as a boy, I regarded any attempt to mix instruction with amusement as being as objectionable practice as the administration of powder in jam; but I think that this feeling arose from the fact that in those days books contained a very small share of amusement and a very large share of instruction. I have endeavoured to avoid this.[25]

If Henty represents a theme that has dated, the period produced one book whose eponymous hero is a cultural icon, and which is 'perhaps the last of the moral tales, the last great first person narrative in the Listen-to-my-life style':[26] Anna Sewell's *Black Beauty, his Grooms and Companions: The Autobiography of a Horse, Translated from the Original Equine* (1877). Despite the potential for bathos, this remains a very forceful first-person narrative, and Sewell gets around the animal-human problem quite neatly. For example:

'My poor Beauty,' he said one day, 'my good horse, you saved your mistress's life, Beauty! yes you saved her life.' I was very glad to hear that, for it seems the Doctor had said if we had been a little longer it would have been too late. John told my master he never saw a horse go so fast in his life, it seemed as if the horse knew what was the matter. Of course I did, though John thought not; at least I knew as much as this, that John and I must go at the top of our speed, and that it was for the sake of the mistress.[27]

Dickens's *A Holiday Romance* (first published in the USA in the magazine *Young Folks*, and in Britain in *All the Year Round* in 1868) is probably the closest thing that he wrote to a children's book—*A Christmas Carol* (1843) is in almost every sense an adult book. *A Holiday Romance* has Dickens's rapidity of wit, and his talent for exaggeration, which has, of course, made his popular writing live on the margins of children's literature, just as it does on the margins of respectable adult literature. One of the four stories, 'The Magic Fishbone', for example, has a sly opening: 'The king was, in his private profession, under government . . .' The heroine, Alicia, looks after eighteen children, and when one cuts himself 'she put the wounded prince's hand in a basin of fresh cold water, while they stared with their twice seventeen are thirty-four and carry three, eyes' and the magic fish-bone is disposed of satisfactorily, but not, perhaps, quite in the way of contemporary Puritan values, thus: 'So she took it from the hand of the Princess Alicia, and it instantly flew down the throat of the dreadful little snapping pug-dog, next door, and choked him, and he expired in convulsions.'

Jean Ingelow's *Mopsa the Fairy* (1869) has survived, if only in the limbo of the unread 'classic'. Carpenter and Pritchard feel that it is 'one of the more successful children's books written under the influence of *Alice's Adventures in Wonderland*',[28] but this delicate fable can be seen as cognate—part of the growing tradition of the fairy-tale, and part of the new freedom in fantasy. The story has traces of the moral tale, and

looks forward to the work of Andrew Lang and Joseph Jacobs
(*English Fairy Tales* (1890)). Something much more like a
follower of 'Alice' was G. E. Farrow's *The Wallypug of Why*
(1895) and its six sequels.

The fairy-tale reached its apotheosis with the twelve anthologies by Andrew Lang, from *The Blue Fairy Book* (1889),
which largely escape the strictures levelled by Tolkien at many
books of the time:

It is true that the age of childhood-sentiment has produced some
delightful books (especially charming, however, to adults) of the fairy
kind or near to it; but it has also produced a dreadful undergrowth
of stories written or adapted to what was or is conceived to be the
measure of children's minds and needs. The old stories are mollified
or bowdlerized, instead of being reserved; the imitations are often
merely silly . . . or patronizing; or (deadliest of all) convertly snigger-
ing.[29]

There is no doubt that, from the beginning, the potency and
crudity of the folk/fairy-tale, a combination of social revolt and
sexual fantasy, has appealed to childhood in so far as childhood
approximates to the state of repressed humanity; and, in the
nineteenth century, it was necessary to domesticate the tale.

An interesting period variant on the fairy/moral tale is Oscar
Wilde's collection *The Happy Prince*. These rather ambiguous
and solemn tales have a kind of literary respectability, but
equally a perfervidness:

So the Nightingale pressed closer against the thorn, and the thorn
pierced her heart, and a fierce pang of pain shot through her. Bitter,
bitter was the pain, and wilder and wilder grew her song, for she sang
of the Love that is perfected by Death, of the Love that does not die
in the tomb.

A comment on these tales by 'Micheál Mac Líammoir' shows
how careful critics have to be not to romanticize childhood:
'Are these stories really intended for children? To me they seem
to have been written for everybody who is or who ever has
been a child in the complete sense of the word, and who is
fortunate enough or wise enough to have preserved something
of what, in childhood itself, is fortunate, wise, and eternal.'[30]

Other writers known primarily for a single book, or whose names are forgotten while their creations live on, include John Meade Falkner, Florence K. Upton, and Helen Bannerman. Meade Falkner, who is distinguished among authors by reputedly having left the manuscript of his last book in a railway carriage, is also remembered for two 'adult' novels— *The Lost Stradivarius* (1895) and *The Nebuly Coat* (1903). But his masterpiece was a book that was adopted after 1924 as a school text, and sold steadily in 'educational' editions for the next fifty years. This is *Moonfleet* (1898), a tale that stands somewhere between *Lorna Doone* (1865), *Treasure Island*, and Kipling's smugglers in *Puck of Pook's Hill*. In helping to create and sustain the haunting literary image of the 'West Country', Falkner produced an exciting novel, but, as Brian Alderson puts it, 'The elegant prose, hospitable to accounts of drastic action and to pleasantries of dry humour, echoes with tolling leitmotifs . . . that are foreign to the racy optimism of the conventional adventure story.'[31]

One of the more contentious creations of children's literature, the 'Golliwogg' first appeared, as a sympathetic character, in *The Adventures of Two Dutch Dolls—and a Golliwogg* (1895), illustrated by Florence Upton (the text was by her mother Bertha). The doll became very popular, and there were five more 'Golliwogg' books up to 1909. The original Golliwogg doll lives, ironically enough, in a glass case at Chequers, but he seems unlikely to survive in a multiracial society.[32] He has, however, made some controversial appearances, as in Brandreth's *Here Comes Golly* (1979), while in 1949 Enid Blyton published a story, 'The Little Black Doll', in which the doll (Sambo, no less) is rewarded for a good deed when magic rain washes his blackness away. That this story was republished in 1976 seems to be a remarkable example of insensitivity.[33]

Another character who has run into the anti-racist sensibilities of the late twentieth century is the hero of Helen Bannerman's *The Story of Little Black Sambo* (1899), a book of world-wide fame, which has been variously reckoned to be innocent, charming, and mystical (it is the pivot of J. D. Salinger's story

'A Perfect Day for Bananafish'), or demeaning, colonial, and racist. It was only her later books—including such titles as *Little Black Mingo* (1901) and *Little Black Quasha* (1908)—that brought the author any money, for the copyright of *Little Black Sambo* had been bought by the publisher Grant Richards for £5 (three years before Arthur Ransome took his first job as an errand boy in that firm). Eric Quayle relates this unedifying story:

Despite the book's continuing success during the next thirty years, Grant Richards refused to pay the author a penny in royalties . . . Due to Grant Richards' claim that . . . he owned the copyright, Mrs Bannerman had lost control of the book's appearances in the United States. Her original sympathetic figures of the coloured family were vulgarised by American illustrators and Sambo was depicted as a capering coon or the idiot of some Nigger Minstrel postcards.[34]

(The practice of buying copyrights outright is discussed in Chapter 5, below.)

The example of *Little Black Sambo* raises the question of racism and other prejudices in books for children in general. As far as other writers (notably Shakespeare) are concerned, some of us may contemplate their deviant attitudes with equanimity, but it is assumed that children are more vulnerable and cannot compensate by contextualizing the book. This attitude has, as we shall see, affected the reputations of writers such as Hugh Lofting, and more recently that of the chronicler of 'Brer Rabbit', Joel Chandler Harris. Harris, a journalist, put together a world-famous book of slave stories, *Uncle Remus: His Songs and Sayings* (USA 1880, UK 1881), which may well have influenced Kipling, Potter (especially *The Tale of Mr Tod*), and Grahame.[35]

Some of their success may lie in the fact that, while they have the resonance of the folk-tales, the telling of them is more particular: we watch a story being told (as in another successful collection of the period, Arthur Ransome's *Old Peter's Russian Tales* (1916)). This may be so, but Moore and McCann have pointed out in an article called 'The Uncle Remus Travesty' that 'At best Uncle Remus is an ambivalent creation.' Their case is that the collection tends to downgrade the culture from which the stories sprang, that it carries a large freight of anti-black patronizing, and that it helped to destroy a story-telling tradition. And behind its success *for children* is a misapprehension by the uncritical adult world of what is suitable for children.[36]

Another outstanding American book of the period is L. Frank Baum's *The Wonderful Wizard of Oz* (1900), which, despite (or perhaps because of) its success, has until recently been ignored by the literary establishment. This may be because, as Perry Nodelman observed (*Oz* did not appear in the 'canon' established by the Children's Literature Association),

The astonishing world Baum describes has no overriding law or principle except variety . . . Baum is hardly the most interesting of stylists; indeed, his prose tends to be perfunctory, so much so that much of the special flavour of his work is the tension in it between the startling inventions and his ploddingly straightforward presentation of them . . . Baum rarely offers any messages at all.[37]

Baum wrote in his 'Introduction' that the book 'aspires to being a modernized fairy-tale, in which the wonderment and joy are retained and the heartaches and nightmares left out', and the book was a great success, with twelve sequels by Baum, and others by other writers; it was a part of American culture long before the 1939 MGM film. Modern literary and popular-culture scholars have found it a very suggestive text in terms of American culture and of the fairy-tale in a utilitarian world.

In many ways, the golden age was the age of women writers, both British and American. Wall suggests that the male and female narrative voices were basically different, the males addressing other males and, very frequently, a double/dual audience, whereas 'most women writers appear comfortable and confident in the familiar role of talking intimately to children, and seem to have experienced less need to turn from a child audience to address an adult audience within the course of a story'.[38]

In England the tradition of Charlotte Yonge and the moralists was continued by writers such as Mrs Ewing and Mrs Molesworth. Juliana Horatia Ewing is chiefly remembered for *The Brownies and Other Tales* (1870), which forty-eight years later inspired Baden-Powell to name the junior branch of the Girl Guide movement after it. She also influenced Nesbit and Kipling, and although some of her books, such as *Jackanapes* (1883), still linger on, the conventional Victorian materials and morals militate against her mature style.

Mary Louisa Molesworth has fared rather better. As Gillian Avery has noted, she 'provided a link between the mid-Victorian family story and the new style. She wrote understandingly of the nursery child; she could be sentimental if they were dreamy, sensitive little boys, but she could also correct their faults sharply (particularly if they were girls).'[39] *The Cuckoo Clock* (1877), for example, is still in print, and the Cuckoo is rather reminiscent of other adult figures in children's books of the period, from the Cheshire Cat and the Red Queen to the Psammead.

'You've a great deal to learn, Griselda,' repeated the cuckoo.

'I wish you wouldn't say that so often,' said Griselda. 'I thought you were going to *play* with me.'

'There's something in that,' said the cuckoo, 'there's something in that. I should like to talk about it. But we could talk more comfortably if you would come up here and sit beside me.' . . .

'Sit beside you up there!' [Griselda] exclaimed. 'Cuckoo, how *could* I? I'm far, far too big.'

'Big!' returned the cuckoo. 'What do you mean by big? It's all a matter of fancy. Don't you know that if the world and everything in it, counting yourself of course, was all made little enough to go into a walnut, you'd never find out the difference?'

'*Wouldn't* I?' said Griselda, feeling rather muddled; 'but, *not* counting myself, cuckoo, I would then, wouldn't I?'

'Nonsense,' said the cuckoo hastily. 'You've a great deal to learn, and one thing is, not to *argue*.'[40]

Mrs Molesworth also—to her critical detriment—contributed to what was known as the 'lisping tradition', that saw the young child as (to use a very expressive word) 'cute'. One of the earliest was John Habberton's *Helen's Babies* 'by their latest victim, Uncle Harry' (1876), and Lewis Carroll followed the fashion with Bruno's dialogue in *Sylvie and Bruno*. This somewhat precious view of the child survived well into the 1920s: A. A. Milne was an exponent of it in *Punch* (Ann Thwaite gives an example in *The Brilliant Career of Winnie-the-Pooh*).[41]

The American tradition combined pious domesticity with a strength of character and a freedom of movement which made the books at least as popular—if not more so—with envious British female readers as with their American counterparts. In some ways, Louisa May Alcott's *Little Women* (1868) was revolutionary in showing the clash between the wilful and energetic Jo and contemporary social standards. 'Alcott had created in the sisters flaws that no writer had previously dared to attribute to fictional characters for children (like selfishness, greed, temper, vanity, and shyness).'[42] In this book and its sequels, *Good Wives* (1869), *Little Men* (1871), and *Jo's Boys* (1886), Alcott explored, sometimes paradoxically, the role of women, but generally escapes the tearfulness endemic in the genre.

The books were much sighed over at the time, but far from forgotten now is Susan Coolidge's *What Katy Did* (1872), despite its conventional plot. As Brenda Niall observed, sardonically enough, 'Spinal injuries must rank a close second to consumption as one of the hazards of nineteenth-century fictional life.'[43] While *Pollyanna* is probably the most cohesive of these books, for slightly older readers the more wordy Kate Douglas Wiggin's *Rebecca of Sunnybrook Farm* (1903) is still readable, and the Canadian L. M. Montgomery's *Anne of Green Gables* (1908) and its many sequels remain popular. The American writers also introduced robust outdoor elements: Gene Stratton-Porter's *Freckles* (1904) and *A Girl of the Limberlost* (1909) are books which contain in equal measure idealism, sentimentality, and the joys of the outdoor life.

These books were paralleled, perhaps not surprisingly, in Australia, most notably with Ethel Turner's *Seven Little Australians* (1894), which, in a singularly unsettling ending, the narrator is obliged to stop writing because she feels so upset at the heroic death of Judy, crushed by a tree. As Brenda Niall has noted, '*Seven Little Australians* looks back to *Little Women*, and improves on it by more realistically observed children and comparatively little moralising.'[44] Norah Linton, in Mary Grant Bruce's 'Billabong' series (1910–42), is even more unfettered.

We can hardly overlook the beginnings of the school story for girls (leaving aside Sarah Fielding), with writers such as Evelyn Everett-Green and L. T. Meade. L. T. Meade's 300 books explored many genres, but 'it was in school stories for girls that she found the story patterns and setting which best suited her emotional romanticism'.[45] Angela Brazil, one of the most influential of writers for girls in the inter-war years, began her long series of school books with *The Fortunes of Philippa* in 1906, and continued to publish through the First World War.

There is, therefore, a rich group of writers who demonstrate a gradual change in attitude to childhood and children's books, and two who mark this change clearly are George Macdonald and Charles Kingsley. Macdonald, who influenced Mrs Molesworth, Burnett, Tolkien, Lewis, and Sendak with his allegorical tales, notably *The Princess and the Goblin* (1872) and *The Princess and Curdie* (1877), was one of the few successful originators of fairy stories. Jack Zipes links him with Wilde and Baum as a subversive innovator.[46] Certainly the books are powerfully symbolic, and have serious things to say about eschatology, mysticism, growth, and, as Macdonald wrote, children 'find what they are capable of finding, and more would be too much'.[47] His Puritanism was diffused through the fairy-tale mode, and through his sense of humour. He was for a time the editor of *Good Words for the Young*; his witty tale 'The Light Princess' (the manuscript of which he showed to his friend Charles Dodgson) could almost have come from the pen of Thackeray.[48] The only other work that has lingered is a grossly sentimental, adult-voiced, perfect-child, curious mixture of social realism and a theology convoluted with sexuality—*At the Back of the North Wind* (book form, 1871). It is difficult to say why it has survived so late into the twentieth century, as it is difficult to imagine to whom it could appeal—if it is not a severe case of publishing inertia.

Humphrey Carpenter has pointed out that the major figures of this period had more in common than 'warped private lives'. Carroll, Kingsley, and Macdonald all began to write for children 'within weeks of each other. Moreover, all three were ministers of religion—if all of very different types—and all three had intense scientific or mathematical interests. A pattern begins to emerge.'[49]

There are certainly common themes—including growth, security, initiation, and challenge to the world, to the world of the child as dictated, and to the world of the children's book. If Macdonald is largely forgotten, a pivotal book is now known as much by reputation or in abridgement as in fact—Charles Kingsley's *The Water Babies: A Fairy Tale for a Land Baby* (1863). This is, by way of a major understatement, an eccentric, unstable text: it contains a strong story, a powerful myth—and it is by turns rambling, erotic, politically and socially astringent, and very high-spirited. Its instability has been neatly summed up by Barbara Wall: 'My own view is that while it succeeds brilliantly in patches on the level of story, and works successfully in symbol on the level of archetype, it is essentially an unshapely and distorted hybrid.'[50]

The Water Babies is a mixture of social comment, redemption theology, satire, Darwinism, and a certain anarchy. As with Carroll, it is possible (should one wish to) to trace Kingsley's phobias and sexuality in the text, but more interesting is the way in which it takes in a huge range of children's book genres. It is certainly appealing archetypally, perhaps in the way that *Black Beauty* or *A Little Princess* are: for all its coyness and sentimentality, Tom's picaresque journey through the world of the water-babies resonates. For the adult, one of the fascinations is that, as Carpenter noted, the narrator 'is really the principal character in the book';[51] for the storyteller, how Kingsley maintains interest through a very ramshackle structure. The ending is characteristic:

And now, my dear little man, what should we learn from this parable?

We should learn thirty-seven or thirty-nine things, I am not exactly sure which . . . Meanwhile, do you learn your lessons, and thank God that you have plenty of cold water to wash in; and wash in it too, like a true English man. And then, if my story is not true, something better is; and if I am not quite right, still you will be, as long as you stick to hard work and cold water.

But remember always, as I told you at first, that this is all a fairy tale, and only fun and pretence; and, therefore, you are not to believe a word of it, even if it is true.

Kingsley's literary and personal progress is undoubtedly interesting for scholars and psychologists—and as far as children's literature is concerned, there is some interest in an early example of the links between an author's mental state and his decision to write 'for children'. Of Kingsley's other works, only *The Heroes* (1856), written in reaction to Nathaniel Hawthorne's *A Wonder Book* (1852), still lurks on the edges of accessible children's literature; his adult novels, *Westward Ho!* (1855) and *Hereward the Wake* (1865), have joined books like Conan Doyle's *The White Company* (1891) or Rider Haggard's *King Solomon's Mines* (1885) in the no man's land of books that were read by adolescents of the last generation, and are now rapidly becoming at one extreme scholarly curiosities, and at the other the stuff of which action movies are made.

It is almost as if, with Macdonald and Kingsley, the limits and uses of the children's book were being explored: as Darton observed, 'It is possible to comprehend why . . . there is in *The Water-Babies* a heavy vein of morality and conventional condescension, as well as plenty of imagination; and yet also why it did not seem outrageous when Lewis Carroll did without open morality altogether.'[52]

4. The 'Landmark' Authors

In some ways it might seem superfluous to write more about Charles Dodgson, Lewis Carroll, and Alice. The 'Alice' books have been the subject of a huge amount of critical exegesis, a disproportionate amount of biographical interest (there have been, for example, two biographies of Alice Liddell), and more than one fictional account (such as Donald Thomas's *Belladonna: A Lewis Carroll Nightmare* (1986)). In terms of the history of children's literature *Alice's Adventures in Wonderland* marked, as Darton said, 'the first unapologetic . . . appearance in print, for readers who sorely needed it, of liberty of thought in children's books'.[53]

But this needs some qualification. Such liberty was far from unprecedented, and it is a subversive liberty of thought. Carroll allied himself with childhood in the sense that the pragmatic and generally stoic Alice moves through a world of mad adults, all with their own irrational logics; she is generally more puzzled than anything else, although occasionally patronizing. Carroll also caught the confusion of growing up, changing size and identity, and coming to terms with self and death and sexuality. All of which means, perhaps (and surveys of readers tend to bear this out), that this book is so successfully of the child's world that children themselves find it of limited interest: it is too true.

Margery Fisher has pointed out that if Carroll 'served children by discarding moral and didactic fetters, his humour was of an exceptionally double-edged kind . . . Ultimately, these are the coruscations of a perplexed and complex mind displaying itself to the young.'[54]

Thus *Alice* and *Through the Looking Glass* are supremely single-focus books; the layers of meaning that Carroll built in are inward-looking. *Alice* has, of course, the characteristic of being written in the first instance for a specific child. (There is, however, a good deal of myth attached to this. It is somehow comforting to find that the day when Dodgson, Canon Duckworth, and the three Liddell sisters took their famous boat trip on the Thames (4 July 1862) was not actually 'a golden afternoon', but a rainy one.[55]) It shares this with a substantial number of other classic books—by Grahame, Ransome, Potter, Stevenson, Tolkien—which has led to a another comfortable myth that books with such a genesis are somehow superior. They are certainly very personal books, and their status says a lot for the way in which children's books are thought about: Carroll's own involvement with pre-pubescent girls, his unusual personality, and his intellectual preoccupations have produced a cult that is at once protective and deeply analytic.

The books were immensely popular, and, after a slow start, had sold over 180,000 copies by Carroll's death in 1898. They have become cultural artefacts, and the extent to which their meanings lie, as it were, below ground is demonstrated by the Disney film, which with only the surface farce available to it is generally considered to be an inferior piece of work. Fundamental to this book, and to children's literature in general, is how far Carroll was writing nonsense at all; how far the books are a repository of profound logic and lateral thinking that is accessible to the child.

The books are unquestionably fruitful for critics. They comment upon Victorian mores and attitudes—Alice is a child in 'luxurious captivity'; they can be said, plausibly enough, to touch on drugs and various states of consciousness; they are heavy with religious symbolism, and Freudians have a lot to work on. They confront semanticist and literary critics (Humpty Dumpty) and the place of humans in life (the chess game); death jokes abound, and, as Martin Gardner has pointed out in *The Annotated Alice*, a good many mathematical ones too. Carroll's prose can be farcical or lyrical, but always demands attention. The White Knight, who escorts Alice to the point at which she will become a Queen, but who constantly falls off his horse in front of her, spends a page of ironic semantics defining the song he is going to sing. Then he pauses in a moment which can easily be seen as poignant in its personal symbolism:

So saying, he stopped his horse and let the reins fall on its neck: then, slowly beating time with one hand, and with a faint smile lighting up his gentle foolish face, as if he enjoyed the music of his song, he began.

Of all the strange things that Alice saw in her journey Through the Looking Glass, this was one that she always remembered most clearly ... she leant against a tree, watching the strange pair, and listening, in a half-dream, to the melancholy music of the song.

'But the tune *isn't* his own invention,' she said to herself; 'it's "I give thee all, I can no more."' She stood and listened very attentively, but no tears came to her eyes.[56]

The books contain some elemental children's book materials, but often subvert them. Just as food can be seen as an important feature of children's books—a substitute, quite possibly, for sex—so the kitchen, as in adult literature, is frequently a stable centre. We will come to Kenneth Grahame's child/adult apotheosis of the kitchen shortly: in *Alice*, the kitchen is a place of violence and revolution and ambiguity. If it were not for Alice's steady gaze and preoccupation with the mysteries of social niceties it might be a nightmare:

The door led right into a large kitchen, which was full of smoke from one end to the other ... [T]he cook took the caldron of soup off the fire, and at once set to work throwing everything within her reach at the Duchess and the baby—the fire irons came first; then followed a shower of saucepans, plates, and dishes.[57]

One of the most striking elements for the late nineteenth-century child might well have been the irreverence with which Carroll demolished the pious poems and songs of the past. Isaac Watts's 'Against Idleness and Mischief' ('How doth the little busy bee'), becomes 'How doth the little crocodile'; and Jane Taylor's 'Twinkle twinkle little star' will never be the same again as 'Twinkle twinkle, little bat', nor will Southey's 'The Old Man's Comforts and How he Gained them' as 'You are old, Father William'. For adults, Carroll parodied the sentimental 'Star of the Evening' and William Mee's 'Alice Gray' ('She's all my fancy painted her ... '). My own favourite is the rather savage mauling that Carroll gives Wordsworth's 'Resolution and Independence'—the parody, however, because of its ingenuity, being quite able to stand on its own.

The secrecy of the books, the endless unravelling, makes them characteristic of the therapeutic, sublimating tendency that can be traced in many children's books, and a good deal of time has been spent in psychoanalysing Carroll, or reflecting upon what children might derive from the hidden agenda. Edmund Wilson's assessment is characteristic:

It is surely the psychological truth of the books that lays its hold on us all. Lewis Carroll is in touch with the real mind of childhood and hence with the more primitive elements of the mind of maturity too—unlike certain other writers who merely exploit for grown-ups an artificial child-mind of convention which is in reality neither childlike nor adult. The shifting and the transformations . . . the mysteries and the riddles, the gibberish that conveys unmistakable meanings, are all based upon relationships that contradict the assumptions of our conscious lives but that are lurking not far behind them.[58]

In the two 'Alice' books, although dreams have several functions—from rather weakly framing the books to raising disturbing possibilities—they probably stay on this side of nightmare; but I doubt whether this is true of Carroll's surrealist poem *The Hunting of the Snark: An Agony, in Eight Fits* (1876). The *Snark* has a dark dual focus, in which the child might perceive nonsense, and the adult a fear of nonsense and nothingness; even the drawings by Henry Holiday (Tenniel had refused to do another book with Dodgson) have a more sinister grotesquerie. Carroll wrote of the *Snark*, in a letter that should be borne in mind by critics in general, 'I'm very much afraid I didn't mean anything but nonsense! Still, you know, words mean much more than we mean to express when we use them; so a whole book ought to mean a great deal more than the writer meant.'[59]

Carroll's other large work, *Sylvie and Bruno*, although available in collected editions of Carroll, shows him losing his empathy with the child, and moving rapidly towards overt self-interest and an accompanying cloying Victorian sentimentality. His narrative stance also becomes very questionable, ranging from Bruno's 'lisping child' ('Oo don't want a *face* to tell fibs wiz—only a *mouf*'[60]) to the sort of self-revelation that we shall also see in Richard Jefferies. Sylvie sings, and the narrator comments, in a tone very like that adopted by Jefferies:

On me the first effect of her voice was a sudden sharp pang that seemed to pierce through one's very heart. (I had felt such a pang only once before in my life, and it had been from *seeing* what, at the moment, realized one's idea of perfect beauty—it was in a London exhibition, where, in making my way through a crowd, I suddenly met face to face, a child of quite unearthly beauty).[61]

Carroll, then, may have been overestimated in terms of historical importance, for it is not until Potter that we find a similar potential for child-sized ironies, or until Nesbit that there is a similarly full-blooded approach to fantasy.

If Lewis Carroll, by a quirk, wrote about displacement and produced a psychological fantasy that addressed the position of the Victorian child, and moved children's literature on, Robert Louis Stevenson did the same for another genre. *Treasure Island*, 'the very apotheosis of the "penny dreadful" ',[62] for all the spontaneity of its composition, brought moral ambiguity into children's literature. It is a genuine landmark; it draws together traditions from the eighteenth and nineteenth centuries and upsets them. As a 'superpotboiler' it was, as Stevenson later admitted, composed of other matters:

No doubt the parrot once belonged to Robinson Crusoe. No doubt the skeleton is conveyed from Poe. I think little of these, they are trifles and details; and no man can have a monopoly of skeletons or make a corner in talking birds. The stockade, I am told, is from *Masterman Ready*. It may be, I care not a jot . . . It is my debt to Washington Irving that exercises my conscience, and justly so, for I believe that plagiarism was rarely carried farther. I chanced to pick up the *Tales of a Traveller* some years ago . . . and the book flew up and struck me; Billy Bones, his chest, the company in the parlour, the whole inner spirit, and a good deal of the material detail of my first chapters—all were there, all were the property of Washington Irving.[63]

And so *Treasure Island* is renowned, or notorious, for its ambiguities—such as the fact that John Silver, the treacherous, cold-blooded murderer, has acquired mythic force[64] (to the extent that he is the hero of Robert Leeson's ingenious and witty parody, *Silver's Revenge* (1979)); while of the other characters, only Captain Smollett (whose name can scarcely be an accident) is in any way admirable. A modern publisher, Julia MacRae, has fastened upon just this point in her dislike of the book, and also that 'much of the revulsion engendered by Stevenson's villains is triggered by his description of physical disability'.[65] But this is just another of the penny-dreadful conventions, as with the villains, the class distinction, and the mythic West Country, and it has the skill of the penny dreadful in creating nightmare moments. Above all this, there is the central ambiguity. Take a simple example, one of the earliest, when Jim's mother is intent upon getting her just money out of the 'dead man's chest':

When we were about half way through, I suddenly put my hand upon her arm; for I had heard in the silent, frosty air, a sound that brought my heart into my mouth—the tap-tapping of the blind man's stick upon the frozen road. It drew nearer and nearer, while we sat holding our breath. Then it struck sharp on the inn door, and then we could hear the handle being turned and the bolt rattling as the wretched being tried to enter. (chapter IV)

Treasure Island also has that other very common feature of the children's book, a local habitation pinned down by the map (which his publishers lost, and which Stevenson had to redraw from the book—rather than the other way around).

Other Stevensons survive. The least of them—although the most popular in its day, as an efficient piece of serial-writing—is what Ransome called (in comparison to *Treasure Island*) a 'poor, machine-made thing',[66] *The Black Arrow* (serialized 1883, published 1888). This novel owes a debt to Marryat, and looks forward to Geoffrey Trease and his kinsmen of the 1930s and onwards, and, whatever its faults as a piece of 'tushery', it has a splendid opening. *Kidnapped* (1886) is perhaps the epitome of the chase novel, again with elements of moral ambiguity, while both it and its sequel, *Catriona* (1893), are fascinating as examples of the use of landscape.

Stevenson's literary status has always been ambiguous, almost certainly because the adventure novel has been regarded as inferior to the 'novel of character'—as Stevenson was well aware: 'Danger is the matter with which this class of novel deals; fear, the passion with which it idly trifles; and the characters are portrayed only so far as they realize the sense of danger and provoke the sympathy of fear.'[67]

A similar ambiguity was found in a contemporary American writer, Mark Twain. In the USA, Thomas Aldrich's *The Story of a Bad Boy* (1869) is sometimes credited with breaking the mould of the Sunday School texts, and Twain followed this lead for *The Adventures of Tom Sawyer* (1876). He had previously written 'The Story of the Bad Little Boy' (1865) and 'The Story of the Good Little Boy' (1870), both anti-Sunday School travesties of real boyhood. *Tom Sawyer*, however, hovers between the two types; originally Twain claimed to be writing for adults, but was persuaded by his wife and his friend William Dean Howells to issue it as a 'juvenile', although, as he wrote in 1871, 'I have no love for children's literature.' He observed in his notebook for 1902: 'I have never written a book for boys; I write for grown-ups who have *been* boys. If the boys read it and like it, perhaps that is testimony that my boys are real, not artificial. If they are real to the grown-ups, that is proof.'[68]

If the narrative stance is very uncertain, sometimes looking down on or back at the characters, it does contain idyllic elements, such as when Tom camps out on Jackson's island. But, like its quasi-sequel, *The Adventures of Huckleberry Finn* (1884), *Tom Sawyer* has a lot to do with adult concerns and affairs; the fictionalized Hannibal is not an innocent place, and Twain was ambivalent about his boyhood. Michael Hearn regards it as 'a subversive and cynical book, perhaps the first in American literature to consider the eternal battle between the generations'.[69] Those critics who bemoan the decline of the adult as an admirable character in contemporary literature might reflect that there is no-one in 'St. Petersburg' who has any respect from the author. As in *Treasure Island* all the adult characters—and the central boy character—are deeply flawed.

Twain's later works 'for children' have had an intermittent life. *The Prince and the Pauper* (1882) is a journeyman fantasy with a republican edge—and again with little time for hypocrisy or parents. Equally, it seems to me that we need not pause over *The Adventures of Huckleberry Finn* (1885) or *A Connecticut Yankee in King Arthur's Court* (1889), both of which have often been marketed for children. (In this respect, Twain bears some resemblance to Kipling, which says a great deal about the insensitivity of publishers—and later critics.) Both these books are savage satires, the one on American society, the other on romanticism; both have curious endings: *Huck* reverts, very disturbingly, to the children's book mode (although it has been suggested that this is simply a case of the American love of complex play); the *Yankee* ends with a massacre, with the hero surrounded by rotting corpses (which were not conspicuous in the Bing Crosby film version).

If Stevenson represents the summing up of the sea story and nineteenth-century adventure story, and looks forward to a new depth in children's books, the country writer Richard Jefferies also looks back to the empire-builders, but looks forward to a totally new type of children's book. Richard Jefferies wrote one novel that was probably intended for children, *Wood Magic* (1881), a very turgid, uneven, and depressive performance, largely a beast fable, not much admired even among Jefferies's devotees. *Bevis, the Story of a Boy* (1882) is, on the other hand, a classic case of a book about childhood that has been adopted by childhood, and, as Carpenter notes, the first two or three chapters contain 'the best pieces of description of a child's imaginative life ever printed'.[70]

Jefferies's great strength was his knowledge of nature and practical gamekeeping and poaching (his best book is probably *The Gamekeeper at Home* (1878)), rather than his story-telling. But in this idealized picture of boyhood, with its complex battle between gangs of boys, its swimming and sailing, he is able to portray, quite probably for the first time, naturalistic children living, plausibly, just outside the control of adults. He showed not only freedom, but the amorality and self-centredness of childhood and the amorality of the nature-lover, with its paradoxical killer instincts. But he also linked the boys to both the classical and the popular literary tradition. Although his boys are wild, and live for two weeks on an island without any 'discipline', they nevertheless apotheo-size the Henty 'manly boy' tradition. This is mixed with an intense practicality which confers realism (in the manner of Defoe) by the sheer weight of detail, and also with a feel for the mysticism of childhood. (Jefferies was one of the few English mystics; he wrote a notable contribution to nature mysticism in *The Story of my Heart* (1883)).

In his narrative Jefferies is very often unconscious of any distance between himself as narrator and the reader; and he stands between the two very different adventure traditions of Henty and Ransome, one outward-looking, one inward-look-ing, and both bound by different concepts of freedom.

In this period, as we have seen, there was a shift in the way in which children were addressed, and among those who made this change most effectively was the ascerbic and individual Beatrix Potter—another writer who has assumed the status of a national institution. Her contribution to the language of children's literature is that of irony pitched at a level that the youngest can understand—for example, Peter Rabbit's fears at the beginning of *Benjamin Bunny* or Jemima's failure to recognize the true nature of the 'furry, whiskered gentleman' in *Jemima Puddle-Duck*. Potter combined this with a straight-forwardness and lack of sentimentality which maintained the basic single-focus contract.

This effect was achieved by a single-minded strength of character. When her publisher, Warne, suggested changing the opening paragraph of *The Tale of Mr Tod* (1912), she wrote:

I cannot think what you are driving at . . . If it were not impertinent to lecture one's publishers—you are a great deal too much afraid of the public for whom I have never cared one tuppenny button. I am *sure* that it is that attitude of mind which has enabled me to keep up the series. Most people, after one success, are so cringingly afraid of doing less well that they rub all the edge off their subsequent work.[71]

As a result, she gave her readers credit for being able to cope unsentimentally with subjects like death (there is a death joke on the second text page of her first book, *The Tale of Peter*

Rabbit); she showed her quasi-children as rebellious and naughty, and does not avoid loneliness or fear. Even a cursory look at her books demonstrates the subtlety of her dry humour, and the carefully constructed prose that reads easily aloud. As she said:

My usual way of writing is to scribble, and cut out, and write it again and again. The shorter and plainer the better. And read the Bible (*unrevised* version and Old Testament) if I feel my style needs chastening . . . I think the great point in writing for children is to have something to say and to say it in simple direct language.[72]

The world she describes and paints may be child- and animal-sized, but the codes of behaviour (as in, for example, *The Pie and the Patty-Pan*) are those of an adult world. This means that she can move between a comment on the adults' concern with polite appearances, to subtle shifts from clothed to unclothed (*Tom Kitten*), all with clear meanings for the child. As Anne Stevenson Hobbes noted,

The stories range from straightforward linear tales to more complicated minor epics—from domestic comedies to romances or more sinister dramas. The drama is increased by a matter-of-fact shrewdness—even toughness—and by a great economy in words . . . She took children seriously, believing that they deserved books written in simple, direct language. For the first time in literature for small children the words are as important as the illustrations.[73]

Potter has been well served biographically and bibliographically but perhaps not so well critically, and her case is instructive. There has been a good deal of debate as to how her work should best be marketed, for she is seen as part of the national heritage. The emergence of her books from copyright in 1993 was preceded by a thorough campaign on the part of her publishers (now Penguin) to pre-empt any unscrupulous exploitation—which has been seen in some quarters as exploitation in itself. However, Potter herself worked on 'spin-offs' virtually from the beginning, designing wallpaper, a board-game, a doll, and several painting-books. The arguments for and against the reissue of *Peter Rabbit* and *Squirrel Nutkin* in Ladybird Books in 1987, illustrated with photographs of stuffed toys and with a new text, polarized opinions sociologically—between the literary haves and have-nots.[74]

And it is in dealing with Potter (and, as we shall see, with the 'Pooh' books) that critics have had problems of scale. Surely the great weight of theory and exegesis has no place when confronting such delicate materials (and, anyway, such common property surely does not need explication)? One of the earliest attempts was by Graham Greene, and no one seems to be quite sure, to this day, whether he was tongue-in-cheek or not. His article on Potter, published in 1933, observes that in her 'selective realism' she 'takes emotion for granted and puts aside love and death with a gentle detachment reminiscent of Mr E. M. Forster', describes her work in terms of 'her great comedies' and 'great near-tragedies' and compares Peter and Benjamin with other great literary double-acts such as Cervantes's Quixote and Sancho or Rabelais's Pantagruel and Panurge. Sceptics will be delighted to know that Greene admitted, in a footnote: 'On the publication of this essay I received a somewhat acid letter from Miss Potter correcting certain details... In conclusion she deprecated sharply "the Freudian school" of criticism.'[75]

The influence of Potter is difficult to establish; overtly, it can be seen in the far more word-bound work of Alison Uttley and Joyce Lankester Brisley's 'Milly-Molly-Mandy' stories, and in several modern commercial enterprises; more subtly, it has probably been very far-reaching.

Peter Rabbit was published in 1902, the same year as J. M. Barrie's *The Little White Bird*, an adult 'novel' that contained the seeds of another national institution, *Peter Pan*. This thoroughly unstable text is one of the rare examples of memorable theatre for children. Originally tapping that vein of preciousness much eschewed by the Bastables, the chapters from *The Little White Bird* were marketed for children as *Peter Pan in Kensington Gardens* in 1906. More significantly, *Peter Pan*, as a play, was produced in London in 1904 in the heyday of Edwardian theatrical trickwork, and some of its most famous characteristics—for example, the character of Smee—were actually developed by actors. (Like another long-running piece for children, *Toad of Toad Hall*, *Peter Pan* had very faithful players.) Other versions appeared before Barrie published a prose version, *Peter and Wendy*, in 1911. As Jacqueline Rose puts it:

J. M. Barrie's *Peter Pan* was retold before he had written it and then rewritten after he had told it. By 1911, *Peter Pan* had already become such a universally acclaimed cultural phenomenon that Barrie himself could only intervene back into its history from the outside . . . *Peter Pan* could *only* go on without him, because it had come to signify an innocence, or simplicity, which every line of Barrie's 1911 text belies.[76]

There is a lot to be said for Rose's view that 'Peter Pan' is the place where a very complex collision of the languages of and attitudes to narrative for children occurs. *Peter and Wendy* is highly ambiguous; an extraordinary mixture of comedy and nastiness, sentimentality and sexuality. And yet the continual changing of the ending of the story (begun by Barrie) has continued with each generation, and this gives the play the status of a folk-tale—it is everyone's property, and the central character is archetypal. But the problem for many readers is that Peter is essentially negative and selfish—and Barrie's own attitude suggests that this is fundamental to childhood. *Peter and Wendy* ends with the suggestion that there is an endless cycle as Peter takes Wendy's daughter's daughter to the Never Land: 'And thus it will go on, so long as children are gay and innocent and heartless.'[77]

Hollindale's comment is perhaps the most charitable:

Barrie is very much a twentieth-century writer for children. He anticipates developments in children's literature which have since achieved more sophisticated, and perhaps more appropriate, forms. At times in the *Peter Pan* stories his narrative commuting between child and adult appears to involve an act of trespass . . . into an emotional terrain which ought to be untouched.[78]

And it might well be that the most definitive version is that by Walt Disney—and even that has been modified since its first release (to cut out the audience participation when Tinkerbell is injured).

These two writers were landmarks in their way, for Potter is a good example of a writer who addresses her audience singly, and designs books for them, looking forwards; whereas Barrie's narrative voice does not seem to relate very closely to any child, and his work therefore looks backwards.

Beatrix Potter has a unique place in literature, but the most influential writer of this period in the long term was the 'advanced woman' and Fabian Edith Nesbit. Julia Briggs sums her up succinctly: 'E. Nesbit is the first modern writer for children. She invented the children's adventure story more or less single-handed, and then added further magic ingredients such as wishing rings and time travel. Her books established a style and approach still widely used today.'[79] And Marcus Crouch, who in 1972 could write a book called *The Nesbit Tradition* dealing with children's books after 1945, observed that she

stands squarely in the doorway between the nineteenth and twentieth centuries. She owed much to the Victorians ... In her hands the Victorian conscience lost its self-consciousness; their insight became sharper and more richly aware of the incongruities which make for humour; above all she threw away their strong, sober, essentially literary style and replaced it with the miraculously colloquial, flexible, and revealing prose that was her unique contribution to the children's novel.[80]

The development of the family story is associated with the change in the status of the child in the family. As the infant mortality rate dropped, so the family became (relatively) smaller and children the more valued; the idea of the (suburban) house and garden as symbols of stability grew. Ironically, perhaps, this unwittingly narrowed the social compass of children's books for the next fifty years.

Perhaps because she was an unapologetic professional, Nesbit has been undervalued by adult critics, for, as we have seen, writers who have chosen a single focus tend to be downgraded by adult commentators. She is part of the complex web of inter-influences at this period, following Kipling in according respect to the child audience, and adapting Grahame's stance of the amused 'Olympian' that he adopted in *The Golden Age*. Nesbit took the idea of the family and the amusing children leading their own secret lives, and later grafted on the idea of magic.

Her most memorable books, which remain alive with little assistance, are *The Treasure Seekers* (1899), *The Wouldbegoods* (1901), and, a lesser performance, *The New Treasure Seekers* (1904). These are all family stories, focusing on the children, and using the first-person voice of Oswald Bastable. The use of Oswald allows Nesbit to produce a voice designed directly for children. As she said: 'There is . . . a freemasonry between children . . . Between the child and the grown-up there is a great gulf fixed—and this gulf, the gulf between one generation and another, can never really be bridged.'[81]

With Oswald Bastable she adopted a mild, child-sized irony. For example, when they are chastised by their father at the outset of *The Wouldbegoods*, the narrator observes:

we felt it deeply in our interior hearts, especially Oswald, who is the eldest and representative of the family . . . But I must not anticipate (that means telling the end of a story before the beginning. I tell you this because it is so sickening to have words you don't know in a story, and to be told to look it up in the dicker).

We are the Bastables . . . If you want to know why we call our youngest brother H.O. you can jolly well read *The Treasure Seekers* and find out.[82]

Her later books are often rather self-indulgent hack-work, and yet, in *The Railway Children* (1905–6), with the strong mother supporting her family by writing in the absence of the father, she produced a classic (sustained, perhaps, by Lionel Jeffries's 1970 film version). Unlike Grahame, who shied away linguistically from confrontation with the lower orders, *The Railway Children* treats the poor but proud porter and the overworked signalman without condescension. And, of course, there is the sentimental climax, perhaps the apotheosis of the Victorian mode:

Only three people got out of the 11.54. The first was a countryman with two baskety boxes full of live chickens who stuck their russet heads out anxiously through the wicker bars; the second was Miss Peckitt, the grocer's wife's cousin, with a tin box and three brown-paper parcels; and the third—

'Oh! my Daddy, my Daddy!' That scream went like a knife into the
heart of everyone in the train, and people put their heads out of the
windows to see a tall pale man with lips set in a thin close line and a
little girl clinging to him with arms and legs, while his arms went
tightly round her.[83]

The strong family relationships are stressed in the books
where magic is involved, the best of which are, arguably, *Five
Children and It* (1902), *The Phoenix and the Carpet* (1904), and
The House of Arden (1908). The irascible magic figures in
these books, the Psammead and the Phoenix and the Mouldi-
warp, are all much the same character, and if Nesbit over-
works the idea of a literal-minded magic, then there are
compensations in her mode of address. Take the end of *The
Railway Children*, where her technique is very modern and
cinematic: on the last pages she changes into the present tense,
pulling back, as it were, from the narrative.

And now I see them crossing the field . . . I see Father walking in the
garden . . . He goes in and the door is shut. I think we will not open
the door or follow him. I think that just now we are not wanted
there. I think it will be best for us to go quickly and quietly away. At
the end of the field, among the thin gold spikes of grass and the
harebells and Gipsy roses and St. John's Wort, we may just take one
last look, over our shoulders, at the white house where neither we nor
anyone else is wanted now.[84]

Far more firmly rooted in the Victorian tear-jerker tradition
is one of the earliest transatlantic writers, Frances Hodgson
Burnett. A new generation might take to the internationalism
of *Little Lord Fauntleroy* (1886), which still reads well as a
fairy-tale, and Cedric Erroll is far from being as nauseating as
his popular image suggests. In book form it was one of the
best-sellers of 1886 (along with *King Solomon's Mines* and
War and Peace)—for adults.[85] It is not a story overtly addressed to children, but has a basic fairy-tale element of youth
overcoming age, as well as rags-to-riches—fulfilling both child
and adult fantasies. The fashion that the book provoked
(Milne and Compton Mackenzie were among its victims, as
well as the illustrator Reginald Birch) of boys dressed in velvet

suits and wearing ringlets is one of the more sobering sociological sidelights of children's literature. Burnett was a con-
sciously commercial writer, and made deliberate play of the
openness and directness of the New World in the characters
of Dick the bootblack and Mr Hobbs the grocer. She was also
(and we have seen a similar talent in *Pollyanna*) a great writer
of confrontation scenes.

But Mrs Burnett, like Nesbit, a hack writer perforce, surrounded by weak men, brings two traditions together, the
American tradition of domestic drama (as in *Little Women*
and *What Katy Did*) and the fairy-tale. Her most blatant
performance is undoubtedly *A Little Princess* (1905) (expanded from the rather less sentimental and over-the-top *Sara
Crewe* (1887)). This plays on basic childhood fantasies: that
parents should be lost (and found); that there will be lonely
times; but that despite evil influences (in this case the
wretched Miss Minchin) the poor heroine will overcome. *Sara
Crewe* was restrained in comparison with its successor, where
scenes such as Sara giving her buns to the starving child are
played, as it were, with full Dickensian orchestra.

Even more successful, for less obvious reasons, has been
The Secret Garden (1911). This too has a basic Cinderella plot,
but this time the achievement is maturity and internal rather
than external riches, with the very satisfying twist that the
heroine, Mary Lennox, is admitted to be unattractive at the
outset: 'When Mary Lennox was sent to Misselthwaite Manor
to live with her uncle everybody said she was the most
disagreeable-looking child ever seen.' It is clear that the major
influences are that essentially adolescent novel *Jane Eyre*,
George Macdonald, and the Gothic side of the Romantics.
The Secret Garden, an expatriate's book, presages the Hollywood version of the north of England: all character actors and
plastic stone walls.

It has perennial themes of sickness, health, and—paralleled
by the garden—regeneration, as the children grow out of
repression of various kinds. It has romantic anti-class attitudes, a series of melodramatic mysteries including the sealed
garden, empty rooms, noises in the night (a mad boy in the

attic), and a romantic hero (a junior version of Heathcliff in Dickon). Like *A Little Princess*, it has serial plotting, and the children are in control and central: the lower-class adults turn to Mary, and she dominates Colin; Dickon is seen as a kind of nature-god.

The book has its weaknesses, in that the authorial voice is inclined to enter and to hector—as when the symbols are explained in chapter XXVII—and there remains a debate whether it is female-repressive or affirming: there is a definite shift of narrative tone in the last three chapters, and Mary is certainly ousted at the end, but is that because she has done her work or is it a concession to male dominance?[86] To many readers, Burnett represents the quintessence of this period: slightly overblown, enthusiastic, sentimental, and having a fundamental belief in fairies.

Such calmness beneath the storms can hardly be said to subsist in perhaps the most famous—and most questionable—of the classics of this period, Kenneth Grahame's *The Wind in the Willows*. Kenneth Grahame was in many ways a displaced person: he had a tragic childhood, he was deprived of his great ambition—an Oxford education—and he worked, with a certain reluctance, in the Bank of England. He spent his weekends with 'muscular Christians' in hearty male expeditions in the Thames Valley, and moved in literary society (ingenuously described in Arthur Ransome's *Bohemia in London*) imbued with fashionable pagan-mysticism. He became, like Robert Louis Stevenson, 'one of W. E. Henley's young men',[87] and began his short but very successful writing career with *Pagan Papers* (1893). He also wrote a number of pieces *about* childhood, collected as *The Golden Age* (1895)—which Swinburne described as 'well-nigh too praiseworthy for praise'[88]—and *Dream Days* (1898), books which have the curious distinction of being landmarks in children's literature while being clearly books for adults. We should not be misled by 'the recent reissuing of these two books ... [which] attests perhaps more to a market of children's literature scholars than to a wider audience'.[89] These were part of the fashionable sentimentalization of childhood, and are very funny—from an adult point of view. For example, in *The Golden Age*, a visiting uncle, in retreat (' "Well, thank God, that's over" '), gives the children a half-crown each as he leaves:

A solemn hush fell on the assembly, broken first by small Charlotte. 'I did n't [*sic*] know,' she observed dreamily, 'that there were such good men anywhere in the world. I hope he'll die to-night, for then he'll go straight to heaven!' But the repentant Selina bewailed herself with tears and sobs, refusing to be comforted; for that in her haste she had called this white-souled relative a beast.

'I'll tell you what we'll do,' said Edward . . . 'We'll christen the piebald pig after him . . .'

And the motion being agreed to without division, the House went into Committee of Supply.[90]

It is the contrast between the children's actions and the elevated style in which they are written that provides the main pleasure. The inset story from *Dream Days*, 'The Reluctant Dragon', has often been reprinted separately as a children's story—but even then it relies a great deal upon fashionable references, and upon the ironic treatment of the myth.

Grahame largely evaded these narrative problems in *The Wind in the Willows* (1908), which was developed from a story written in letters for his only son, 'Bertie's Escapade'.[91] At first it is Mole's story, as he moves from his suburban, Pooter-like existence, to being an accepted member of the upper middle classes. Then it is the rollicking farce of the child-*nouveau riche* Toad. Between these are sandwiched neo-pagan, Pre-Raphaelite excursions—'The Piper at the Gates of Dawn', 'Dulce Domum', and 'Wayfarers All'—with very different, much slower structures.

What is for children and what is for adults on a child level and adults on an adult level is far from clear. 'The narratee and the implied reader in this story may change from paragraph to paragraph,'[92] the language switchbacks from the simple to the arch, from the poetic to the parodic—which, it seems sometimes, is a way of evading issues. (How could Otter and Mole, or Toad and the Engine Driver, cross their social divides without the help of an evasive narrative?) Thus *The Wind in the Willows* is and is not a children's book, and the narrative voice and stance is not necessarily conterminous with the episodes—hence we get adult parody in those slapstick episodes generally thought to be 'for' children.

In many ways, *The Wind in the Willows* summarizes the golden age: it uses a concept of childhood, but there is nothing childish about the characters except that they are dressed as animals and have no responsibilities. It also sums up a lot of the shifting features of the period, and Grahame's reaction to them—which are only distantly the concern of children. While the River Bank (a personal pun from the Secretary of the Bank of England, surely) is a safe, middle-class bohemia, full of rural conservatism, not far away is the Wild Wood. There are the seeds of urban, working-class revolution. Not far away either, over the hills that Rat fervently urges Mole not to explore (and Mole, indoctrinated, 'saves' Rat from exploring) is the Wide World, where there are motor cars and, worse, women. To compensate for this there is Mole's secure home, the reclaiming of Toad Hall, Toad's (apparent) conversion, Badger's underlying authority.

Despite these adult readings, there is no denying the place of *The Wind in the Willows* in English culture, but, as with 'Peter Pan', we have to ask, just what is it? Is it an idyll about animals, a *Bildungsroman*, a sociological document on class warfare, a high comedy of anarchy, a burlesque, an essay in nostalgia or neo-pagan sentimentalism, a sexist conservative tract? And the answer has to be—by fits and starts, all of these.

It certainly has elements common to many established children's books—the sense of place, of initiation, of learning skills, of establishing boundaries. But its ambivalence might be summed up by its use of animals. It is, after all, only about animals in a symbiotic sense: the Badger is given squirearchical characteristics and hence we think of badgers as squirearchical. Animals can stand for the helpless or displaced child, or for freedom and examples of adult/human oppression, while retaining their independence. For adult writers like Grahame, it is an attractive device for carrying allegory or social satire and fantasy—in *The Wind in the Willows*, there is only one Rat, one Mole, one Badger, and one Toad—but a great many undifferentiated sans culottes, the Stoats and Weasels.

The appeal of this book to children may be the farce, or the image of Toad as anarchic child or trickster; it may be the outsider/insider situation; it may be the opposition of threat and security (as in Mole and Rat, lost in the snow in the Wild Wood, finding the security of Badger and his ultra-cosy kitchen). It may be the structure: the first five chapters are classically balanced as Mole joins the society, reaches his nadir in the Wild Wood in the exact centre of the section— and finally returns home, temporarily, having matured.

All of this can be attractive or off-putting: and there are moments of immense brilliance, when scales and expectations are confronted with a staggering sleight of hand. For example, Toad, the country gentleman lately escaped from prison, takes a lift on a canal narrowboat, and pretends to be a washer-woman. His disguise is soon penetrated, and the bargewoman laughs at him.

Toad's temper, which had been simmering viciously for some time, now fairly boiled over, and he lost all control of himself.

'You common, low, *fat* barge-woman!' he shouted; 'don't you dare to talk to your betters like that! Washerwoman indeed! I would have you know that I am a Toad, a very well-known, respected, distin-guished Toad! I may be under a bit of a cloud at present, but I will *not* be laughed at by a barge-woman!'

The woman moved nearer to him and peered under his bonnet keenly and closely. 'Why, so you are!' she cried. 'Well, I never! A horrid, nasty, crawly Toad! And in my nice clean barge, too! Now that is a thing that I will *not* have.'

. . . One big mottled arm shot out and caught Toad by a fore-leg, while the other gripped him fast by a hind-leg. Then the world turned suddenly upside-down, the barge seemed to flit lightly across the sky, the wind whistled in his ears, and Toad found himself flying through the air, revolving rapidly as he went.[93]

Two very illuminating glosses have been written on the book: one is A. A. Milne's play *Toad of Toad Hall* (1929), where Milne strips out the mysticism and much of the ambiguity (although retaining—and increasing—the sentimentality); the other is Jan Needle's deconstructive parallel text *Wild Wood* (1981), in which the story is seen from the point of view of the 'invisible' working classes, who both manipulate and are manipulated by Toad.

The Wind in the Willows is a complex, uneasy book, whose place in children's literature is ambiguous and yet definitive. It certainly deals with change in the world in general, and, as Darton points out, 'in the world of younger children something like a change of mental outlook was also becoming visible . . . Rudyard Kipling . . . is once more a valuable index of what was happening.'[94]

If Grahame was a 'one-book' man, Rudyard Kipling touched more children's book genres, more profoundly, than any other writer except William Mayne. 'It can be offered as a pseudo-Euclidean proposition', John Rowe Townsend wrote, 'that any line drawn between books for adults and books for children must pass through the middle of Kipling.'[95] I would argue that Kipling's best work was for children, and that he stands as a landmark author in at least four distinct fields. That he is still in print with some of his books in several editions may once again smack of homage to a classic; but Kipling does encapsulate a remarkable number of the central characteristics of the children's book.

In *The Wouldbegoods* the Bastable children despise a visitor who skips the Mowgli stories in *The Jungle Book* (1894) and, one assumes, *The Second Jungle Book* (1895), probably because they address so many of the unspoken codes of childhood. These are the most un-childish of Kipling's 'children's' books, and are really no more about animals than is *The Wind in the Willows*. They are in the tradition of the fable, the symbolic story; above all, they are serious, and it is significant that of all the films that Walt Disney has made, this is the one that relates least to the original texts. Here Kipling, writing out of his own background, is dealing with a powerful myth, with a dominance fable, a *Bildungsroman*, the education and acculturation of Mowgli (through Baloo and Bagheera), with egocentricity, and with very crude and deep motivations, such as revenge. All this is held within Kipling's concern with 'the inner ring', the initiation process, and the system of the jungle, where all the animals are given (quasi-military) ranks. Kipling's 'Law of the Jungle' therefore represents the kind of enlightened self-interest that children should acquire.

But all of this is abstract in the context of Kipling's powers as a story-teller. His force may be demonstrated by this extract from 'Kaa's Hunting', where the damned are the monkeys who live outside the law.

Kaa glided out into the centre of the terrace and brought his jaws together with a ringing snap that drew all the monkeys' eyes upon him.

'The moon sets,' he said. 'Is there yet light to see?'

From the walls came a moan like the wind in the tree-tops: 'We see, O Kaa.'

'Good. Begins now the Dance—the Dance of the Hunger of Kaa. Sit still and watch.'

He . . . began making loops and figures of eight with his body, and soft, oozy triangles that melted into squares and five-sided figures and coiled mounds, never resting, never hurrying, and never stopping his low, humming song.

Baloo and Bagheera stood still as stone, growling in their throats, their neck-hair bristling, and Mowgli watched and wondered.[96]

His concern with codes and order led Kipling, naturally enough, to the school story, in a book that told his truth about the United Services College at Westward Ho!, *Stalky and Co*. If there are many examples of authors working out their problems in children's books, here is Kipling getting revenge. It makes anarchic reading, was roundly condemned when it was published, and has been questioned ever since. As John Rowe Townsend points out, 'a great deal of Stalky makes uneasy reading today. The exploits of Study Number Five occasionally take place in the worrying twilight zones of human conduct in which Kipling seems a peculiarly blinkered guide.'[97] In a period when the school story had settled into its comfortable conventions, *Stalky* came as a shock. '*Tom Brown* had become a lonely deserted rock in the distance. *Eric* was a kind of immovable moral jelly-fish left behind by the tide.

Baines Reed and his imitators were the regular ripples in a smooth sea. No wonder that when *Stalky and Co* appeared in 1899 there was an outcry.'[98]

Kipling's ironically realistic picture sometimes comes close to the intensely personal, as in the notoriously drawn out bullying of the bullies in 'The Moral Reformers'. Beetle (alias Kipling) is beating one of the bullies: 'In his excitement Beetle had used the stump unreflectingly, and Sefton was now shouting for mercy.'[99] The book says a great deal about Kipling and class and war, but it also says a good deal about childhood: Kipling was very much aware of the 'secret places' of the children he wrote about, a characteristic that marks all his children's stories.

In the oral tale, Kipling contributed a very rare, perhaps unique, instance of tales told to his children and transposed meticulously into print, with the *Just So Stories*. Highly personal, immediate, and whimsical, they are a stylistic *tour de force*. The prose is full of patterns, exact repetitions, and family dialect: one of the family, Angela Mackail, wrote that 'The *Just So Stories* are a poor thing in print compared with the fun of hearing them told in Cousin Ruddy's deep unhesitating voice. There was a ritual about them.'[100] The stories are based on South African and Indian legends mixed with parodies of Victorian instructional texts. Elements in them have passed into oral tradition—another measure of the classic.

Hear and attend and listen; for this befell and behappened and became and was, O my Best Beloved, when the Tame animals were wild. The Dog was wild, and the Horse was wild, and the Cow was wild, and the Sheep was wild, and the Pig was wild—as wild as wild could be—and they walked in the Wet Wild Woods by their wild lones. But the wildest of all the wild animals was the Cat. He walked by himself and all places were alike to him.[101]

But Kipling's triumph is a remarkable pair of books, *Puck of Pook's Hill* (1906) and *Rewards and Fairies* (1910), that grew out of his love for his Sussex home, Bateman's. Digging a well, Kipling's workmen found 'a Jacobean tobacco-pipe, a worn Cromwellian latten spoon and, at the bottom of all, the bronze cheek of a Roman horse-bit'. Cleaning out a pond, they found an Elizabethan 'sealed quart', and 'its deepest mud yielded us a perfectly polished Neolithic axe-head with but one chip on its still venomous edge'. Nearby was an ancient forge

supposed to have been worked by the Phoenicians and Romans and, since then, uninterruptedly till the middle of the eighteenth century.

Then, it pleased our children to act for us, in the open, what they remembered of *A Midsummer-Night's Dream* . . . And in a near pasture of the water-meadows lay out an old and unshifting Fairy Ring . . . You see how patiently the cards were stacked and dealt into my hands? The Old Things of our Valley glided into every aspect of our outdoor works. Earth, Air, Water and People had been—I saw it at last—in full conspiracy to give me ten times as much as I could compass, even if I wrote a complete history of England, as that might have touched or reached our valley.[102]

This book is highly allusive. The central characters, Puck, and the children Dan and Una (based on Kipling's own children), are the still points that link two sequences of stories, of the rise of England from pagan god to Magna Carta, and the decline of the Roman Empire—both of which had contemporary political relevance.

As the historical figures conjured up by the eternal spirit, Puck, tell their stories, what we see is a very advanced weave on a simple frame. The sense of place (rather than the abstract jungle) is very strong here. Sussex—and the Englishness of it—is central. In one sense the book is defining Englishness and patriotism; Hobden the labourer represents the spirit of the land and craft. The idea of 'insidership', secrecy, and initiation is represented not only by craft but by the cult of Mithras, by freemasonry, and by Judaism; the military structure provides a balance of power and freedom; and the book is full of the mutual respect of the young and old—of the children for the 'old things', and vice versa; within the stories, young and old work together, as with Richard and De Aquila, and Pertinax, Parnesius, and Maximus. And there are plenty of links to the literature of childhood—notably Puck's scornful attack on the Pre-Raphaelite fairies (who may well have originated in Shakespeare): 'little buzzflies with butterfly wings and gauze petticoats, and shiny stars in their hair, and a wand like a school-teacher's cane for punishing bad boys and rewarding good ones. *I* know 'em!'[103]

Perhaps, above all, these books speak to the child's intelligence—which, paradoxically, leaves them on the borderline of books for children. Kipling himself said of *Rewards and Fairies*, the more complex and sombre sequel to *Puck* (which has the repeated, ominous motif 'What else could I have done?'), 'Since the tales had to be read by children, before people realized that they were meant for grown-ups ... I worked the material in three or four overlaid tints and textures, which might or might not reveal themselves according to the shifting light of sex, youth, and experience.'[104]

Kipling, then, brought together triumphantly several strands of children's literature, and looked forward to a century in which children could comfortably be addressed as intelligent beings without condescension. His feel for childhood was such that it is hardly surprising to find that the structure of *Puck of Pook's Hill*, with its stories linked directly to a central core and more loosely to each other, bears a striking similarity to the way in which children think about stories. (See Arthur N. Applebee's *The Child's Concept of Story*, where the concept of story structures is based upon the ideas of the developmental psychologist Vygotsky.[105])

As the First World War approached there were other notable works, in both Britain and the USA. Apart from *Pollyanna*, Rackham's *Mother Goose*, and others that we have noted, 1911 saw John Masefield's *Jim Davis*; 1912, Howard Garis's *Uncle Wiggly's Adventures*, Heath Robinson's *Bill the Minder* (his ground-breaking *The Adventures of Uncle Lubin* had appeared in 1902), and a book first published in the *Ladies' Home Journal*, but soon appropriated by adolescents, Jean Webster's *Daddy-Long-Legs*. And in 1913 came 'an unpretentious little book, with plain blue covers and no illustrations',[106] Walter de la Mare's strange, quirky, sometimes nightmarish collection of poetry, *Peacock Pie*. This is the kind of text that is central to any debate as to whether there is such a creature as 'poetry for children': can a verse like this fit into, or be excluded from, any category?

> Who said, 'Peacock Pie'?
>   The old King to the sparrow:
> Who said, 'Crops are ripe'?
>   Rust to the harrow:
> Who said, 'Where sleeps she now?
>   Where rests she now her head,
> Bathed in eve's loveliness'?—
>   That's what I said.[107]

And then the world was plunged into what A. A. Milne called 'that nightmare of mental and physical degradation, the War'.[108] The comics and the popular press, which had been fighting skirmishes for some time, went into the fray with writers like Percy F. Westerman, and 'the editorial policy of Lord Northcliffe's Amalgamated Press . . . was to involve its girl characters and readers unreservedly in the war',[109] but the 'respectable' writers for children were silent, and only several generations later was the subjected treated—and then often peripherally (as in K. M. Peyton's 'Flambards' trilogy (1966–9)).

Milne published the Thackeray-like pastiche of the fairy-tale *Once on a Time* in 1917, himself uncertain of its audience. Eleanor Farjeon, whose work was to dominate, in some ways, the inter-war years, published her first book, rather strained explanations of London place-names, *Nursery Rhymes of London Town*, in 1916. Arthur Ransome, who, after a few youthful neo-pagan whimsies and forgotten (and unregretted) pieces such as *Highways and Byways in Fairyland* (1907) was in Russia reporting the revolution, chastening his style, wrote one of the most atmospheric and authentic of collections of folk-tales, *Old Peter's Russian Tales* (1916).

However, even more than with the Second World War, the reality of carnage seems to have temporarily defeated the resilience of fantasy. Serious writers of more realistic books for children may also have found that the war was intractable as a setting, highlighting as it did the failure of adults and the vulnerability of childhood. And so, as the world emerged into the 'long weekend' of the 1920s and 1930s, the war had little direct influence on children's books—but, indirectly, it set the tone for those twenty years.

5

The Long Weekend, 1920–1939

Mary Poppins, Bilbo Baggins, Biggles, Winnie-the-Pooh, Little Tim, Babar, Wurzel Gummidge, the Cat in the Hat, William, Dr Dolittle, Superman, the Swallows and Amazons . . . and Rudolph the Red-Nosed Reindeer. Why, one recent critic has asked, did the 'interwar period see the creation of so many modern mythical heroes?'.[1]

One answer is that children's books reflect the world as we would like it to be; they react to the adult world. Just as, after the trauma of the Second World War, children's books reacted by turning to fantasy, so, after the First, they looked towards various kinds of freedom. It may have been an effect of the change in attitudes to childhood; but, more concretely, there had been a sea-change, and the world after 1914 is much closer to ours than the world before. Certainly—although there are many exceptions—the tone of voice, the mode of telling, and the narrative contract between narrator and implied child reader of the children's book that we recognize today were fully established.

But the period between the wars was one of contrasts. The *Library Association Review* observed that there were 'a few admirable books, submerged in an ocean of terrible trash . . . unreal school stories, impossible adventure, half-witted fairy-tales . . . in every respect disgraceful'.[2] This judgement may well say more about critical attitudes than the state of the books, but it was certainly the age of the overblown 're-wards'—prizes and presents—whose basic materials (and illustrations) harked back to the end of the nineteenth century. As Geoffrey Trease observed, 'A new story in 1920 or 1930 tended to be a fossil in which one could trace the essential characteristics of one written in 1880 or 1890 . . . Serious reviewing hardly existed.'[3]

This view is echoed by Eleanor Graham: in 1927 there was 'No reviewing ... by and large [children's books] were regarded as trash ... No one, of course, would stop to consider critically the work of Angela Brazil ... but there were many people then who assumed that *all* children's books were on that level,' and even by 1939, only 40 per cent of libraries had children's sections.[4]

Looking back, the gap between the mainstream and the popular becomes blurred. The post-war paper shortages did not affect the boys' magazines very greatly, and they were increasingly supplemented by—and eventually supplanted by—the comics. At the beginning of the period, the Amalgamated Press (the name had changed in 1902) dominated the field. The *Gem* (1907–39), with a peak circulation of 200,000 copies (down to 16,000 at its close), and the *Magnet* (1908–40) (from 200,000 to 40,000) supplied readers with a diet of improbable adventures and endless school stories. Dominating these was Charles Hamilton, whose lifetime output of around 72 million words—an estimated 5,000 stories under twenty-six pseudonyms, including, of course, 'Frank Richards'—cannot be underestimated in terms of influence. George Orwell's famous attack in 1939 (which was somewhat undermined from the start by the assumption that the stories could not be the work of one man) took the boys' stories to task for being out of touch with the world. As Richards had the advantage over Orwell of having a sense of humour, he easily won the contest on points: 'Mr Orwell would have told [the reader] that he is a shabby little blighter, his father an ill-used serf, his world a dirty, muddled, rotten sort of show. I don't think it would be fair play to take his 2d. for telling him that!'[5]

Girls' journals also bloomed, even though most of them, like *School Friend* (1919–29) and the *Schoolgirls' Weekly* (1922–39), were produced by men. 'The twenties and thirties have been described as the heyday of girls' fiction, a time when girls drove fast cars, chasing spies and jewel-thieves and smashing smugglers' rings; it was the age of the resourceful, high-spirited heroine.'[6] It was also the age of the girls' public school story, established since the 1880s by writers like

L. T. Meade; only the post-war British girl was a good deal more like her pre-war American counterpart: healthy, hearty, and regarding boys only as 'chums'. Although the books are very much 'of their time', several long-running series have survived with their own intricate mystiques. Elinor M. Brent-Dyer's fourth book was *The School at the Chalet* (1925) and it was followed by fifty-seven sequels, the last, *Prefects of the Chalet School*, published in 1970. Angela Brazil, whose influence was immense, continued to write, although her books became increasingly formulaic. Elsie J. Oxenham, who had begun writing in 1904, wrote sixteen books before *The Abbey Girls* (1920) began a series that lasted into the 1960s. Her mixture of romanticism and correctness, and the following of her girls into adulthood, necessitated an even greater degree of fantasy than the other writers. But, as Cadogan and Craig point out in their definitive study *You're a Brick, Angela!*,

In writers like Elsie Oxenham, the tendency to emphasise the joys ('the fun') of childhood was part of a deliberate attempt to counter teenage precocity, noticeably more widespread since the rise of Hollywood. . . . Girls' writers were in the artistically awkward position of having to deny, by implication, the nature of adolescence: they were far more concerned with their effects on readers than with the realities of their theme.[7]

(Enid Blyton did not begin writing this kind of story until *The Naughtiest Girl in the School* (1940) and *The Twins at St. Clare's* (1941). Malory Towers is a post-war creation.)

A certain immortality must also be accorded to Nancy Drew, a creation of Edward Stratemeyer's syndicate, which had produced the Bobbsey Twins (1904) and the Hardy Boys (1927). The first adventure of this asexual mistress of coincidence and the lucky guess was in 1930, and one could write a history of fashion as well as of attitudes to sexuality from the subsequent covers of her books. She represents a huge industry, much refined since the 1960s, and Cadogan and Craig make the key points about such series:

Nancy has a genuine heroic quality unconnected with the literary value of the series. A product of commercial expediency, planned to exert the maximum appeal for the greatest number of readers, she was tailored to correspond to the child's wish for excitement and entertainment. Didacticism and sentimentality were not part of the package. Social and moral observation is contained in the stories only in the form of the preconceived idea: certain values are taken for granted, including a view of femininity which actually conflicts with Nancy's behaviour . . . Nancy has never had to waste time wishing she were a boy; for all practical purposes, she *is*.[8]

Another change was that children's books now existed not simply in the context of magazines and comics, but beside non-print media: the BBC Children's Hour began in December 1922, and on it appeared S. G. Hulme Beaman's playlets *Tales of Toytown* (1928 onwards). Ten of them were rewritten as *Stories from Toytown* in 1938. Walt Disney's first 'full-length' feature production, *Snow White and the Seven Dwarfs*, appeared in 1937—with one, perhaps surprising, link with the past: Arthur Rackham 'provided wild wood and old witch effects'.[9] Disney represents an interesting example of the clash between popular/commercial values, and 'establishment' values, for his images are often condemned as vulgar and destructive of the originals. His films have obviously had a huge influence on generations of children and there is no doubt that Disney moulded his whole ethos to his own (Middle American) tastes: but, for the fairy-tales, there is no particular reason why he should not have done so, when all other interpreters have done the same thing. As a general rule, the less substantial the book or tale on which it was based, the better the film: thus, as we have seen, his version of *Peter Pan* (1953) is probably the definitive version of that unstable text. Similarly, *Cinderella* (1950) is an excellent and ingenious rendition (if the endemic sexism is overlooked). On the other hand, *The Jungle Book* (1967) is totally at odds with the spirit and intent of Kipling, while the necessity of concentrating on the surface/farcical/comic aspects of the books has severely hampered his versions of *The Sword in the Stone* (1963), *Alice in Wonderland* (1951), and the 'Winnie-the-Pooh' stories. Only with a middle-range book, such as Dodie Smith's *The Hundred and One Dalmatians* (1956, filmed as *One*

Hundred and One Dalmatians (1961)), are the honours about even

Meanwhile, the comics continued. The first real adventure strip cartoon was 'Rob the Rover', serialized in *Puck* for twenty years from 1920: this introduced the hand-lettering that characterizes modern strips. Some of these have had remarkably long lives, such as 'Rupert Bear', born 1920, an individualistic, and sometimes frighteningly grotesque, strip, which has survived to be a television cartoon. Others, notably 'Desperate Dan' (from 1937), originated with the Amalgamated Press's main competitor, D. C. Thompson. Thompson were successful with adult magazines, such as *My Weekly* and the *Sunday Post*, which are still with us, and comics such as *Adventure* (1921), *Rover*, *Wizard* (1922), and *Hotspur* (1933) ran into the 1960s. Peak circulation of the *Wizard* was well over 500,000 copies.

Some famous names in 'comic' strips were born in this period: the earliest was the *Daily Mail's* 'Teddy Tail' in 1915. 'Pip, Squeak and Wilfred' ran in the *Daily Mirror* from 1919 until 1955, and J. F. Horrabin's characters Happy, Japhet, and the Noah family (which continued through the Second World War), from 1919 in the *News Chronicle*. The latter two, and Rupert, each had their own readers' clubs for children. Notable comics were *Chicks' Own* (1920–57), *Rainbow* ('The children's paper that Parents Approve Of') (1914–56), and *Sunbeam* (1922–40). Over the next two decades the influence of the USA grew steadily, with the import of strips aimed initially (as was the tradition in the USA) at a family audience: Tarzan appeared as an 'action' strip from 1929, Flash Gordon in 1936; also in the late 1930s came Superman (created by two teenaged boys), Captain Marvel, Captain America, and finally Batman (1939).

The 1920s were heralded by two books written in reaction to the memory of the war. One was the Australian masterpiece *The Magic Pudding* (1918) ('this little bundle of piffle', as its author Norman Lindsay called it), a thoroughly eccentric comedy, which follows Bunyip Bluegum and his friends, and Albert the pudding, across the outback. The other sprang from Hugh Lofting's grim experiences with horses in the First World War; *The Voyages of Dr Dolittle* won the second Newbery Medal (awarded by the American Library Association) in 1923. It is interesting to note that Lofting changed his narrative stance from *The Story of Dr Dolittle* (USA 1920) to *The Voyages of Dr Dolittle* (1922), using a child narratee (even though Tommy Stubbins is a grown man, reminiscing), which allows a direct address to the reader. The Dolittle saga has raised, once again, the problem of racism in books that have remained popular: whether the Jolliginki tribe or Prince Bumpo (with his desire to be white) should be expunged to suit modern sensibilities, or whether (as with 'adult' literature) they should be understood as products of their time.

Also characteristic of the 1920s were the verses and fairy-tales, some original, some adapted, of Eleanor Farjeon. A typical title from her huge output of verse in the 1920s and 1930s is *Singing Games from Arcady* (with music by the author) (1926). Her Arcady was located somewhere in Sussex, and her romanticism and whimsicality have not worn well; many of her books have a 'feyness'—a kind of intense charm and allusiveness, seen at its best (or worse) in *A Nursery in the Nineties* (1935). She was undoubtedly very influential—along with her friend Walter de la Mare—but relatively few of her poems have survived (with the notable exception of one that became both hymn and pop song: 'Morning has Broken'). Thus it should be remembered that her *Martin Pippin in the Apple Orchard* (1921), a highly romantic tale, embedding fairy stories in a quasi-erotic, quasi-troubadour, quasi-Arcadian Sussex, was originally published for adults—occupying much the same ambivalent position in the literary/cultural hierarchy as most of Disney's animated films. The sequel (for children), *Martin Pippin in the Daisy Field* (1937), escapes much of the sticky romanticism, and contributes authentic-sounding folk-tales.

Some indication of Farjeon's reputation is the fact that the Children's Book Circle named their annual award after her; characteristic samples of her work, appropriately illustrated by Ardizzone, are *Eleanor Farjeon's Book* (1960) and *The Little Book-room* (1955). Farjeon, then, is very much of her time, and a good many books from the 1920s seem more distant from the modern reader than those of earlier decades. Basil Blackwell's annual *Joy Street* (from 1926), with contributors such as Rose Fyleman, Farjeon and de la Mare, Houseman and Belloc, is famous in children's book history for attempting to raise standards—but it is little known elsewhere. And we might consider that those same years saw the publication of *Ulysses*, *Kangaroo*, *The Great Gatsby*, and *The Hollow Men*, and, among the best sellers, Michael Arlen's *The Green Hat*, P. C. Wren's *Beau Geste*, and Mary Webb's *Precious Bane*. In those same years, the most famous figure of the children's book world was a popular West End playwright and *Punch* light-versifier, A. A. Milne.

'There is', Milne wrote in his autobiography *It's Too Late Now*, 'no artistic reward for a book written for children other than the knowledge that they enjoy it. For once, and how one hates to think it, *vox populi, vox Dei*.'[10] That ironic reluctance sums up Milne, a man who was not really a writer for children at all, and whose four most famous books, which have been phenomenal world-wide sellers, are aimed at both adults and children—which in part accounts for their longevity.

The success of *Winnie-the-Pooh* (1926) can also partly be attributed to its strengths as domestic fantasy. It posits a secure world of the Hundred Acre Wood (shrunk from the less manageable 500-acre wood of reality in Sussex), a coherent secondary world of toys, a mystic/guizer/child figure (Pooh) with whom readers can identify, and a controlling/wizard/ *deus ex machina* figure (Christopher Robin) with whom readers can identify as well. There is animism and anthropomorphism. There is, in little, the everyday conflict between the grown-up world of irrationality and conflict (represented by Owl, Rabbit, and Eeyore) and the childhood world with its different kinds of children (Pooh, Piglet, Tigger, and Roo).

It comes as little surprise that Owl and Rabbit were Milne's 'own unaided work',[11] rather than the creations of his son and wife, or that Milne had little real sympathy with childhood. He was a meticulous craftsman, and his two books of verse for children, *When We Were Very Young* (1924) and *Now We Are Six* (1927), are, as he said, 'technically good. The practice of no form of writing demands such a height of technical perfection as the writing of light verse . . . *When We Were Very Young* is not the work of a poet becoming playful, nor of a lover of children expressing his love . . . [I]t is the work of a light-verse writer taking his job seriously even though he is taking it into the nursery.'[12]

The first of the verses written, 'Vespers', was first published, it might be noted, in *Vanity Fair*, and it has been widely misunderstood and mercilessly parodied (notably by 'Beach-comber', who attacked 'Woogie-Poogie-Boo' verse with a sample called 'Now We Are Sick': 'Hush, hush, | Nobody cares! | Christopher Robin | Has | Fallen | Down-| Stairs').[13] Milne has been written off as a sentimentalist (notably by Dorothy Parker),[14] but—as he was a man well able to defend himself—he pointed out that in fact 'Vespers' is a poem about the amorality of childhood, not its cuteness. Christopher Robin, ritually saying his prayers, is really thinking about 'And what was the other I had to say?' and the bath, and the dressing-gown, and, of course, his own position of power: '*God bless Nanny and make her good.*'[15]

The books of verse, which have been marginally less pop-ular than the two 'Pooh' books (although with such large sales figures that can hardly be said to be significant), have dated rather more, and I doubt whether many adults can read the opening poem of *When We Were Very Young* (1924) with any comfort. (It is 'Corner-of-the-Street' in which Percy's slippers go 'Tweet-tweet-tweet'.) But presumably the poems *of* child-hood—'Happiness' ('John had | Great Big | Waterproof | Boots on . . .'), 'Rice Pudding' ('*What* is the matter with Mary Jane?')—and the poems *for* children—'The King's Breakfast' and 'Bad Sir Brian Botany'—outweigh the more precious poems that read like the worst of Robert Louis Stevenson. Some, like 'Disobedience' ('James James | Morrison Morrison | Weatherby George Dupree . . .'), seem close to de la Mare's surrealism. Much the same might be said of *Now We Are Six*; but, apart from the only partially satisfactory suggestion that there is a good deal of cultural inertia in the continued success of these books, criticism has, as yet, little to offer by way of explanation.

The Pooh books themselves betray Milne's ambivalence, notoriously in the opening chapters of *Winnie-the-Pooh*, where the narratee, Christopher Robin, is built into the book, marked by the second person: 'When he put it like this, you saw how it was, and you aimed very carefully.' Also, the first two jokes are directed at adults: 'Once upon a time, a very long time ago now, about last Friday, Winnie-the-Pooh lived in a forest all by himself under the name of Sanders.'

But where Milne caters for a dual audience, he succeeds magnificently. For example, Pooh often stands for the child, watching the adult Owl attempting to hide his ignorance from the adult Rabbit, or not worrying about noises in the night, as long as Christopher Robin knows about them. Rabbit, on the other hand, bossy and vindictive, is the serpent in Eden: 'You know how it is in the Forest. One can't have *anybody* coming into one's house. One has to be *careful*.'[16] Similarly, the child figures tend to ignore the pathological depressiveness of (the adult) Eeyore: ' "Hallo, Eeyore," they called out cheerfully. "Ah," said Eeyore. "Lost your way?" '[17] Another reason for the books' longevity is the appeal of Shepard's drawings, which, like Tenniel's for the 'Alice' books, seem to have withstood recent rivals. (Milne certainly thought that the success of the books was attributable to Shepard—and rather resented it.[18]) Both the pictures and the Pooh stories certainly lay less stress on the middle-class nursery that dates the books of verse, and produce, to some extent, an Arcadia. It may seem that, in such an Arcadia, adults are not required, and yet the distant and condescending adult, who 'might' watch his son having his bath, does intrude, does try to manipulate. Again, it comes as no great surprise to find that, whereas A. A. Milne thought that the family was not affected by the cult of 'Christopher Robin', the real Christopher Robin carried the scars for life: 'I vividly recall how intensely painful it was to me to sit in my study at Stowe while my neighbours played the famous—and now cursed—gramophone record remorselessly over and over again."[9]

The 'Pooh' books, then, far from being innocent, represent another collision between adult writer and child reader—the central conundrum of children's literature. It is for historiographers to point out that Cotchford Farm, around which the books were set, was also the place where the Rolling Stones' guitarist Brian Jones was drowned, or to debate the *Pooh Cookbook* or *Winnie Ille Pu*, or *The Tao of Pooh*, or *The Pooh Perplex*. Small wonder that the 'Pooh' books remain a potent cultural symbol, and that many adults, as well as many children, have an uneasily intimate relationship with them.

In stark contrast to the Milne/Shepard beautiful children in their rural idyll, William Brown, born into *Home Magazine* in February 1919, and into book form as *Just—William* in 1922, was scruffy and anarchic. His longevity, through thirty-eight volumes containing well over 300 short stories, may have been helped by the occasional topicality (*William—the Dictator*, for example, published in 1938) and by latter-day updating of details. But these books are fundamentally dual-focus situation comedy; William's parents, sister, and brother are types who suffer from an adult's as well as from a child's point of view, just as William and the outlaws are seriously wild children. Richmal Crompton also wrote thirty-nine adult novels, now almost entirely forgotten.

But no figure of the 1920s and 1930s can match the phenomenon of Enid Blyton, a name almost synonymous with children's books—and a certain kind of children's book. It is easy to overlook the fact that her first full-length story, *Adventures of a Wishing Chair*, was published in 1937 and that it was at least her eighteenth or nineteenth book: she began writing in 1917 and her first pamphlet was published in 1922. From that date, she produced well over 600 books, several hundred of which are still in print in the UK—more than sixty 'Noddy' titles alone. At her peak, in 1951, she published thirty-seven titles. In 1974 she was the 'fourth most translated author in the world, following on after Lenin, Marx and Jules

Verne, with 149 translations being made in fifteen countries'.[20]
One small indicator of her popularity might be that when I
surveyed groups of university students in 1992 in Britain, *The
Magic Faraway Tree* (1943) was by far the best-remembered
book of their childhoods.

With such an output and popularity, it would be idle to
ignore her; like the comic, Blyton and her many cohorts
represent the 'real' reading of childhood. The problem has
been summed up succinctly by Sheila Ray: 'Blyton has been
criticised for her impoverished vocabulary, her undemanding
style, her stereotyped characters, her incredible plots, her
attitudes towards minority groups, her sexism and her snob-
bishness' (which seems to be a fairly comprehensively damn-
ing roll-call). But, as Ray shrewdly goes on: 'The faults of
plot, characterisation, and style for which she is criticised by
adults contribute largely to her popularity with children.'[21]
The fact that her stories are set as firmly as A. A. Milne's in
a 1920s–1930s middle-class social ethos seems to be irrelevant
to children, but that is not surprising. At this level, most
readers are reading for plot; anomalies of setting or dress or
attitude such as afflict any long-running popular series, from
'The Saint' to 'Nancy Drew' (which originated in 1929 and
1930 respectively), are not important.

The books can also be racist, and there is no doubt that, as
Bob Dixon put it, in a swingeing attack, 'golliwogs [are]
normally cast in "naughty", evil and menacing roles . . . Blyton, in her simple way, found their blackness a sufficient cause
for dislike.'[22] Dixon, in his simple way, perhaps, overlooks the
view that Noddy himself is a particularly unlikeable caricature
of the white middle-class child. Blyton herself suggested that
children like Noddy because 'he is like themselves, but more
naïve and stupid. Children like that—it makes them feel
superior.'[23] And the children are also superior to the working
classes—one does not have to look far to find Julian of the
Famous Five sneering at the lower orders—or, indeed, to
parents and authority figures. Blyton clearly appeals to some
basic needs of the child reader, which are a good deal less
admirable than she might have supposed.

The most usual explanation of Blyton's popularity is that she is 'on the side of the child', but what precisely does this imply? Certainly, there is a good deal of wish-fulfilment of the crudest kind (as Eileen Colwell memorably put it, 'What hope has a band of desperate men against four children?'[24]); the morality is simple; and the prose very oral and conversational—if in the manner of a certain period. And yet Blyton was no mean stylist, and she very often used 'mind style' or 'free indirect discourse' which blurs the distinction between what the narrator and the characters are thinking and saying. There is therefore no 'gap' or, if there is, there is a clear context of a comfortable story-telling situation.

She subordinated all adult concerns to what she saw as the needs and interests of children, and in so doing developed a narrative manner which bridged the gap between adult teller and child reader in a new way—a way which in its apparent endorsement of reprehensible childish attitudes many critics have found deplorable. The voice that is heard most consistently in Blyton's stories is not the voice of the adult narrator, but the voices of children. The pervading tone of the dialogue becomes inescapably blended with the narrative voice.[25]

It seems inevitable that Blyton will continue to represent the polarization between the popular and the prestigious. Her books, now being reissued in edited versions, to tone down racism and sexism (although they will remain fertile ground for Freudian analysts), are part of the public domain, part of myth that can legitimately be 'retold'. If her sales have been perpetuated by the system of popular cultural acceptance, she is, in a very real sense, a true 'classic'.

In the 1930s Blyton's growing success was the exception. In general, it was not a good time to be a children's author, as Geoffrey Trease explained:

Of fame there was none for the living. Children's books were in the doldrums, with a handful of exceptions such as A. A. Milne, no writer enjoyed public esteem. 'You can't beat Henty and Ballantyne' was the cry. Everyone looked backwards . . . If there was no fame, there was not much fortune. Children's books were commonly published under the old system long abandoned for other types of

book. The author sold his copyright for a single payment of perhaps
£50. There was nothing to be done then but begin another. He was
on a treadmill. It was small wonder that so much of children's
literature was hackwork.[26]

The trend, unconsciously reflecting the times, was towards
freedom through realism; a few minor fantasies have survived,
such as Patricia Lynch's *The Turf-Cutter's Donkey* (1934) and
Professor J. B. S. Haldane's *My Friend Mr Leakey* (1937), but
four fantasies stand out. (We can discount T. H. White's *The
Sword in the Stone* (1938), which, although sometimes marketed for children, falls outside our general category, and
Alison Uttley's essentially backward-looking series of books
that borrowed from Beatrix Potter, her own country childhood, and the sense of 'pre-war' Arcadia, beginning with *The
Squirrel, the Hare, and the Little Grey Rabbit* (1929).)

The first two unique combinations of adventure, legend,
and magic were by John Masefield (appointed Poet Laureate
in 1930): *The Midnight Folk* (1927) and *The Box of Delights*
(1935). As Margery Fisher says, 'Masefield's narrative method
in *The Midnight Folk* must be accepted for what it is—seemingly discursive, even rambling, like a surprise Christmas
stocking full of brightly coloured unrelated objects.'[27] Masefield's two books throw together what might seem to be
dissonant elements of the historical novel, the thriller, and the
farce; post-war, only Joan Aiken approaches his range of
imagination. (Not many authors would contemplate having
their villain kidnap a bishop and all the cathedral clergy down
to the canons minor, as Masefield has Abner Brown do in *The
Box of Delights*.)

The third fantasy was the forerunner to one of the major
best sellers of the century, J. R. R. Tolkien's *The Hobbit*
(1937). Although a little stilted at the outset compared with its
successor (it was revised several times), *The Hobbit* has the
classic 'circular' plot of the adventure story for children, a
shape echoed by the gradual change of tone as Bilbo gets
further from home and meets trolls and dragons. The creation
of the hobbits—child-like adults—and the feeling of complete-
ness in the world that surrounds them made the book a hard

act to follow. This is demonstrated by the hundreds of imitations of *The Lord of the Rings* in the 1960s and 1970s, where Tolkien's manner was imitated but no one was able to match the depth and detail of his invention.

P. L. Travers's *Mary Poppins* (1934 and sequels), is another example of a book at least matched, and perhaps excelled, by the Disney version of it. The book was not included in the Children's Literature Association's 'Touchstones' list, because, as Perry Nodelman noted, 'so much of its fantasy is, despite its inventiveness, finally unconvincing. And it is unconvincing because Travers undermines our experience of it by insisting on its great significance . . . *Mary Poppins* sometimes reads less like a novel than a public relations release for its star performer.'[28] Some of Mary Poppins's ascerbity was certainly lost in the film, but then so was the goddess-element in Mary, and Travers's own concept of heavenly inspiration.

As before, children's books largely ignored the contemporary political scene of slump and war and impending war in Europe. Geoffrey Trease's *Bows against the Barons*, published by the left-wing publisher Lawrence & Wishart in 1934, was an attempt—though it now reads very crudely—to bring political awareness to comfortable legends. Even in its revised edition *Bows against the Barons* retains a certain bitterness and brutality in its accounts of battles in Sherwood Forest, and its communist attitudes seem naïve. When the central character, Dickon, meets Robin Hood, the outlaw says: '. . . don't call me "sir". We're comrades in Sherwood, all equal. What's the sense of getting rid of one master and taking a new one?' Both the evil Earl and Robin express the same thought, that the cause of the peasants is just, and that they will win, *one day*, and when Robin is treacherously killed, the despairing comment is: 'So they got him in the end. They always do.'[29]

Trease's later career, as a middle-range, journeyman writer, touched on many genres in the course of over a hundred books including a series dealing with day-school children in the Lake District (beginning with *No Boats on Bannermere* (1949)). In his later years he has preferred the historical novel on the grounds that he was no longer able to reproduce the current argot of children.

Noel Streatfeild began the 'career' books with *Ballet Shoes* (1936) and *The Circus is Coming* (1938), which won the third Carnegie Medal. Here we have the characteristic voice of modern children's literature: clear, uncomplicated, and generally neutral—but occasionally revealing the problems of adult–child communication. Consider the opening of *The Circus is Coming*: 'Peter and Santa were orphans. When they were babies their father and mother were killed in a railway accident, so they came and lived with their aunt. The aunt's name was Rebecca Possit, but of course they called her Aunt Rebecca.'[30] Not only is this a blatant use of a brutal (although generally unnoticed) device for ridding fictional children of their parents, but there are two subtle linguistic indicators: 'came' and 'of course'. These echoes of the story-telling situation indicate not so much an intimacy between the narrator and the narratee as the subtlety of the power-relationship between the two. How times have changed might be indicated by the ironic opening of Nina Bawden's *Humbug*, written just over fifty years later:

Alice and William and Cora lived with their mother and father who were no better and no worse than most parents. Their father picked his nose when no one was watching and since children are 'no one' he picked his nose in front of them. Their mother told lies; she had given up smoking but sometimes when they came home from school the windows were wide open . . . and they knew she was hoping to get rid of the smell before anyone could come home and catch her.

Although their parents were not perfect, Alice and William and Cora were used to them and quite fond of them, and so they were sorry when their father told them that the bank was sending him to Japan for six months and he wanted to take their mother with him.[31]

There is a good deal of ambivalence about this tone: now the parents are faintly patronized and they are given recognizable characteristics, instead of simply being dismissed. There has been a subtle shift of power—perhaps of respect—and the collusion is of one intelligent person talking to another.

That tone of mutual respect, the voice of the neutral, competent adult addressing, so far as it is possible, equals, was exemplified in the 1930s in two authors widely separated in experience, but close in their attitude to childhood and realism. In the USA, the most distinguished successors to the family books of the turn of the century were the seven volumes by Laura Ingalls Wilder, beginning with *Little House in the Big Woods* (1932), and best known collectively by the title of the third book published, *Little House on the Prairie* (1935, UK 1957). The series has all the family virtues, the omniscient Pa, the intimate, private life in the context of the huge Midwest, survival, the quarrels with other children, and, in keeping with the *Pollyanna* tradition, a tragedy, in the form of Mary's blindness. Most of all, it is unsparing of detail and uncondescending, and in many ways sums up the characteristics of the American novel. For example, as the family moves further west, the prairies begin:

The endless waves of flowery grasses under the cloudless sky gave her a queer feeling. She could not say how she felt. All of them in the wagon, and the wagon and team, and even Pa, seemed small.

All morning Pa drove steadily along the dim wagon track, and nothing changed. The farther they went into the west, the smaller they seemed, and the less they seemed to be going anywhere. The wind blew the grass always with the same endless rippling, the horses' feet and the wheels going over the grass made always the same sound, the jiggling of the board seat was always the same jiggling. Laura thought they might go on for ever, yet always be in this same changeless place, that would not even know they were there.[32]

(Another pioneering book, Carol Rylie Brink's *Caddie Woodlawn* (1935), is less well known in Britain.)

Wilder's British counterpart in terms of language and attitude was the recipient, in 1936, of the first British Library Association Carnegie Medal, Arthur Ransome. (The presentation was a rather low-key affair, and Ransome remarked that 'it would have been better to send the blessed thing by post'.[33])

Arthur Ransome's books, largely 'realistic' when they were written, are now undeniably 'historical'; but, because of their status, there is no question of their being updated, or even of his last, unfinished book being completed by another hand. It may be that his books have reached the stage where adult nostalgia is taking over from children's enthusiasm, but there is no doubt that their influence and popularity have been international.

Ransome, a distinguished, if somewhat maverick, foreign correspondent, produced twelve books in the 'Swallows and Amazons' series between 1930 and 1947 to add to around twenty-eight volumes of travel, novels, and political writing. Nine of the books are set in the English Lake District, on the Norfolk Broads, and around Harwich; all are concerned with the same families of children, with traditional outdoor activities—sailing, fishing, camping—all lovingly and expertly described. In a context of a popular literature that specialized in the improbable, Ransome dealt in probabilities. His children are civilized, on holiday, almost invariably nice to each other; their world is secure, and the places—although enviably empty—are recognizable. Like Jefferies, Ransome gave his children an ingrained knowledge of children's books, so that they can move easily between the real and the imaginative. It was, and is, a remarkable mixture.

But, as a good many imitators through the 1940s and 1950s found, there was no 'Ransome formula' for success. One recent critic has suggested that Ransome created 'something resembling a childhood mythology . . . his . . . children are *magical* characters'.[34] The characterizations are understated, the plots generally low key. Ransome allows his children holiday freedoms, practical adventures, plausible, absorbing activities, within a secure family framework. The common themes of outsider/insider, of skills, of national and literary heritage, of a sense of place, of firm codes, of family groups, of mutual respect between adults and children are all there. His earlier literary lives as critic and folklorist allowed him to structure his books in a way that makes recognizable use of folk-tale patterns. For example, the main action of *We Didn't Mean to Go to Sea* (1937) follows four children as they drift out into the North Sea on a yacht, in fog and darkness, and how they take control and sail safely to Holland. But, just as in many folk-tales, the first third of the story is given over to preparation; the children acquire skills that they will use later, just as the heroes and heroines of folk-tales acquire gifts or magic devices that they later use.

The set of twelve books functions as a *Bildungsroman* as the characters gradually develop towards adulthood: the first book, *Swallows and Amazons* (1930), is a perfect example of a 'circular' story, beginning and ending in the same place, with the same characters. As the series progresses, the endings become less 'closed', and more adult. The characterization becomes more perfunctory, and the children's personal behaviour more improbable, as the books go by, and Ransome's functional, Defoe-like prose, concentrating on primary features of things rather than on emotive or value-laden words, reflects his limitations as well as his strengths as a writer. But he was capable of a low-key lyricism, often celebrating places—such as this description of the hound trails in *Swallowdale*.

The white spots far away, slipping into sight and out again among the screes and heather, dropping away into a dip, showing again now startlingly nearer on the moorland slopes, disappeared. Farther away one or two white spots, hounds wavering and at fault, could still be seen. Then these, too, vanished, and it was as if all the hounds had fallen over a precipice or been swallowed up in some hidden chasm in the fells. 'We shan't see them any more,' said Titty. But Nancy knew better.[35]

Ransome made major contributions to the genres of the sea story (*We Didn't Mean to Go To Sea*) and the detective story (*The Big Six* (1941)), but he epitomizes those writers who used the 'middle style', who exercised a quiet censorship of certain kinds of realism, and who dominated writing for children in the immediate post-war decades.

Ransome's series ran through the war, and he was advised by his publisher, Jonathan Cape, to 'steer clear of the war at all costs'.[36] This was ostensibly easy, as his fictional series was set in the early 1930s, but both *Secret Water* (1939) and *The Big Six* have elements that can easily be read as paralleling the political situation. Success is achieved by teamwork, by the most unlikely person, by perseverance, by preparation.[37]

Ransome's 'realism', for all his democratic protestations, and the unpatronizing presentation of working-class characters, was essentially middle-class (one family has a cook and a car and a telephone!), and few attempts were made to write about life from a different angle. One was Eve Garnett's *The Family from One-End Street* (1937), which won the Carnegie Medal that year—possibly on the grounds of its political correctness. This, and its sequels, sound to the modern ear a little patronizing, but, rather like the BBC radio interview of the period, the problem is a matter of technique, and Kate Ruggles does emerge as a three-dimensional heroine. Garnett's books have survived at least as well as similar attempts such as John Rowe Townsend's *Gumble's Yard* (1961) and *Widdershins Crescent* (1965)—and her illustrations are distinctive.

In picture-books, the increased use of lithography had been in part encouraged by Jean de Brunhoff's 'Babar' series (France 1931, UK 1934, with an introduction by A. A. Milne). Before that there had been distinguished examples such as Sir William Nicholson's illustrations for Margery Williams's *The Velveteen Rabbit* (1922) and his own *Clever Bill* (1928).[38]

Edward Ardizzone's *Little Tim and the Brave Sea Captain* was one of the first picture-books to use photo-offset litho, 'although initial drying problems in the hot, humid summer of New York in 1935 meant that the resulting 64-page folio had both the hand-lettered text and colour pictures printed on one side only of each leaf'.[39] Ardizzone followed *Little Tim* with *Lucy Brown and Mr Grimes* (1937) and *Tim and Lucy Go to Sea* (1938) (both hand-lettered), setting a trend for the interweaving of text and pictures.

Other survivors from this period include Kathleen Hale's bold large-format books about Orlando, the Marmalade Cat (1938), and many influential American imports. Among those which are still popular are Wanda Gág's *Millions of Cats* (1928, UK 1929), Marjorie Flack's very stylish *Angus and the Ducks* (1930 and three sequels) and *The Story about Ping*

(1933), and a strong group published in the late 1930s including Munro Leaf's *Story of Ferdinand* (1936, UK 1937), Ludwig Bemelmans' *Madeline* (1939), and Dr Seuss's revolutionary *And to Think that I Saw it on Mulberry Street* (1937) and *The 500 Hats of Bartholomew Cubbins* (1938). These books, present a challenge to the adult; as William Feaver put it, illustration in children's books is 'suspended in [a] welter of imagery, occasionally bobbing into fine-art waters but more often drifting into commercial shallows'.[40]

However, war was approaching. The adult literary world seemed to be in retreat; as Graves and Hodge wrote, 'Was it dying, or merely in hibernation?'[41] Children's books, in contrast, had just completed a very rich period, from Hergé's 'Tintin' (Belgium, 1929), to notable bears such as Mary Plain (Gwynneth Rae, *Mostly Mary* (1930)), a twentieth-century Black Beauty (Golden Gorse, *Moorland Mousie* (1929)), and a major poet's whimsies—T. S. Eliot's *Old Possum's Book of Practical Cats* (1939) . . . and *Rudolph the Red-Nosed Reindeer*. This is another surprising text, which seems to have been always with us, but was in fact written by a copywriter for the Montgomery Ward company as a 'give away' item. The company issued 2.5 million copies for Christmas 1939 and a further 3.5 million for Christmas 1945 before giving the copyright to the author, Robert L. May. The famous, or infamous, song was not written until 1949.

'The decade before the outbreak of war in 1939', Marcus Crouch wrote, 'had been an exciting period, with interesting experiments, much fine writing, stimulating influences from abroad, and a growing awareness of standards in children's books among teachers, librarians, and parents.'[42] There was to be a delay of more than ten years before these influences came to fruition, for during the war years much that was good and bad in children's books was destroyed.

However, if the war interrupted 'quality' writing, the magazines were ready, while W. E. Johns had a hero who had been fighting the First World War since 1932, and was ready to fight another. Captain James Bigglesworth had been invented because, as Johns wrote: 'I was the editor of an aviation magazine [*Popular Flying*] and needed an air story to counter-blast some of the war-flying nonsense that was being imported in the cheap papers.'[43] The career of 'Biggles' from 1939 on-wards sums up, as we shall see, the development of popular fiction for children for the thirty years that followed.

6

Equal Terms: 1940 to the Present

1. Overview

The last fifty years have seen children's literature established
as a major commercial area of publishing. Since economic
stability was restored in the 1950s, children's books have
weathered the economic storms at least as well as their adult
counterparts. Four things have been very noticeable: the first,
the move into fantasy in the 1950s and 1960s, and, since then,
a swing towards a 'new realism': streetwise, multiracial literature, often written from the 'inside'. The second has been
the spectacular growth of high-quality picture-books (under
virtually any definition). Thirdly, although each generation
rewrites the rules, the problem of balance between adult and
child within the book has to some extent been solved—partly
because writing for children is a much less anomalous activity
than it used to be. And, finally, a very distinct 'teenage' market
has emerged, crossing every genre and every section of publishing; how writers and publishers have solved the problems of
what Frank Eyre called 'in between' books is a central issue.

Commercially, children's books have been affected in much
the same way as other books. In the 1960s and 1970s virtually
every mainstream publisher established a children's list (a far
cry from the immediate post-war situation), but since then the
market for hardbacks has declined with educational and
library cuts; the tendency to reprint and repackage well-selling
authors has increased (rather more than in other areas, given
the long shelf-life of children's books); and conservatism
in marketing has ruled. Children's lists have been merged
and amalgamated with bewildering speed; although, since the
mid-1970s, there has been a reaction, and smaller publishing
houses have re-emerged from the corporate wreckage. 'Popular'
literature has taken on other media—TV, cinema, video,

music, and, latterly, computer-related materials; American marketing techniques and American products have assumed a much greater importance than ever before.

As far as reviewing and public recognition are concerned, children's literature may not have escaped from what Wallace Hildick called 'the habits formed in the workhouse of the popular press',[1] but more and more the books are surrounded by informed discussion. The Children's Book Circle, a publisher's group, was founded in 1962, with some of the most forward-looking publishers, such as Anthony Kamm, Julia MacRae, and Kaye Webb (of Puffin), on its committee. Among the journals dealing with children's books in Britain are, or have been, *Books for your Children* (1965–), Margery Fisher's remarkable one-person reviewing journal *Growing Point* (1962–92), *Children's Literature in Education* (1970–), *Signal* (1970–), and *Children's Book Review* (1970–6); among the organizations, the Federation of Children's Book Groups (1986–) has taken books into the community; and among the many awards, The Other Award (1975–) has been given for books that are 'progressive in their treatment of ethnic minorities, the sex roles and social differences'.

While 'mainstream' books flourished, comics rose at the expense of the traditional word-filled magazine; *BOP* closed in 1967, having survived rather longer than might have been expected. It was replaced in popular esteem by *Eagle*, whose editor Marcus Morris had much the same ideals as his nineteenth-century predecessors, and whose front-page hero, Dan Dare, had much the same clean-cut image and square jaw as *his* predecessors. It is no doubt a sign of the times that *Eagle* lasted only from 1950 to 1969, overtaken by brasher, more worldly (and, it must be said, more violent) comics. A similar sign was that BBC Radio's 'Children's Hour' died in 1961, while BBC TV's 'Jackanory' began in 1965.

If distinctions between media became blurred, so did the distinction between the mainstream/respectable/literary texts and the successors to the penny dreadfuls. Some of Enid Blyton's books, for example, appeared under the imprint of such major publishing houses as Macmillan; W. E. Johns had

had twenty-three titles published by Oxford University Press between 1935 and 1943, *Biggles Flies Again* appeared as a Penguin Book (348) in 1941, and he was published after the war by Hodder & Stoughton and Brockhampton Press. Children's books have continued to be commissioned and sold through major retail chains; but such 'commercial' texts are nothing new: Marks & Spencer produced 'Marspen' books during the 1930s, and many of today's 'check-out' books are produced by leading publishers.

2. The Second World War and Children's Literature

'At the end of the war', Cadogan and Craig have observed, 'the bulk of children's fiction was still located in a dream world of boarding school, ponies, the prevention of crime, impossible reversals of fortune and holiday high-jinks.'[2] Why was this so? During the war, paper shortages raised prices and reduced book sizes and production runs (one of Enid Blyton's series, 'Mary Mouse', was printed on magazine off-cuts), although the first volumes of two very influential series—Puffins and Picture Puffins—were produced in 1940. But on the whole it seems that the 'middle-class' books avoided direct confrontation. As we have seen, writing about the child in war (especially during wartime) involves facing the loss (rather than the convenient suspension) of adult order, and an edgy kind of realism that necessarily emphasizes helplessness and seriousness.

Thus although there were some respectable examples few are remembered or reprinted. Among them are two studies of evacuees, Kitty Barne's *Visitors from London* (1940), P. L. Travers's rather sober story of a journey to the USA, *I Go by Sea, I Go by Land* (1941), and a very distinctive example of the pony book, Mary Treadgold's *We Couldn't Leave Dinah* (1941). For the war years, this account of Caroline Templeton's adventures on an occupied Channel Island is remarkable for its tolerance towards the Germans.

Otherwise relatively few books have survived. Alison Uttley's 'Sam Pig' stories (1940) looked back to rural peace, William Croft Dickinson's very intelligent fantasy *Borrobil*

(1944) looked forward to developments a decade ahead. And one highly thought of book demonstrates the woolly thinking of some critics. *The Little Grey Men* by 'BB' (D. J. Watkins-Pitchford's pseudonym is itself suggestive of violence, albeit 'sporting' violence), about the last gnomes of England, has been much praised as a 'country' book, precise in scale and observation, instructive and serious: as Margery Fisher has said, 'These are heritage stories.'[3] This kind of classification tends to ignore the leaden prose of the books, and overlooks the rather unsavoury murder by the gnomes of the game-keeper (by blocking the barrels of his shotgun).

The Arthur Ransome 'tradition' of outdoor stories was carried on by Malcolm Saville and Aubrey de Selincourt; from America came Esther Forbes's *Johnny Tremain* (1943, UK 1944), Virginia Lee Burton's *Mike Mulligan and his Steam Shovel* (1939, UK 1941), and Robert McCloskey's *Make Way for Ducklings* (1941, UK 1944), and from France, André Maurois's anti-war fantasy *Fattipuffs and Thinifers* (written in 1930, but not translated until 1941), which, like *Gulliver's Travels* before it, and S. A. Wakefield's *Bottersnikes and Gumbles* (1967), exploits the comic possibilities of total contrasts.

The only author who was not greatly affected by the war in terms of output was Enid Blyton, who produced over seventy books between 1940 and 1945, including *The Naughtiest Girl in the School* (1940) and the first 'Famous Five' adventure, *Five on a Treasure Island* (1942). Apart from a good deal of mild propaganda writing in magazines, Blyton also wrote a war story, *The Adventurous Four* (1941), which involved the finding of an enemy submarine base in Scotland. (She also produced *The Babar Story Book*, 'retold by Enid Blyton', which provoked the *Junior Bookshelf* to comment: 'What in heaven's name can she have done to it? Did de Brunhoff's fine prose need rewriting?'[4])

The war had an immediate impact on the 'comics' and popular literature in other ways. W. E. Johns swung into action with books such as *Biggles Defies the Swastika* (1941), and invented a WAAF pilot in the surprisingly non-sexist 'Worrals' series (1941–50) and a commando (more in the mould of Rockfist Rogan of the *Champion*) in 'Gimlet' (1943–54). Johns is an interesting case, because his books are a throwback to the nineteenth-century adventure writing tradition of Henty, and quite how its sentiments and style have survived is not clear. *The Rescue Flight*, published by Oxford in 1939, was a timely account of First World War heroics, with a hero, Captain Bigglesworth, who smokes and twitches: 'Slight in build, his features were as delicate as those of a girl . . . a pale face upon which the strain of war, and the sight of sudden death, had already graven little lines.' What are more difficult to accept (the book is still in print, apparently unedited, in the 1990s) are scenes like the encounter between schoolboy and headmaster:

'Come in, my boy,' he said, in a curiously husky voice . . . looking down into the keen, questioning face . . . 'Since you have been at Rundell, whatever your failings may have been, you have always played the man . . . Thirty bowed his head so that the Head should not see his face . . . 'I won't blub,' he told himself fiercely, '*I won't*.'[5]

Johns's wartime writing inculcates a sense of English 'fairplay'. After the war, Biggles became a routine character of pulp fiction. As Fisher says: 'Biggles as the enemy of the Hun can be accepted in historical perspective: as the bloodthirsty, self-righteous opponent of thriller-villains, he deserves no critical charity.'[6] For all that, Biggles lives on, and dramatized versions of some of his wartime adventures, notably *Biggles Defies the Swastika*, are currently available on tape.

The war—as adventure—cropped up in the work of the major girls' school story writers Dorita Fairlie Bruce, with *Nancy Calls the Tune* (Oxford University Press, 1944), and Elinor Brent-Dyer, with *The Chalet School in Exile* (1940). Although this latter book contains scenes of anti-Semitism, 'serious' treatment of the war has been rare, despite what might seem to be a disproportionate featuring of war books on the Carnegie Medal lists since 1945. One of the most durable adventure stories to use the war as a setting was Ian Serraillier's *The Silver Sword* (1956), which had a long run of popularity as a school text.

Otherwise, the war had to wait for the generation that experienced it as children to grow up. (I consider the portrayal
of aspects of the war in picture-books in Chapter 7.) Characteristic are Jill Paton Walsh's *The Dolphin Crossing* (1967),
about Dunkirk, and *Fireweed* (1969), about the London blitz,
both of which are worthwhile attempts to give self-respect to
children in the ultimate adult world. Paton Walsh epitomizes
this post-war school of writers; careful, intelligent, and positive in its attitude to writing for children. As she has written,
of children,

To reach their possibilities without stumbling over their limitations,
one . . . must find the ultimate structure of what truth one is dealing
in . . . Not everything can be said for children; not everything can be
explained to them. But once it is not clogged up by hesitation and
pretension almost anything can be *told* to them as a story.[7]

The English translation (from the Danish) of Anne Holm's
I Am David (1965), a book about refugees, found a role for
children in war that was both realistic and manageable, but
in Britain at least the most memorable book has been one
that uses the war only as a backdrop. Nina Bawden's *Carrie's
War* (1973) looks very closely at the experience of evacuee children, coming up against Bawden's customary not-quite-normal
adults. When the war does crop up, it is a puzzle: 'Carrie
thought of bombs falling, of the war going on all this year
they'd been safe in the valley; going on over their heads like
grown-up conversation when she'd been too small to listen.'[8]
Such a book makes later attempts, such as Michelle Magorian's *Goodnight Mr Tom* (1981) and David Rees's *The Exeter
Blitz* (1978), both of which won the Carnegie Medal, seem
very ersatz—based more upon British war films than on the
war itself.

Certainly the British comic seems to have been preoccupied
with the Second World War until very recently, and one
attempt to counteract it was the uneasy comedy of Andrew
Davies's *Conrad's War*, which won the *Guardian* Award for
children's books in 1978. Susan Cooper contributed a low-
key, suburban novel, where children's gang-fighting is over-

laid by the air raids and death, *Dawn of Fear* (1970), but the most notable writer on the war has been Robert Westall, beginning with *The Machine Gunners* (1975). Westall was an exponent of the 'new realism', and *The Machine Gunners*, which deals with the breakdown of communication between adults and children under the stress of war, is genuinely atmospheric and ambiguous. His later books about the war seem to owe more and more to film and to nostalgia—which perhaps explains their popularity: readers may be relating to literary rather than genuine experience. The war is being rewritten, with all the attendant ideological implications. *Blitzcat* (1989), which, notoriously, won the Smarties Prize 'for the most outstanding children's novel for 9–11 year-olds', is a tapestry of violence, sex, and horror which seems to be ultimately, if inadvertently, nihilistic. Westall, however, has made his position clear in several talks—that out of death and destruction the writer must find some balance, some hope.[9]

Westall's is an instructive case in other ways. His account of his early career, when he won the Carnegie Medal for a book written for his son, *The Machine Gunners*, raises an interesting point:

I began writing books for the children of publishers, librarians and the literary gent of *The Times* ... Now that I am at last conscious of what I was doing, I look round and see so many 'good' children's books written for the same bloody audience. Books that gain splendid reviews, win prizes, make reputations and are unreadable by the majority of children.[10]

Two latter-day and rather less bloody examples of writing about the war are Judith Kerr's semi-autobiographical *When Hitler Stole Pink Rabbit* (1971) and Bette Greene's account of a German prisoner of war in the southern states of the USA, *The Summer of my German Soldier* (1973, UK 1974).

After fifty years, the Second World War is still with us in fiction for children, and whether this is because it has now become an area in which a country that is no longer a world power can show its heroic side, or because it has become a site for parables, or whether it has ceased to have much reality outside fiction, is not clear. What is clear is that one of the main immediate results of the war was a strong trend towards fantasy of various kinds.

3. Fantasy

Immediately after the war Graham Greene wrote the first of his small books for children, *The Little Train* (1946), but the most enduring character created in this period was Thomas the Tank Engine, who first appeared in *The Three Railway Engines* in 1945. Marcus Crouch demonstrates the ambivalence of the critic, for it is not easy to account for their success:

Enid Blyton's came from a highly professional, even if unconscious, assessment of the lowest common denominator in her audience. The Rev. W. Awdrey was essentially an amateur, whose naïve stories, crudely illustrated, spoke directly to some primitive element in his readers. Few books have inspired greater devotion. *Thomas the Tank Engine* and the others must rank with *Little Black Sambo* among the great bad books of children's literature.[11]

Naïve, perhaps, but not innocent. The books were the target of a scathing attack by Bob Dixon, for their conservative and classist attitudes—trucks are working class, diesels threateningly modern. More recently, Thomas has been recruited as fodder in the academic wars surrounding critical theory (not the first time that such a thing has happened). In his *In Defence of Realism*, Raymond Tallis demonstrates (most convincingly, incidentally) that the books can be read as quintessential postmodernist texts, although he concludes, with the clear implication that it is churlish to use texts in this way:

My use of the Rev. W. Awdrey's work must not be construed as placing it on the same plane of worthlessness as that of Donald Barthelme . . . The trouble is . . . the criteria that place . . . Barthelme on the side of the angels will also put A. A. Milne, Rev. W. Awdrey and a host of other writers of children's books in the forefront of the *avant garde*. Once you start reading anti-realist theory into the practice, you can find it everywhere and in children's literature most of all.[12]

This little excursus can act as a warning to those of us in the field of children's literature who are inclined to look for allies in the realms of literary theory. But, despite this, Thomas has acquired a mythological status alongside Peter Rabbit, and his commercial exploitation seems almost as far-reaching. But Thomas, along with Mary Norton's first books, *The Magic Bedknob* (New York 1943; UK 1945) and *Bonfires and Broomsticks* (1947), was the forerunner of a wide range of fantasies, from science fiction to latter-day Nesbit-like mixtures of domesticity and magic, to books that mixed legend and the modern world, and which explored, often with remarkable sophistication, theories of time.

Certainly in much the same league as Thomas in terms of popularity, but in a far higher one in terms of respectability, is C. S. Lewis's 'Narnia' sequence from *The Lion, the Witch and the Wardrobe* (1950) to *The Last Battle* (1956). With some exceptions they continue Lewis's proselytizing, which began in his (still successful) *The Problem of Pain* (1940) and *The Screwtape Letters* (1942). The strand of respectable faith which underlies these books, sometimes allegory, sometimes fairy-tale, has been, for adults, a short cut to making the books a 'safe' choice. *The Lion, the Witch and the Wardrobe* re-enacts Christ's passion; *The Last Battle* is eschatology made easy (although scarcely clear). Those readers are also happy to accept the borrowing of a very disparate set of elements; the first book, notably, includes Father Christmas, fauns, talking animals, Norse-influenced witches, and, of course, the lion/ Christ figure of Aslan.

On one level, these books combine many attractive elements and a widely imaginative range of incidents, and they are held together by a religious conviction very rare in the twentieth-century children's book. Academic critics have been very interested in the way that Lewis has contrived to transmute his materials, and children have, it seems, found them consistently bright.

The opposite camp, however, holds that the picture of Christianity that Lewis propagates is one of violence; that the books are riddled with his own prejudices; and that they are ultimately unhealthy. The most trenchant statement of this has been, notoriously, David Holbrook:

Most children probably read the stories as spooky yarns, and probably little harm is done. But under cover of his apparent religious intentions and his mask of benignity C. S. Lewis conveys to his readers a powerful unconscious message that the world is full of malignancy; that one must be continually alert; that aggression is glorious, exciting and fully justified; that tenderness, cowardice, and reticence are weak; that one may easily be assured as to one's righteousness; that magic works—and these messages are sometimes conveyed with undertones of a sadistic-sexual kind, or with powerful phantasies rooted in hate. This must surely raise doubts as to the wisdom of exposing children to them, from a writer of such clarity, persuasiveness and power.[13]

As might be expected, there has been a good deal of heated reaction to this attack—but it seems to be based largely upon the naïve religious premiss that to speak against Lewis is to speak against religion and the imagination. On the second point, J. R. R. Tolkien, Lewis's contemporary at Oxford, disliked his 'secondary world' partly on the grounds of its paucity of imagination, while critics have wondered over the books' popularity when the omniscient Aslan denies, in effect, free will in adventure. However, as Margaret and Michael Rustin observe in their psychological study *Narratives of Love and Loss*, 'Lewis's religious views may be in accord with the simplifying moral preferences of the child';[14] whether the concomitant violence is in accord with modern concepts of behaviour is another matter.

At an opposite extreme lie the secular books that have explored time, among them Lucy M. Boston's books about her ancient manor house, beginning with *The Children of Green Knowe* (1954). As Aidan Chambers says, it is 'intelligently arguable that this book directly influenced a number of the writers who began work in the 50s and 60s. (Philippa Pearce's *Tom's Midnight Garden*, Alan Garner's *The Weird-*

stone of Brisingamen and the work of William Mayne owe a considerable debt to Lucy Boston. Discuss.)'. What are distinctive about these books are the ambiguities as to whether what has happened is real, or dream, or imagination, and the 'strong sense of alliance' between the characters through whom the story is mediated, and the narrator. 'All Miss Boston requires of her reader is a willingness to enter into the spirit of sensuous discovery'; and the conservative middle-classness underlying the fantasy may well have added to the appeal.[15]

One of those books arguably influenced by Lucy Boston, Philippa Pearce's *Tom's Midnight Garden* (1958), has received probably more critical praise than any other post-war book. Pearce began with a leisurely rural treasure hunt, *Minnow on the Say* (1955), which demonstrates her capacity for atmospheric writing. *Tom's Midnight Garden*, after a rather wooden and conventional beginning, chronicles Tom's dream-like visits to a Victorian world and raises many questions about time, dream, and psychology. Margery Fisher's view is characteristic: 'The style is impeccable—loose-jointed and flexible, colloquial when the occasion demands, at other times rhythmical and poetic.'[16] Rather more precisely, as Wall observes, Pearce's success 'raises questions, for perhaps the comforting consoling voice and the presence of an overt narratee are a valuable, even perhaps necessary, part of writing for the majority of children'.[17]

A writer who confronts this issue, perhaps to the detriment of a good initial idea, is Mary Norton, with *The Borrowers* (1952 and four sequels). The books, which aim to convince partly through the minutiae of the daily lives of the under-floor inhabitants of houses, are provided with increasingly labyrinthine 'frames' to prove (or disprove) the existence of the characters. These have provided critics interested in narrative structure with a good deal of material, but it can equally be argued that the books are encumbered by a very unwieldy framework (and they were omitted from the 1992 British television serialization of the books). The beginning of the second book, *The Borrowers Afield*, for example, describes how Kate, who was told the story in *The Borrowers* by Mrs May, reflects on its authenticity.

The original story had smacked a little of hearsay: Mrs May admitted—in fact, had been at some pains to convince Kate—that she, Mrs May, had never actually seen a borrower herself; any knowledge of such beings she had gained at second hand from her younger brother, who she admitted was a little boy with not only a vivid imagination but well known to be a tease.[18]

Norton's earlier books, *The Magic Bedknob* (1945) and *Bonfires and Broomsticks* (1947; both books revised as *Bedknob and Broomstick*, 1957), are cheerful farces, unencumbered (or unenhanced) by such intricacies.

Among the most influential fantasies of this period was a curious book that seems almost obligatory reading in American schools, E. B. White's *Charlotte's Web* (1952). Initially a story of Fern's saving of the runt pig Wilbur, it slowly becomes an animal fantasy as the spider, Charlotte, takes over Wilbur's education and makes him famous. The book has been very fertile ground for symbol-hunters and is distinguished by one of the most striking opening lines of any book: ' "Where's Papa going with that axe?" said Fern to her mother as they were setting the table for breakfast.' Like White's earlier fantasy *Stuart Little* (1945)—which begins with Mrs Little being delivered of a mouse—*Charlotte's Web* is an uneasy mixture, which moves simultaneously from innocence to experience and (paradoxically) from naturalism to fantasy.[19]

But the writer of fantasy who has been as much a darling of both academic and child-orientated critics as of the children is Alan Garner. He began his career with two breakneck-paced thrillers, *The Weirdstone of Brisingamen* (1960) and a rather poorer sequel, *The Moon of Gomrath* (1963), both of which superimpose figures and creatures from a liberal selection of mythologies upon the real (or slightly edited) Cheshire landscape, which, as one reviewer remarked, becomes positively cluttered with svarts, dwarfs, trolls, and apparatus from Welsh, Manx, Norse, Scandinavian, and Arthurian legend. Whatever weaknesses the books have—primarily those caused by conforming too closely to children's book conventions—they are chilling, and although Garner has dismissed them, he also edited them slightly to tighten the prose. Critical opinion is divided over *Elidor* (1965), which posits a parallel world, but one whose symbolism is ambiguous.

Garner, whose more recent work has been in folklore, produced two books that have received the highest critical attention—and in the case of the first, sales and educational endorsement to match. *The Owl Service* (1967) is a remarkable exercise in oblique narration. In an isolated Welsh valley, a story from the *Mabinogion* of adultery and murder is re-enacted generation after generation. The current re-enactment also involves upper/lower-class tensions as well as Welsh/English, and the improbable magical and traditional elements are conveyed more subtly than perhaps in any children's book before it.

Garner's next book, greeted by one reviewer as 'a bad attack of gimmicky self-indulgence brought on by over-praise' and by another as 'probably the most difficult book ever to appear on a children's list',[20] was *Red Shift* (1973)—and those comments surely reflect a very conservative attitude to what 'children' can and should be offered. This three-layered or parallel text deals with two atrocities (a massacre by and of Roman legionaries, written as if the Romans were US marines; a massacre during the English Civil War) and the unhappy loving of two adolescents in the present day, and shifts between them. The stories are bound together by being enacted on the same piece of ground, and by symbols and artefacts and similar characters. The narrative, often in long stretches of untagged dialogue, is spare to the point of being skeletal, and frequently brutal. As John Rowe Townsend observed: 'I cannot see that there is anything in it for a child, or much for an early teenager. It is just a novel, and more adult than most "adult" novels.'[21]

There are American connections here. Fantasy in the USA has not generally been as strong as in Britain—with rare exceptions such as Natalie Babbitt's work (for example, *Tuck Everlasting* (1975)), but outstanding is Ursula Le Guin's

'Earthsea' trilogy (1967–72), the work of a philosopher, and 'primarily concerned with the meaning of death and immortality'.[22] Le Guin creates a secondary world, and provides a densely layered quest story in which Ged's story parallels children's search for identity. But, in comparison with, for example, *The Lord of the Rings*, it is a very American work. As Peter Dickinson observed of Le Guin in an interview: 'Have you noticed what an *American* writer she is? The basic myth! The boy in *A Wizard of Earthsea* did the fastest spell in the West! Her books are perfect examples of the American myth translated. *The Tombs of Atuan* is *Shane*: here is this girl on this great ranch, and she is oppressed . . . and here is this tall stranger, wounded, comes riding in.'[23]

The books are also, like much fantasy, sexist. Le Guin has written a fourth volume, *Tehanu* (1990), which to some extent redresses the balance, and discussed her position in a lecture given in 1992, *Earthsea Revisioned*:

Since my Earthsea books were published as children's books, I was in an approved female role. So long as I behaved myself, obeyed the rules, I was free to enter the heroic realm. I loved that freedom and never gave a thought to the terms of it. Now I know that even in fairyland there is no escape from politics, I look back and see that I was writing partly by the rules, as an artificial man, and partly against the rules, as an inadvertent revolutionary.[24]

Fantasy, then, is bound by the same politics as rule the primary world, whether it links to past legends directly or not. Other books that have built on or exploited older materials include another, perhaps rather less philosophical, distinguished trilogy, Lloyd Alexander's *The Book of Three*, which is a respectful gloss on T. H. White and Welsh legends. This seems also to be part of an attempt, perhaps especially by Americans (Nancy Bond's *A String in the Harp* (USA 1976) is another example), to recapture their roots.[25] Some attempt was made to consider a mythology of pre-Columbian America by Jane Curry in *The Daybreakers* (1970).

An Englishwoman who has moved to the USA, Susan Cooper also made use of myth, transposing it very successfully into contemporary England. The nightmares of not knowing whether ordinary-looking people are of this world or not, and of having to resolve huge problems within the everyday, are strikingly followed through. *Over Sea, Under Stone* (1965) might be taken as the paradigm for post-war children's novels: in its four sequels Cooper broadens her range and refines her effects. In *The Dark is Rising* (1973), for example, the chilling opening describes curious happenings in the bleak winter fields, and the hero, Will, meets a farmer: ' "The Walker is abroad," he said . . . "And this night will be bad, and tomorrow will be beyond imagining." ' Will then goes to bed, and outside the storm breaks.

He switched off the light again, and instantly everything was even worse than before. The fear jumped at him for the third time like a great animal that has been waiting to spring. Will lay terrified, shaking, feeling himself shake, and yet unable to move. . . . Outside, the wind moaned, paused, rose into a sudden howl, and there was a noise, a muffled scraping thump, against the skylight in the ceiling of his room. And then in a dreadful furious moment, horror seized him like a nightmare made real; there came a wrenching crash, with the howling of the wind suddenly much louder and closer, and a great blast of cold; and the Feeling came hurtling against him with such a force of dread that it flung him cowering away.[26]

The range of fantasy produced in the 1960s and 1970s is remarkable; it was a period of fresh and intricate ideas. An outstanding example is the Booker prizewinner Penelope Lively, who began her career with a series of witty and increasingly difficult books, some, like *The Whispering Knights* (1971), appearing on the surface to follow the early Garner, some, like *The Ghost of Thomas Kempe* (1973), providing high comedy, and others, like *The House in Norham Gardens* (1974), looking forward to her adult work. *The Ghost of Thomas Kempe*, typically, is 'a book about layers—not only . . . layers of artefacts . . . but also layers of recorded time', and it conveys its sense of the past 'through attention to the changes in a language'.[27]

Helen Cresswell is another writer who has covered several genres most competently. Her initial humorous, nostalgic books like *The Piemakers* (1967) and *The Signposters* (1968) took on a more sinister element with *Up the Pier* (1972) and *The Nightwatchmen* (1969); she has also had a considerable impact with several humorous series, notably the 'Bagthorpe Saga', beginning with *Ordinary Jack* (1977), which raise many questions, just as poetry does, as to how far adults and children can share humour.

This period also saw Joan Aiken's series of books set in a fictitious nineteenth century, with King James III on the throne, wolves (who have migrated through the Channel tunnel), and the Hanoverians waiting in the wings, beginning with *The Wolves of Willoughby Chase* (1962). Notable single fantasies were Pauline Clarke's story of what happened to the Brontës' toy soldiers in *The Twelve and the Genii* (1962); Catherine Storr's remarkable psychological nightmare *Marianne Dreams* (1958), and probably the best of many books in which children exchange identities with children in the past, Penelope Farmer's *Charlotte Sometimes* (1969).

Similarly, although science fiction has been successful 'downmarket', only a few British writers such as Donald Suddaby, John Christopher, and Nicholas Fisk have made it respectable—along with several American imports such as Robert E. Heinlein, André Norton, and Madeleine l'Engle, and one highly successful British all rounder (like A. A. Milne assistant editor of *Punch* for a time), Peter Dickinson.

Peter Dickinson's 'The Changes' trilogy began with a dream of an England in which everything had reverted to medieval times, *The Weathermonger* (1968), an idea elaborated more seriously in *Heartsease* (1962) and *The Devil's Children* (1970). These books are part of a large genre in children's publishing, not so much science fiction as future-speculation. His 'very "iffy" books', as he has described them, have also stemmed from issues: they are ways of making points, of propagandizing—a form of writing somewhat frowned upon elsewhere. *Tulku* (1979), winner of the Whitbread Award, is an adventure set around the Boxer rebellion, although it seems to be actually about manipulation (and has been accused of racism), while *City of Gold* (1980) consists of retellings of Old Testament stories. Both these books won the Carnegie Medal and Dickinson's success has continued—*AK* won the Whitbread in 1990.

Dickinson writes comfortably for two audiences; it is rather rarer to find a book that attracts two distinct audiences. *Watership Down*, a first novel by Richard Adams, must, as Elaine Moss notes, 'surely be the supreme example of a freak success that resulted in self-perpetuating sales stimulated partly by the non-book media'.[28] Adams began a revival of the animal story, and was an object-lesson to publishers. *Watership Down* was rejected several times (it is said that one reason was that the hero—a male rabbit—is called Hazel) before becoming a best seller for both adults and children, briefly holding the record for the fee paid for paperback rights, and going on to become an animated film with a title song that became a hit record. Apart from its careful rabbit's-eye view of the world, *Watership Down* is a classic example of the male-oriented 'quest' book, with a highly conventional range of characters, from the sensitive mystic to the bone-headed strong man. Fantasy it must be, but underneath the fur is an archetypal set of humans.

4. The Maynestream: Forms of Realism

Of course, many authors, like Dickinson, crossed these notional boundaries. Leon Garfield's work is unique in that his writing is essentially pastiche. At his best, he full-bloodedly pulls the reader into an eighteenth- or nineteenth-century world of narrow alleyways and fog and Dickensian or Fieldingesque plots and grotesques, carried on a verbally aware and ingenious language. One of the problems for child-oriented critics has been that his morality is about as foggy as his books, and in books like *The Pleasure Garden* (1976) he provides virtually no signposts. Townsend's comment about his style, that 'he heels his craft at a spectacular angle and looks as if he may capsize at any moment into a sea of bad writing; but he never does',[29] is rather generous, but it makes the key point. Garfield needs very strong material to allow it to survive. His best work may well be in the humour of the Regency *The Strange Affair of Adelaide Harris* (1971) and with ghost stories, notably *The Ghost Downstairs* (1972).

If Garfield's style is distinctive because of its echoes of past writers, William Mayne's is perhaps the most distinctive of all children's writers because it is unlike any other. Mayne is a paradox, or a conundrum; he has published over 100 books since *Follow the Footprints* in 1953, and yet he is not a household name, and, where he is known, is often accused of not being a children's author at all: perhaps the epitome of that 'adulterated' side of publishing for children in which the more a book appears to be like an adult book, the more highly it is valued. And yet, with rare exceptions,[30] he is also unappreciated by 'adult' critics. This in itself says a great deal about both the standards of the literary establishment, and the standards of the children's literature establishment. As Wall has pointed out:

Mayne's commitment to children is so intense and so strong, and is borne out so forcibly in all his writing that it is extraordinary that there can be a doubt about his intended audience. That there is such doubt . . . [is] the result of some widely held but little discussed assumptions about literature for children. A book for children is not a good book unless it is enjoyed by the majority of children; pace and drama are essential in fiction for children; complexity is out of place—these are some of the assumptions that underlie attacks on Mayne's work.[31]

Indeed, as publishers are not notoriously charitable, Mayne can clearly look after himself, and in a rare interview he observed, 'It might be a comfort to some child to know that *its* way of thinking is not necessarily wrong because it's not the "right" way—I don't want them to think that the accepted way has any more value at all than their own way.'[32]

This may account for the style that 'operates as a form of continuous subdued recoil against the narrative shape and impetus which his plots demand'.[33] Mayne's books require thoughtful, careful reading and there are two opposed critical views: one that he is a close ally of the reader, the other that he is a watcher, alienated from character and audience alike.[34] I would say rather that stylistically he is an original: because he stands so close to his characters, and frequently close to their dialect, readers of all ages are inclined to misinterpret him. Thus he is also close to the child narratee, if the real reader can read slowly enough.

Take this example from a picture-book text for young children, *Barnabus Walks* (1986):

Barnabus walks when all the scholars have left the schoolroom and gone hip-hooraying home.

When the black-board chalk-dust floats in the setting sun and the desks are still; when the ink is silent and the clock asleep; then Barnabus comes out of his house on a shelf.

Scholars call it a hutch, but to Barnabus it is a house, with a front door, a dining room with hay, a bedroom with straw.[35]

Or, to choose at random from Mayne's output for older children, here is the opening of *The Twelve Dancers* (1962). Mayne's remarkable eye for reproducing childhood perceptions, and the gap between childish logic and adult schemata, is neatly demonstrated. Note also that Mayne's primary stylistic trick is to subvert our expectations of sentence structures.

Blue is the colour of the sky. Marlene was in bed still when she thought that. It was the colour of the sky in a chalk drawing or a painted drawing, but it was not the colour of the sky this morning. The sky now was green over the hills, with silver clouds lying tarnished above it. Higher still the sky was bruised with overhanging morning.

There was a foot out of bed. Marlene brought it in and put it bitter behind the other leg's warm knee. It lay cold and clammy, because the dew of the room had settled on it just as it settled on the window, hanging like a mask on each pane. They were green masks, because of the hills beyond. The hills were a different green from the sky. Miss Williams, down at the school, would never allow a green sky into a drawing. Marlene thought Miss Williams must be an artist, to see things differently from ordinary people. She could look at the sun, and make people draw it yellow. Marlene had never looked at the sun, except once. It had looked white at the moment, then black for the rest of the day. Nobody else thought the sun was black.

Mayne is, it seems, frequently misread (by adults) because readers, unused to his demands, try to read him for plot. His earliest books, from *Follow the Footprints* to *The Member for the Marsh* (1956), lay great emphasis on plot, but even then there is a tendency to cloud, to be looking somewhere else. Thus books like *A Parcel of Trees* (1963) or *The Battlefield* (1967), although they have mysteries to solve, are seemingly more concerned with place and character. He has touched many genres: the quartet about a choir school (*A Swarm in May* (1955 and sequels)) combines atmospheric writing with mystery and the dynamics of the public school. Although *Earthfasts* (1967) has been praised as a contribution to the fantastic, Mayne seems to be uncomfortable with the mechanics of fantasy (*Over the Hills and Far Away* (1968) is another example). However, over the last decade he has broadened his range from political satire (*Tiger's Railway* (1987)) to quasi-myth (*Drift* (1985) and *Antar and the Eagles* (1991)). The critical success of these later books suggests that Mayne is still a writer to be reckoned with: his *Low Tide* won the 1993 *Guardian* Children's Fiction Award—thirty-six years after *A Grass Rope* won the Carnegie Medal.

Another reason why Mayne has not been accorded major status (as opposed, say, to Garner) is that he has not obviously written about, as it were, portable themes. His folklore is not derivative. And he chooses a single focus, a single audience, which, of course, makes him suspect. Equally, while other writers demand 'knowledge and experience', Mayne 'presupposes intelligence and a willingness to think hard'. As Wall puts it: 'Mayne chooses—and he chooses children.'[37] This is why Mayne is worth considering at length: his very invisibility despite his huge output may well make him the true children's writer—true to his audience.

One of the few genres not touched by Mayne is the curiously unprestigious 'historical novel'. This may be a critical association with adult light reading, or a suspicion that we must necessarily be dealing with the covertly educational, but any account of children's literature cannot sensibly omit Hester Burton, or a writer of the status of Rosemary Sutcliff with her

Roman trilogy *The Eagle of the Ninth* (1954), *The Silver Branch* (1957), and *The Lantern Bearers* (1959). More domestically, there are the eight 'Mantlemass' novels of Barbara Willard, beginning with *The Lark and the Laurel* (1970), in which 200 years of history are seen from the point of view of a sequestered country house.

Which brings us to the 'new realism', a genre perhaps originating in William Mayne, but which has developed steadily towards dealing with serious (and often brutal) social problems. Characteristic is Berlie Doherty's 1992 Carnegie Medal winner *Dear Nobody*, a series of letters to an unwanted unborn child. The problems over such books are summed up by the chair of the selection committee: 'Where would it go in the library? Too old for the younger teenager, might it become lost on the adult shelves?'[38]

It is this vexed question of 'content' which led librarians in the USA to introduce the category of 'young adult'; however, in the media context of today, where readers are exposed to all kinds of material, such issues may seem superfluous.[39] What was felt to be missing in the early 1970s was 'the literary novel with an adolescent hero or heroine seen coming to terms with the world and self'.[40]

There are several strands here that have produced novels of great sociological and literary interest. In the British tradition, the 'domestic' novel has continued, and some of the authors, notably Jane Gardam, have produced books that have found an adult market; they are as much about childhood as for or of it. *A Long Way from Verona* (1971) and *Bilgewater* (1976) are characteristic; *A Few Fair Days* (1971) could stand beside classics about childhood such as Laurie Lee's *Cider with Rosie*. So could Alan Garner's latest non-folklore book, generally reckoned to be a masterpiece of children's fiction (and, thus, almost by definition inaccessible to children), *The Stone Book Quartet* (1978-9). Here Garner has refined his language even further, to a remarkable succinctness, and making great use of West Mercian dialect. Each novella presents one notable day in the life of a child from four generations of the Garner family. Like many very successful

children's books, it is about the relationships between generations, but it is also about craft and its loss, about tradition
and time. That there have been many questions about whether
children can cope with the text reflects more on attitudes
in teaching than on Garner. It is eminently quotable. Here, in
the second story, Joseph, the 'Granny Reardun' (i.e. brought
up by his grandmother), decides to get out from under the
shadow of his grandfather Robert and to become a smith.

'Will you set me on?' said Joseph. 'I'll be prenticed to you.'

'Shall you?' said the smith. 'Come up, then.'

He was a big man, in his shirt sleeves; a leather brat, tied round his
waist, reached below his knees. He bent and put his arms under the
farrier's anvil, lifted it from its bed, carried it across the yard and set
it down.

'Now take it back,' he said to Joseph . . .

'I can't shift it,' said Joseph.

'A smith carries his anvil.'

'Well I can't yet.'

'You can't shift an anvil,' said the Smith, 'yet you want to join the
generous, ingenious hammermen? . . . Give me one reason why I
should set you on . . . You're old Robert's lad, aren't you?'

'Ay.'

'The granny reardun.'

'But me mother's coming up our house for her dinner.'

'You're still a granny reardun.'

Joseph said nothing.[41]

Others have approached the everyday lives of children, and
almost certainly the best of these (although her range is wide)
is Jan Mark. Mark won the Carnegie Medal in 1977 with her
first novel *Thunder and Lightnings*, and demonstrated the
subtle understanding of children's relationships which makes
her a writer who can simultaneously be appreciated by adults
and by children. Her short stories about school life, in particular
Hairs in the Palm of the Hand (1981), show a rare appreciation
of the subtle realities of contemporary schooling. Jan Mark
won a second Carnegie Medal with *Handles* (1983), a low-key
exploration of identity; in some senses, she has successfully
reworked several well-mined genres.

It is interesting to see that the religious/didactic element in children's books has been replaced by a movement to be 'politically correct'—socially and racially aware. This need has been answered by hundreds of books clearly designed to be bibliotherapeutic (or, if we are cynical, to exploit the market). Foremost among those who would probably claim to be writers first, and propagandists—if at all—second, are Bernard Ashley, with books about working-class/multiracial life seen from the inside, such as *The Trouble with Donovan Croft* (1974) and *High Pavement Blues* (1983); Jean Ure whose teenage novels face up to such matters as blindness, terminal illness, homosexuality—as well as the embarrassment of a boy becoming a ballet dancer (*A Proper Little Nooryeff* (1982)); and Catherine Sefton with books about Northern Ireland, such as *Starry Night* (1986). (Sefton is the pseudonym of Martin Waddell.) A good many well-intentioned books have run into trouble with those concerned about racism, for example Jan Needle's anti-racist *My Mate Shofiq* (1978), which, for dramatic purposes, may have presented the racist position too vividly. Janni Howker's *The Nature of the Beast* (1985) pushes back the frontiers of acceptable material to raw working-class political comment; Anne Fine, in a series of edgy comedies, has explored the relationships between youth and age, and the discomforts of divorce (as, for, example, in *Goggle-Eyes* (1990)). Michele Landsberg has commented on this genre that 'while not all British problem novels are works of genius, most seem to exercise a tactful reticence on the subject of teenage sex, rarely confusing it for the ultimate meaning of life'. Unlike, she implies, the Americans.[42]

It is certainly true that (although, as we have seen, there have been some distinguished fantasies) the main thrust of post-war American children's and teenage fiction has been in 'realism'. The quality and range of American output has been remarkable, and, in the freedom (spatial as well as sexual) accorded to the children, as much an influence on British fiction as were the American writers of the late nineteenth century.

The family-centred tale, which was continued during the Second World War in the old tradition by Eleanor Estes

(*The Moffats* (1941; UK 1959)), still flourishes for younger children, but has been displaced for adolescents by books that acknowledge the difficulties of late twentieth-century life. Writers as diverse as Virginia Hamilton, Cynthia Voight, Catherine Paterson, and Betsy Byars have explored with varying degrees of rigour (and symbolic intent) issues of race, death, and displacement. The underlying element of moving westward (as opposed, in the English tradition, of digging deeper) has been replaced by concepts of survival in a corrupt world. The most distinguished of these are Hamilton's explorations of racial questions (*Zeely* (1967), *M. C. Higgins, the Great* (1974)); Voight's 'Tillerman' series, beginning with *Homecoming* (1981); Paterson's *Bridge to Terabithia* (1977) and *The Great Gilly Hopkins* (1978); and Byars's rather lighter *The Pinballs* (1977).

It is very common in American texts to find that even books which are apparently comic have disturbing undertones, and three writers stand out for their sustained wit and intelligence, outpacing any British equivalents. Elaine Konigsberg, whose books, such as *From the Mixed-Up Files of Mrs Basil E. Frankweiler* (1967, UK 1969) and (*George*) (1970, UK 1974), confront displacement and race relations and illness in an oblique way, is consistently experimental—as was Ellen Raskin. Her first picture-book, *Nothing ever Happens on my Block*, is still successful, while her 'puzzle-mystery' *The Westing Game* (1978), a battle of wits between narrator and reader, but with a gallery of essentially sad characters, won the Newbery Medal. The third author dealt with city life: Louise Fitzhugh's *Harriet the Spy* (1964) seems at first to be a comedy, but is slowly revealed to be an exploration of the child as victim of rich metropolitan life—indeed, of a whole life-style.

It is hardly surprising that these themes have emerged in more popular fiction, in what have been called, perhaps unkindly, the 'anorexic' novels: that is, novels designed to illustrate problems. A good many of these cannot be lightly dismissed; a random sample might include Paul Zindel's *The Pigman* (1968), Ursula Le Guin's *A Very Long Way from Anywhere Else* (UK 1976), or a characteristic example of a 'lightweight' book tackling adolescent problems, Paul Danziger's *The Cat Ate my Gymsuit* (1974, UK 1986).

Much fire has been levelled at the most popular of these writers, Judy Blume, whose books of adolescent ponderings, such as *Are You there, God? It's Me, Margaret* (1970, UK 1978), have been dismissed by critics and welcomed by children. The biggest divide is illustrated by *Forever*, the first book to feature explicit teenage sexual activity; and the anti-Blume movement is well summed up by Landsberg, who, in a comment that rather undercuts her own criticism, but contextualizes modern children's literature, observes: 'Innocence, if it ever existed in the sense of sexual ignorance and/or purity, is a vanished quality.' She goes on: 'How is it possible to devote an entire novel to teenage love without conveying one tremor of rapture, joy, delight, intensity, sadness, dread, anxiety or tenderness? Blume's "love" is all fumbling and bra hooks, semen and birth-control pamphlets.'[43]

The attacks upon the book have not, on the whole, centred on the explicitness of the sex (in many ways it is too clinical to be called salacious), nor on the fact that the adolescents are acting outside the adult moral code. Rather, it is the *lack* of excitement and mystery; perhaps the gap between the reading generation and the criticizing generation is at its widest here, as witness John Rowe Townsend, writing on *Are You there, God? It's Me, Margaret*: 'This story . . . is a sad one, really. To an adult it seems a shame that the competitive jostle towards maturity should force itself into the child's consciousness at such an early age.'[44] Thus Blume's books, by turns edgy and bland, dramatic and displaying the small change of daily life, have been undervalued by critics. The fact that she appeals to a huge audience means, of course, that she may be setting as much as reflecting the trend. However we view her, it is salutary to think that *Forever* was designed for an audience of the same age as were the readers of *The Fifth Form at St. Clare's*, *Swallows and Amazons*, or *Little Women*—or, indeed, Beverley Cleary's innocent (if sexist) novel *Fifteen* (1956, UK 1962).

A similar distance between readers, writer, and critics is found in the case of Robert Cormier, whose novels, as Ann

Scott Macleod has observed, have had an impact on the field of adolescent literature well out of proportion to their number. He began by demolishing the school story in *The Chocolate War* (1974, UK 1975)—a grim novel in which a school mafia and a corrupt teacher succeed in defeating (and very nearly killing) the apparently upright 'hero' figure. Cormier (amid a good deal of dispute) moved on to governmental brainwashing (*I Am the Cheese* (1977)), terrorism, betrayal, and highly graphic murder (*After the First Death* (1979)) and voyeurism, sadism, and sexual deviancy in *Fade* (1988). Curiously, Cormier's stated views are very similar to Edward Ardizzone's: that adolescents should be told the truth; the reaction to him is most often that he sells hopelessness.[46]

Equally revealing are S. E. Hinton's books, the first of which, *The Outsiders* (1967, UK 1970), was published when she was 17. It is a fascinating mixture of formulaic gangster scenes from the cinema: this, it might be said, is the image of life perceived by the child from the media, reflected back into books—and, ultimately (as the book was itself filmed), back on to the screen. The whole process has been made rather easier, one feels, by the fashion for the demotic first person, perhaps derived from J. D. Salinger's *The Catcher in the Rye*.

Commercially, these books shade into formula writing[47] in most genres, with romance being the most popular. Series have been 'manufactured', notably by the publishers Bantam and Scholastic, where the chaste world is full of good guys called Mark, solid second-lead nice guys called Thad, bad girls (who wear make-up) called Pam, and 'plain but interesting' girls called Jenny. The prose is nothing if not workmanlike (if not entirely grammatical):

How white his teeth were, how straight and black his hair, but it was his eyes that fascinated her. They flickered with all sorts of emotions, flashed with humor, smouldered with a tinge of anger, then grew gentle when they looked at Pam. It tore at Jenny's heart. If only there was some way to escape.[48]

The current picture of novels for children and adolescents across the world provides a spectacular range, from the formulaic to the metafictional. At one point of the compass are difficult, experimental novels, such as Aidan Chambers's *Breaktime* (1978), *Now I Know* (1987), and *The Toll Bridge* (1992), which deal seriously with matters of narrative, philosophy, religion—and sex, and violence. Justifiably famous is the scene in *Breaktime* when the hero makes love with his girlfriend; the pages divide into three: one column consists of a first-person narrative of what is happening, and, on alternate lines, an internal monologue (in italics); the other column is an extract (on sexual intercourse) from Dr Spock's *A Young Person's Guide to Life and Love*.[49]

At another extreme is the hugely successful 'respectable' romance such as K. M. Peyton's 'Flambards' trilogy (1967–9). At yet another are Robert Leeson's attempts to secure a new, or at least a continuing, audience for books by being innovative within the context of the middle-range—rather than middle-class—reader (*Time Rope* (1986) and *Slambash Wangs of a Compo Gormer* (1987)), or subversive (*Candy for King* (1983)), or realist (*It's my Life* (1980)).

In the last forty years books from Australia, New Zealand, and Canada have increased their influence on children's literature in the USA and the UK, and all three have high-quality book-production and world-class authors, backed by a very strong academic and public awareness. For example, a study by the Australia Council found that of all the books bought in Australia, '30 per cent were children's books, and 30 per cent of those were Australian'.[50] The names of the pioneering librarians Lilian H. Smith (*The Unreluctant Years* (1953)) in Canada and Dorothy Butler (*Cushla and her Books* (1979) and *Babies Need Books* (1980)) in New Zealand are known world-wide.

Among Australian authors, Ivan Southall and Patricia Wrightson have perhaps had the greatest international success. After writing ten books about an Australian 'Biggles', Simon Black, Southall produced a group of award-winning books, often of the harshest realism, with groups of children pitted against the Australian elements. There is a bush fire in *Ash Road* (1965), children trapped in a flying aeroplane with a dead pilot in *To the Wild Sky* (1967), while *Finn's Folly* (1969) brings together a fatal crash, cyanide, a reservoir, and other unpleasant devices. His best book may well be *Josh* (1972), an intense semi-autobiographical novel which won the Carnegie Medal.

Patricia Wrightson has forged a new mythology for Australia, which, while taking into account aboriginal thinking, has produced an original synthesis. Books like *The Ice is Coming* (1977) and *The Nargun and the Stars* (1973) are haunting evocations of strange landscapes, but her contribution to urban realistic fiction, *I Own the Racecourse!* (1968), is just as distinguished. It is beyond the scope of this book to do justice to the talent emerging from Australia, but outstanding writers over the last ten years who have acquired international reputations include Libby Gleeson, Victor Kelleher, and Nadia Wheatley.

Margaret Mahy dwarfs other writers from New Zealand, with around one hundred books, some of which originated in the pages of a unique publication, the *School Journal*, published by the Department of Education. This began in 1907, and since the 1940s has been largely fiction, and, as Betty Gilderdale has observed, 'the quality of the *Journals* ensures the attention of the young reader and affords a favourable impression of indigenous art and writing for children'.[51] Mahy has had considerable success as the writer of texts for picturebooks, such as *A Lion in the Meadow* (illustrated by Jenny Williams, 1969), and high comedy, such as *The Great Piratical Rumbustification* (1978). However, her two Carnegie Medal winners, *The Haunting* (1982) and *The Changeover* (1984), which explore the supernatural impinging on the contemporary world, and the naturalistic and highly quirky *The Catalogue of the Universe* (1985) and *Memory* (1987), have moved her into the forefront of writers for teenagers. Her oblique view of the world, and her humour that keeps tragedy at bay, are a potent combination, and she has found favour with academics, as well as in the popular market-place.[52]

Mahy has contributed a good deal to books marketed for lower age ranges—along with Chambers and Blume and the whole spectrum of writers. New bears have appeared beside Pooh—notably Michael Bond's Paddington (from *A Bear Called Paddington* (1958)). Characteristic of the best of these books are Russell Hoban's successful small-scale domestic dramas *Bedtime for Frances* (1960) and its four companions. Hoban is an excellent example of a writer whose range allows him to write as strikingly for children as for adults; his partnership with Quentin Blake has produced one master-piece—*How Tom Beat Captain Najork and his Hired Sports-men* (1974)—which combines child-centred drawings (words do not help to explain the pictures), a satire on adult discip-line and cautionary tales, and a *Bildungsroman* structure. As with his adult novel *Riddley Walker* (1980) or the book that lies between the two lists, *The Mouse and his Child* (1967), some of Hoban's work seems destined to take on the status of myth.

5. Picture-Books and Verse

If, however, there is any one area in which children's books have found their own individual voice, and have influenced literature in general, it is in the picture-book. Illustrations for novels have become unfashionable since the first two decades after the Second World War, when distinctive work was done by Charles Keeping, Margery Gill, Pat Marriott, Anthony Maitland, C. Walter Hodges, Lynton Lamb, Robin Jacques, William Stobbs, Shirley Hughes, Pauline Baynes (most not-ably for Lewis's 'Narnia' series), and others.

The picture-book built to some extent on the pre-war tradition. There was a strong stylistic influence of the Poles Jan Lewitt and George Him, whose most famous book is probably Diana Ross's *The Little Red Engine Gets a Name* (1942), and many individualistic contributions, notably from Mervyn Peake, with the eccentric grotesques of *Captain Slaughterboard Drops Anchor* (1939; reissued 1945) and *Ride-a-Cock-Horse* (1940), a collection of nursery rhymes using stencilled colour with aniline dyes. He memorably illustrated *Treasure Island* in 1949.

Landmarks in illustration include the biennial Hans Christian Andersen Award (1953–   ), and the Kate Greenaway Medal (1955–   ) which was first presented to Ardizzone for *Tim All Alone* in 1956. Ardizzone's major—pioneering—achievement in children's books began, as we have seen, with the first version of *Little Tim and the Brave Sea Captain* (1936). Ardizzone was a Royal Academician and later a war artist, and his illustration of many books is characterized by a pre-1914 golden age nostalgia mixed with a rather tough and unsentimental approach, despite the fact that his books are designed for the younger reader.

Little Tim began as a tale made up to amuse his children, and was one of the first books to be colour lithographed (in the USA). In 1949, with *Tim to the Rescue*, he adopted a standard format of pen and colour drawings on one opening and pen only on the next, and his previous books were redrawn to match. Ardizzone's mature style contrived to intermingle the words and the text, even using the occasional speech balloon, but he was a master of lighting effects, of shadow and suggestion, as can be seen from his work in, for example, *Eleanor Farjeon's Book*, *The Little Book-room*, and *Peacock Pie* (1946). *Little Tim* remains, as Marcus Crouch observed, 'a major landmark in English picture books, for its fine colour, vigorous action drawings, beautifully simple and vivid prose, and profound understanding of children and their dream fantasies'.[53]

From the 1950s onwards, the picture-book, in all forms from the very junior board-books to books which are actually for teenagers or adults, increased in quality and quantity. The refinement in offset litho meant increased quality in the books, and Brian Wildsmith is generally credited with spearheading this new development with his *ABC* (1961). As Whalley and Chester note, 'Wildsmith's use of rich masses of textured colour flooding off the page initiated the "painter's" style that has recently threatened to extinguish the art of illustration by a dependence on its own qualities and a lack of concern for textual integration and the design of the book as a whole.'[54] To the impartial observer, these seem at first to be books for the artistic adult, although it could be equally argued that they are actually books which appeal directly to children, but only those children trained towards such a static concept of art.

Charles Keeping's work is more inclined to narrative. Some of his best work, like *Joseph's Yard* (1969), is heavily symbolic, and some of his later work crossed over into the adult sphere, with his illustrations to *The Highwayman* (1981) and *The Lady of Shalott* (1986). Keeping also illustrated the contentious attempt by Edward Blishen and Leon Garfield to retell the Greek myths, *The God beneath the Sea* (1970), and the opinion of many is that the illustrations are far better than the text.

Another illustrator whose preoccupations have enabled him to work across the age range is Raymond Briggs. His career began with illustrations to Hamish Hamilton's 'Antelope' series, and he made his name with the 897 illustrations to *The Mother Goose Treasury* (1966). Since then, he has been simultaneously more inventive and more depressive. He has made the cartoon strip not only a speciality but respectable, notably with his iconoclastic (and occasionally vulgar) *Father Christmas* (1973) and the wordless *The Snowman* (1978). His pessimism and brutal realism within the context of the cosy-looking cartoon strip developed from the sad fatalism of *Gentleman Jim* (1980) to the apocalyptic and merciless account of nuclear war, *When the Wind Blows* (1982). This, although published for adults, was often to be seen (predictably enough) in the children's section of bookshops—as was his direct and bitter political satire on the Falklands war, *The Tin Pot Foreign General and the Old Iron Woman*. However, he has also contributed to the success of some classic picture-books, notably Elfrida Vipont's *The Elephant and the Bad Baby* (1969), and produced a cult classic of existentialism and scatology, *Fungus the Bogeyman* (1977).

If Briggs is a writer whose pessimism may seem to some to be a dubious contribution to children's reading, John Burningham has pushed back the frontiers of the picture-book in a rather more cheerful fashion. His first work was rather leaden (*Borka: The Adventures of a Goose with no Feathers*

(1967)), but he became one of the foremost experimenters in the form with *Come away from the Water, Shirley* (1977), which explores the contrast of adults' views and the child's view. *Granpa* (1984), with its multiple narrative patterns and sophisticated use of layout, colour, and type-styles to indicate different kinds of material, presented a distinctive and ambiguous approach to death—one which was considerably smoothed out in a cartoon-film version (and, oddly, a book of the film). Burningham's *Where's Julius?* (1986) is a counterpoint to *Shirley*, where the parents involve themselves in the child's fantasy world.

Of the 'realist' artists, who chart day-to-day lives of children, Shirley Hughes stands out. Hughes began as a book-illustrator, working in fine line (in the tradition of the Brocks) on books by Mayne and others, but her later work has been largely in colour. She chronicles with a very perceptive eye the lives of respectable urban and suburban Victorian-terrace streets with her 'Lucy and Tom' books, beginning with *Lucy and Tom's Day* (1960), and the Alfie and Annie Rose series, beginning with *Alfie Gets in First* (1982). The wordless *Up and Up* (1979), and the experimental *Chips and Jessie* (1985), which combines the cartoon strip with standard text, stand beside classically rounded family tales such as *Dogger* (1977) and the six remarkable miniatures of the *Nursery Collection* (1985–6).

A pervasive presence in picture-books as well as in illustrated books is Quentin Blake, who has worked on nearly 200 books. His 'apparently spontaneous art . . . springs from exacting working methods';[55] he is able to produce very fine nuances of human expression from what seems to be casual drawing. He has been particularly successful with books of 'performance' verse, where the reading act matches the controlled anarchy of his drawing, such as *Mister Magnolia* (1980) and *We All Join In* (1991), as well as producing what is to all intents and purposes an adult novella of great wit and sympathy, *The Story of the Dancing Frog* (1984).

At this point, the catalogue of distinguished, inventive, and talented artists could become extensive: Helen Oxenbury,

Anthony Browne, Jan Ormerod, Julie Vivas, David McKee . . . McKee's work is noteworthy both for its political dimension, and for his attempt to reproduce the child's-eye view of art by flattening perspective: indeed, *I Hate my Teddy Bear* (1982) has become a classic of surreal, 'anti-adult' writing. Most successful of all is Janet Ahlberg (and her husband Allan), who has produced two texts designed to be read by children that are both of the child's world and of the child's mindset— *The Babies' Catalogue* (1982) and *Starting School* (1988)—and others which require a good deal of contextual knowledge of nursery texts, such as *Each Peach Pear Plum* (1978) and, more experimentally, *The Jolly Postman* (1986) and *The Jolly Christmas Postman* (1991)—with which we have come nearly full circle to John Newbery, for if it does not contain a ball and pincushion, it contains a jigsaw puzzle and a board game.

While the havoc created by the war almost brought children's book publication in Europe to an end, in America a new tradition was built. Pre-eminent has been Maurice Sendak, whose first children's book was Marcel Aymé's *The Wonderful Farm* (1951) and whose first big success was Ruth Krauss's *A Hole is to Dig* (1952). Sendak's work is highly allusive, as in *Outside Over There* (1981)[56] (although the quality of his written text is questionable), and highly aware of the spatial codes available to the picture-book artist—notably in *Where the Wild Things Are* (1963, UK 1967). The broadness of the American tradition can also be seen in the great diversity of styles in such artists as Marcia Brown, Ezra Jack Keats, and Chris Van Allsburg.

From the British point of view, the American contribution has been most striking in cartoon-related materials, from Tomi Ungerer, Richard Scarry, Roger Duvoisin, the anarchic Dr Seuss, whose *The Cat in the Hat* (1957) began a long series of 'easy readers', and, more recently, Sandra Boynton and Rosemary Wells. Wells was a pioneer of the short picture-book, and her texts are wry and understated, allowing even the smallest child to join in (as with *Stanley and Rhoda* (1978, UK 1980)). She addresses those things that adults tend to bury. Consider the matter of going to school for the first time:

working in a direct line from Beatrix Potter in producing spare, ironic, single-audience-oriented texts, Wells has treated this in *Timothy Goes to School*. For the first three days, whatever Timothy wears to school is wrong, according to the execrable Claude:

[Left opening]
  After school, Timothy's mother could not find Timothy. 'Where are you?' she called.
  'I'm never going back to school,' said Timothy.
  'Why not?' called his mother.
  [Right opening]
  'Because Claude is the smartest and the best at everything and he has all the friends,' said Timothy.
  'You'll feel better in your new football shirt,' said Timothy's mother.
  [Page turn: left opening]
  Timothy did not feel better in his new football shirt.
  [Right opening]
  That morning Claude played the saxophone.[57]

This is very subtle, careful writing, and it is not surprising that some adults, remembering their own schooldays, rapidly reject the subject-matter and hence the book. But the first line of this extract depends on the build-up of the pattern (a traditional feature) being broken; the whole text depends on the ironic treatment of both the mother and Timothy—child readers can see the characteristic practicality and helplessness of the mother on the one hand, and the innocent optimism running into despair of Timothy. And the whole matter is paced carefully within the small confines of the 'young child's' picture-book. All of this is too subtle to be discarded lightly.

  I have left poetry to the end of this survey. It epitomizes the difficulties of judgement, for it seems to be most *of* childhood when seeming to be least acceptable to adults. The tradition of the playground rhyme, collected by Iona and Peter Opie in *The Lore and Language of Schoolchildren* (1959), is essentially anarchic, a thing made of tags and fragments from the adult culture—and a good deal more scatological than the Opies were able to print then. (Iona Opie's *The People in the*

Playground (1993), and Michael Rosen's *Inky Pinky Ponky: Children's Playground Rhymes* (1982) has since redressed the balance.) Poetry for children seems to be essentially rhymic or narrative, rather than static and contemplative. Perhaps most of all, it is (again in contrast to the views of high culture) accessible to childhood—it becomes part of what children *write*, and it becomes interactive. Brian Morse, introducing a selection of nearly 150 in-print books of poetry for children in 1992, advised teachers trenchantly:

Poetry that's good enough for children ought to be good enough for you too: if the poetry you are introducing makes you uneasy (maybe because it's only jokey, maybe because it's the heritage sort that's handed down as the best and you've never really liked it), then trust your own judgement. Dump it ... Read children poetry you feel happy with ... Enthusiasm is contagious.[58]

Curiously, the fact that poetry is very much a minority occupation in the adult world has had its effects in education. The way in which poetry has been treated in schools—which are the pivotal point—has changed under the influence of a few pioneers. In 1978 Michael Benton wrote: 'Poetry has had bad luck. It has suffered a double misfortune: neglect where it most needs attention and concern where it is best left alone.' He went on to point out that books on children's literature invariably neglect it, and that the Bullock report on language and literature in schools, *A Language for Life*, devoted only 3½ of 600 pages to poetry.[59]

Into the 1990s poetry is probably more visible in children's publishing than in adults'; there has been a great deal of colloquial, more ephemeral, squibbish verse published by poets such as Kit Wright, Michael Rosen, and Roger McGough, but all of these can move from the slight to the serious. McGough, particularly, is the master of the joke which has a sting to it, and the same poems are printed in his books for adults and for children.

Verses tend to be freer and more graphic. One example, by Allan Ahlberg, can stand for all: a sad joke, pitched at a level that allows a genuine dual focus: 'Slow Reader':

I—am—in—the—slow
read—ers—group—my—broth
er—is—in—the—foot
ball—team—my—sis—ter
is—a—ser—ver—my
lit—tle—broth—er—was
a—wise—man—in—the
in—fants—christ—mas—play
I—am—in—the—slow
read—ers—group—that—is
all—I—am—in—I
hate—it.[60]

But poetry remains a very potent weapon, which emphasizes a fact which will have become evident from this historical survey. The world portrayed by the poetry of the last quarter of the century is very different from that of the first; as with the novel, and, as we shall see, even the picture-book, a reality that is harsh and unidealized is pervasive. Poems about children being killed in Northern Ireland are a far cry from Robert Louis Stevenson's peaceful garden of verses, or Isaac Watts's optimistic and pious songs, and for many adults that is a very uncomfortable thought.

7

Uses and Abuses, Themes and Variations

The picture of children's literature that emerges from 300 years of history is one of a literature divided between entertainment and edification, and criticism today is divided along the same lines.

As we have seen, the idea that children's books should be, or can be, as free of ideological 'taint' as an idealistic concept of childhood might wish is obviously naïve. What complicates the simple distinction between 'pure' and 'applied', or *dulcis et utile*, is the paradoxical cultural status gap that has opened up between them.[1] Literary studies have for many years been seen as 'superior' to educational studies, and yet 'realist' texts have generally been seen as superior to 'fantasy'. This chapter explores some of these dichotomies, and some of the ways in which this most democratic of literary forms can be read, both practically and theoretically.

1. Censorship and Social Engineering

Children's literature, more than most literatures, is susceptible of control at all stages of its production. As Alan Garner put it,

There are three principal human beings between a story and the child reader: the writer, the editor and the adult who makes the book available. If they go down like dominoes, if the adult can dictate to the editor and the editor commandeer the author, then where is the story? Where is the child?[2]

But this is inevitable in any literary system, and it is only because of a romantic sense of responsibility to childhood that it seems unusual or undesirable. And such an attitude (which is common) may carry a subtext which questions the expertise of those involved.[3] Nevertheless, it focuses on the knotty problem of adult authorial freedom, and the adult control of childhood: once again, everyone can be involved, and on an equal footing.

In the USA there are many examples of books banned by local or state legislatures, of books being burned, of teachers and librarians being victimized. Many of the examples may well seem absurd, as when Garth Williams's *The Rabbit's Wedding* was banned because the marriage was between a black rabbit and a white rabbit.[4] In the UK, the procedure tends to be more covert, with teachers, school library services, publishers, and retailers responding, as it were, silently, to a complex web of reactions.

The polarization is easily summed up. One camp holds two basic unspoken premises: first that children can and should be protected, and secondly that anyone within the system may exercise restraint. The other is that any censorship is, *per se*, a bad thing, and all that can be done is to exercise a very local control over the reading of a child or group of children. Both groups start from the assumption that books are an important influence (although that is, in itself, questionable). Because the book is held to be more involving and interactive than, say, a video, then its impact is supposedly stronger. The book also has a culturally mythic status (whatever the reading statistics): what it describes it may also be supposed to endorse.

However, as Gillian Klein has pointed out in her survey of children's books and learning materials, *Reading into Racism*, 'the producers of books for children have assumed that the messages in them are very important indeed', and, as often as not, those messages will operate subliminally. There is, as Klein concedes, 'No such thing as an unbiassed book',[5] but she suggests that it is the reader who must be educated to deal with the books, rather than that the books must be changed. Political correctness may be a movable feast, but the printed word inevitably plays a part (if a diminishing one) in shaping as well as reflecting society. Thus a survey in the USA showed

that, between 1973 and 1975, only 14.4 per cent of books published for children featured a black character, which reflects
quite accurately power in society rather than demography,
and does not necessarily (or probably) reflect attitudes of
authors or the audience that they address.[6]

A rather less book-centred view is that both these camps
overestimate the effect of books. Children are, increasingly, subjected to a mass of information and entertainment, of which
books are (with rare exceptions) a relatively small part. Children who do read a lot are likely to have a very varied diet,
which may well not appeal to the adult's conception of childhood. Thus a competent early teenage reader at the beginning
of the 1990s is quite likely to be reading anything from Enid
Blyton school stories to violent, surrealist texts such as those
based on the 'Twin Peaks' film/television series, and from Judy
Blume and Paula Danziger (rather lightweight books specifically designed for the teenage market) to *Romeo and Juliet*.
Solemn discussions of what readers should know are very
often mocked by what they do know.

Another important point is that, as reader-response theory
and practice shows, what children understand from texts is far
from clear. They may find the structure of adult taboos quite
contradictory: for example, the facts of sexual activity and
death are surely not in themselves objectionable; it is any
violence accompanying them which makes them questionable,
and yet violence itself is far from taboo. Thus, until recently,
the approach to the death of children in children's books has
been avoided (parents, grandparents, and pets have not been
so sacrosanct); those deaths which have appeared have done
so, as it were, under adult escort.[7]

As Cadogan and Craig noted, since the 1970s, 'the sense of
moral obligation, which governs all writing for children, has
acquired an new bias. It used to entail keeping your stories as
anodyne as possible; now, if anything, the opposite holds true.
Painful topics have become virtually *de rigueur* as far as
children's fiction is concerned.'[8] What is lacking is a sense of
perspective and an ability to perceive what books are actually
doing and saying. As Gillian Klein put it:

At no stage have campaigners against racism, sexism and class bias in books suggested that our entire vast heritage of children's literature be discarded. That awesome body of books, however, asserts overall that only white people exist, only the middle class matter, and that boys will be boys and girls will be good.[9]

The awareness of the potential effects of the subtexts of Enid Blyton or the 'Janet and John' series must be put beside the changes in society which allow children to see, literally as well as figuratively, far more extreme forms of prejudice as the norm. This collision between world, book, and child is most strikingly demonstrated by the picture-book.

2. Realism and the Picture-Book

One of the paradoxes of children's reading is that a verbal text, while it may have immense interactive potential, may also disguise by virtue of the inexperience of the reader: whether realism in words alone is discerned by the readers will depend upon their experience. Picture-books have a more immediate affect; they are more accessible, they literally show as well as tell.

Realism in literature is an interesting concept. After all, '[Literature] first tries to reflect reality as faithfully and as fully as it can, and then, despairing of the attempt, tries to evoke the feeling of a new reality of its own.'[10] Children's literature is often identified with forms of fantasy; escapism, wish-fulfilment, the dreams and ambitions of the weakest and most dependent seem to be best fulfilled in books that explore possibilities rather than describe actualities. A good many parents and teachers I have spoken to betray a certain lack of delight in ordinary life, and feel that they are depriving children if their imaginations are not allowed to go beyond it (a curious reversal of pre-1850 views on the matter). Realism is for adults. As the *Westminster Review* wrote in 1853, 'a scientific, and somewhat sceptical age, has no longer the power of believing in the marvels which delighted our ruder ancestors',[11] and the marvels were, in Tolkien's memorable phrase, 'relegated to the nursery'.[12]

So effective has been this process that, as we have seen, after 1945 there was a period when books in which the laws of the ordinary world are *not* suspended (to take the broadest possible definition of 'realism') were in the minority, especially among British books. As John Rowe Townsend wrote: 'since the second world war the realistic has continued to be the dominant mode in American and Australian fiction for children. In Britain realism has lacked prestige, and until recently has not attracted anything like its share of the ablest writers.'[13] This may be attributed initially to an adult reaction to post-war drabness, but Michele Landsberg's opinion was that 'some of the best writers for young people deal in fantasy precisely because the power of young sexuality, the urgency of life and death questions, are diminished and shrivelled into lifelessness by too direct a representation'.[14]

Equally, could it be that the adults are more afraid of reality than the children? How do we present the unpleasant truth about humanity? Ardizzone, as we have seen, thought that 'If no hint of the hard world comes into these books, then I am not sure that we are playing fair,' but how naïve was Ardizzone? A lot of recent books that deal with 'realism' deal with some very hard aspects of the world indeed, from the horrific (child abuse, mass destruction) to the taboo (sex and death).

Realism sits uncomfortably between fantasy (where the rules of the world are suspended) and romance or adventure (where the rules are bent). Fantasy has the advantage that it can handle large, rather than local, problems; it can overcome difficulties (evil, death) by changing the rules; the romance and the adventure, on the other hand, are set in a recognizable world, but one which simplifies or ignores the problems. Fantasy is sometimes discredited (by, perhaps, a puritanical turn of mind) as being a cheat, but it can deal with the universal. Romance/adventure may mislead and confuse because of its ostensible relationship to the 'real' world: Enid Blyton's 'Famous Five' and other adventure series are best read as 'romances'; Roald Dahl gets away with much worse violence, sexism, and vulgarity, because he is obviously writing fantasy.

As a consequence, realism is a poor relation. As Michele Landsberg observed: 'The pitfall of the realistic novel, when it is based in a one-dimensional contemporary reality, is that it is by definition too specific to be of much use.'[15] This is true of form as well as content, and such 'localization' may work against the need for the child readers to expand their horizons, and can reduce the texts to bibliotherapeutic aids.

Two questions have to be asked at once. Can you have realism in fiction at all; and then, can you have realism in children's fiction in particular? The second is a question of social practicalities, which are discussed in the next chapter, while the first is a matter of theory, and its investigation can lead into some very arcane philosophical areas. The argument against 'realism' in fiction is that all fiction is fantasy. However, as Raymond Tallis has persuasively argued in his *In Defence of Realism*, life is only understood in terms of storying (what Barbara Hardy memorably called the 'primary act of mind');[16] 'events' only exist in the telling or description of them; stories only 'falsify' reality in so far as all orderings of reality necessarily falsify it. Having said that, we can then say, as Tallis does, that 'Realism takes up the challenge of all literary art most directly and most compendiously: to discover a significant order (or disorder) in common experience; to deepen and sharpen our sense of reality; and, ultimately, to mediate between the small facts that engage us and the great facts—that we are unoccasioned, that we are transient, that we nonetheless make sense of the world—that enclose us.'[17]

The question then becomes another: can an acceptable illusion be created? To begin with, this seems to be a technical point, as reference to a standard dictionary of literary terms shows (although almost every aspect of this description raises interesting points with regard to children's literature):

Realistic is the label we apply to those novels that seek to provide a convincing illusion of life as we normally think of it . . . Realistic novelists are often moralists . . . In talking about a realistic novel, however, we should resist the temptation to discuss it as if it is real life . . . The realistic novel attempts to reproduce something of the complexity of life itself . . . Realistic novels sometimes end unconvincingly, because the aim of providing a full picture of life cannot really be reconciled with the order that is often established in the closing chapters of a book.[18]

The point about moralists is particularly pertinent. Because the adult writer or mediator has power over the child reader, the image of the world presented may have a particular force or influence. We want to select what the children may or may not know, and at which stage in their development they may know it. As adults, we might be able to make allowances for, say, Hugh Lofting's racism, but can the child? And we may have plenty of other prejudices that an unselected, realistic snapshot of the world might uncomfortably reveal. As Westall put it, 'Because we adults are upset by children's real thoughts, we regard them as being unsuitable material for children's books. . . . You don't even have to go as far as death to find taboos in the children's book world. We need go no further than the loo.'[19]

Of course, the 'lower' human functions are not germaine to story; but is this true of children's books? The case of Arthur Ransome's books springs to mind—where the omission of such details (amid the welter of other practicalities) is, if not conspicuous, a minor niggle to modern readers. And there is a good parallel here with the mechanics of sex in Judy Blume's *Forever*; there is plenty of evidence from teachers that copies are bought for straight informational rather than, or as well as, erotic purposes.

Thus, one of the major differences between realism and fantasy is not that, in the latter, the physical laws of the world are suspended; certain moral or ethical ones are too. I find it hard to imagine that violence is encouraged by the cartoon violence of, say, 'Tom and Jerry', because I find it hard to imagine a viewer who cannot distinguish between realism (even realism as seen on a TV screen) and that kind of fantasy—but also because the viewer can distinguish between what is morally or socially acceptable in those different worlds.

'Realistic' books for children fall into several categories. The first is a category rarely found outside children's books: books where the characters are not human, but everything they do, and the way they live, is quintessentially so. Jill Murphy's *Five Minute's Peace*, Russell Hoban's 'Frances' books, and Margaret Gordon's deadpan 'Wilberforce' books fall into this category. The use of bears, or elephants, or badgers (or whatever-Frances-is) does universalize and avoids problems of race sufficiently, perhaps, to short-circuit the limitations of realism that we have already discussed. A second category raises questions of whose reality we are dealing with; and the two key examples, Julie Vivas's version of *The Nativity* and Sarah Moon's photographic version of *Little Red Riding Hood*,[20] may at first seem a long way from realism as conventionally defined.

Julie Vivas's angels have moth-eaten wings and large boots; Gabriel discusses things with Mary over a cup of hot something, and holds the baby while Joseph shoves her on to the donkey; Mary gets hugely pregnant. Despite its caricatured form, this book struck me as bringing to the story a curious modernity (the text is from the Authorized (King James) version, which comes over as deadpan rather than poetic in the context). It challenges us to rethink the images we may have in our minds, of whatever kind of reality the text deals with: it is subversive in a way in which children's books have been prevented from being for too long. (Perhaps needless to say, the book has had a frosty reception from some religious groups.)

Sarah Moon's *Little Red Riding Hood*, with the Perrault text, is a bleak set of very dark photographs, with the little girl running through grim and shadowy city streets, meeting an unseen wolf in his shadowy wolf-like car, and finally (as in the original) undressing, getting into bed, and (in shadow) being eaten. This is realism of the sleazy kind, pinning down an ultimately frightening and frightened tale, and questioning whether it should have ever been in the children's canon.

Indeed, many of the most interesting examples of realism lie on the borderline between realism and fantasy; each contributes to the life of the other. John Burningham is a master here, but Anthony Browne's work, pushing towards surrealism (*A Walk in the Park* (1977)) or dream (*Gorilla* (1983)) or reverie (*Look What I've Got* (1980)) or allusion (*Hansel and Gretel* (1981)), is another rewarding example; even a humble joke such as Jill Murphy's *On the Way Home* (1982), where the heroine retells the story of her scraped knee in several ways, takes us into a fascinating borderland, rarely acknowledged by mainstream fiction.

The borderland may also be marked by visual style. David McKee's masterpiece is probably *I Hate my Teddy Bear* (1984) but he has made the same point with *The Sad Story of Veronica who Played the Violin* (1987) and *Who's a Clever Baby, Then?* (1989). McKee's art is deceptive; he challenges the very way in which we organize our concepts of reality, as compared with a child. By flattening out whole complex landscapes he deals with the way in which the child (the innocent, the guru) sees all parts of the world as equal. Perspective has to be learned.

From this point, it could be said that realism is a matter of degree, a matter of where the lens is pointed. There is, as I have suggested, a very strong British school of what might be called 'domestic' realism—realism restricted to what the child might see and comprehend, but which does not duck the implications of what is seen. Shirley Hughes has provided almost a guidebook to Victorian-house urban life; the Ahlbergs (*Starting School*, *The Baby's Catalogue*) have an orbit perhaps a little further into the suburbs. And there have been excellent contributions from Bob Graham (*First there was Frances* (1985), *The Wild* (1986), *Pearl's Place* (1983)), Jan Ormerod (*Sunshine* (1981) and *Moonlight* (1982)), and Philippe Dupasquier (*Our House on the Hill* (1987)).

Yet the difficulties remain: the Hughes houses are surrounded by a savage world, and we have seen the difficulties that arise with a writer like Cormier. *The Chocolate War*, as the critic Betsy Hearne observed, 'manipulates readers into believing how rotten things are by loading the dice', and Norma Bagnall drew the general conclusion that 'We can teach hopelessness to our young if they are taught that no matter how hard they struggle they cannot win.'[21] But Cormier is writing fiction. What of that group of books which deal with very harsh realities, such as the Jewish Holocaust or the bombing of Hiroshima?

A common first reaction is that this cannot be the stuff of picture-books, but as books which treat of the Holocaust, such as Abells's *The Children we Remember* (1986), Wild and Vivas's *Let the Celebrations Begin* (1991), or Innocenti and Gallaz's *Rose Blanche* (1985)[22] have demonstrated, the picture-book is a potent form. The questions of whether what we are shown is falsified, whether such falsification is productive or unproductive, or what subtexts are inevitably expressed are very complex. Hamida Bosmajian has suggested that Holocaust narratives for children 'show the limits of language . . . all are selective and self-censoring';[23] they also, perhaps, show the limits of thought.

Picture-books which have dealt with Hiroshima, such as Toshi Maruki's *Hiroshima no Pika* (1982) or Junko Morimoto's *My Hiroshima* (1987),[24] are mercilessly graphic examples: the latter shows the dead and the dying with their skin hanging from their fingers. They clearly raise both direct and indirect political questions. *My Hiroshima*, for example, was published in Australia, and includes a brief paragraph on 'The Facts about Hiroshima'; the sentence describing the event omits one, arguably salient, fact: 'At 8.15 a.m. on August 6, 1945, an atomic bomb was dropped on the Japanese city of Hiroshima.' Many doubts have been expressed about their appropriateness to the age range which usually uses the picture-book, and certainly to their uncontextualized use.[24] In reply, Barbara Harrison has observed that 'in postponing discussion, we must be careful that we are not also saying, ask me no questions about indifference, about fear; ask me no questions about my own responsibility for action and for change'.[25]

3. Children's Literature in the Classroom

'Creating in children a love for literature is a basic part of the educational process'; so begins *Children's Literature: Strategies of Teaching*, which is characteristic of the vast library of texts that have been created around children's literature in education.[26] Children's books are used not only as a way of teaching the dominant culture, but as the bases for a huge range of educational projects. (As an example, Charlotte Huck's *Children's Literature in the Elementary School*, which, in its fourth edition (1987), runs to nearly 800 pages, has a 300-page *Instructor's Manual* of more practical ideas to go with it.[27]) Of these, I would like to consider, as an indicative example, the attitudes that have developed towards the use of 'literature' in reading education.

As before, there are two views, polarized between those who support the 'reading scheme'—the carefully graded text—and those who support the use of 'real books' in the classroom. It is as much an ideological argument as an educational one. Consider this view:

I am sure that, in spite of their modern forward-looking teachers, quite a lot of bright middle-class children, with parents working feverishly in the background, are still learning to read. But what about the ordinary working-class children and those from educational priority areas, whose parents don't know how to make up for classroom deficiencies? What about the inexperienced teachers influenced by statements that reading is best taught through language experience and ungraded reading books.[28]

The contrary argument is that 'literacy' means more than 'functional literacy'. As Jill Bennett puts it: 'Getting the words right is only a small part of knowing how to read; and to get the most from a book the reader must learn the rules that the maker is inviting him or her to play, the crucial matter being the nature of the bond with the author.'[29]

It is easy to see why there is a conflict; even though two theories are being propounded, the language is hardly neutral. Take Liz Waterland, the successful advocate of the 'apprenticeship approach to reading', who adopts Elaine Moss's distinction between 'free-range' and 'battery' books, the latter being 'the product of a factory-like approach to literature, exemplified, I think, in the fact that so much reading-scheme material comes shrink-wrapped in sets. There is a hint of unnatural practices, of confinement and restriction, of a lack of fresh air and room to spread one's wings; even a suggestion of the mechanical and automatic.' As she observes, reading schemes (as opposed to primers of various kinds) date from the late 1800s, and they were 'brought in to enable the untrained monitor to teach reading. These youngsters [a good example is seen in *Little Town on the Prairie*], themselves often only a very little older and wiser than those they taught, needed something which would deskill the reading process . . . The saddest thing is that this view of the teacher as being unable to teach without some prop . . . should still have such currency.'[30] Again, this evades the patent point that, sad though it might be, and unskilled as the teachers might be, this is reality. Rather functional literacy than no literacy. Waterland's credo is easily seen as élitist; after all, who is to say that the 'reading scheme' is necessarily devoid of skill, or of literary value (despite C. S. Lewis's view: 'I will not say that a good story for children could never be written by someone in the Ministry of Education, for all things are possible. But I should lay very long odds against it.').[31]

An American text, while not criticizing 'basal readers' directly, does so by implication, devoting scarcely two pages to them out of a 200-page book. It distinguishes the questions: 'What skills do I want my students to learn?' and 'What attitudes about reading and books do I want to promote?' Even-handedly, it goes on: 'We cannot tell you what the best answers to these questions might be, because in our experience . . . in some communities there will be a strong emphasis on preserving a heritage . . . in others an emphasis on skills and preparation for later education; in others an emphasis on individual creativity and the imagination.'[32]

Clearly some compromise is required, such as Robert Protherough's suggestion that 'Ideally any sort of programme should be firm enough to exemplify some identifiable pattern at the children's level, yet flexible enough to be modified in the light of changing needs and interests.'[33] Factually, there is little question: Huck *et al.* cite a good deal of research to indicate the value of reading to children and a 'literary' background, but understand the problems involved:

Teachers who want to incorporate more literature into their reading programs need to experiment with ways that are comfortable for them and still meet the expectations of the schools. If they are willing to risk new approaches, they may find their children are enjoying reading more and becoming real readers, rather than children who simply know the skills of reading.[34]

Lurking behind this debate may well be the suspicion that children's literature is not actually 'work', and this relates to one of the underlying themes that can be traced through the history.

4. Work and Play: Adults and Children

As we have seen, children's literature can be related to concepts of childhood, and childhood can be defined in terms of responsibility versus lack of responsibility—and that, at least in some cultures (including the British), can be defined as work versus play.

Consequently, children's books are, almost by definition, NOT concerned with work; they are concerned 'merely' with play: a lesser activity, and the modes adopted, such as fantasy, consequently become lesser modes. The typical person whom Ursula Le Guin accused of being afraid of dragons is that 'hardworking, upright, responsible citizen, a full-grown, educated person'.[35] It is interesting that Le Guin begins her definition of an adult with the word 'hardworking'. But the utilitarian might say that there is a falsity here; work is part of life, and children are surrounded by it and are being prepared for it: can it, should it, be ignored?

Of course such a split is characteristic of the majority of imaginative texts. In Thackeray's *The Virginians*, the narrator comments (at the opening of chapter lix) that 'The real business of life, I fancy, can form but little of the novelist's budget . . . All authors can do is depict men *out* of their business.' Even the school story does not actually deal with school*work*. Children's books, after all, are fun and work is not. Work, then, forms a contrastive subtext to the golden play-world of the child. In one way, the concept of work becomes a class-specifier: childhood, from the mid-nineteenth century, and perhaps before, is something only the middle class could afford; not only work but the workers who clear up after the jolly nursery children are invisible. Who serves the breakfast at Toad Hall?

This defining aspect is shown in the characteristic reading matter fed to the Victorian working-class child. As J. S. Bratton says in her *The Impact of Victorian Children's Fiction*, describing books circulated by the SPCK: 'The message repeated over and over again . . . is "remember your time is your employer's": servants exist to serve, and if their souls are their own [many] SPCK writers seem to find that their least important dimension.'[36]

Consequently, work is marginalized. Macdonald and Kingsley, for example, acknowledged the fact of work, but saw escape only through fantasy, and salvation only through death. Others either treated work as a scarcely imagined and repressive ritual (Carroll) or virtually ignored it (Grahame). Nesbit used it as a framework, and although she is less culpable than most of her contemporaries her attitude (despite her Fabianism) is not far from Wilde's 'Really, if the lower orders don't set us a good example, what on earth is the use of them?' More recently, work settings have been used primarily to link generations as in Berlie Doherty's *Granny was a Buffer Girl* (1986), to act as initiation (William Mayne's *The Incline* (1972)), or as both (Leon Garfield's *The Apprentices* (1977–9)).

Fortunately, some exceptional texts locate the child in a more complete world. Kipling, for example, celebrates for children the importance and continuity of work and craft. 'Contrivance, conjuring, craft: through such characteristic code-words he almost too easily acknowledges their dignity and worth, and at the same time assimilates himself as craftsman to their world.'[37] In the 'Puck' books Kipling relates the children to their heritage, not only in place and history, but in the context of work, and with it craftsmanship, dedication, and achievement. Thus when, in the Romano-British story 'On the Great Wall', the Emperor Maximus says, 'It is always one man's work—always and everywhere,'[38] he is alluding not just to inspired leadership, but to real work. Although Dan and Una are privileged, they share the work ethic. Thus the farm-labourer, the hop-pickers, the smith, the milkmaids, the carters, and the men on the timber-tug all give and receive respect. Hal o' the Draft, the master mason, interrupts his story to give Dan some advice, after Dan has cut himself: ' "That came of not steadying your wrist," said Hal calmly. "Don't bleed over the wood. *Do* work with your heart's blood, but no need to let it show." '[39] All the occupations are meticulously, even lovingly described, as when Weland makes the sword for Hugh.

He had worked for his living, and he paid his debts before he left ... Then he made a sword—a dark-grey, wavy-lined sword—and I blew the fire while he hammered. By Oak, Ash, and Thorn, I tell you, Weland was a Smith of the Gods! He cooled that sword in running water twice, and the third time he cooled it in the evening dew, and he laid it out in the moonlight and said Runes (that's charms) over it.[40]

In Kipling's books, children are taught to respect codes and craft, and to understand that work is all around them and that they are part of it. Curiously, this is also true of Arthur Ransome, who is usually credited with having invented the fictional holiday, and who, it is sometimes supposed, gave his children a freedom to play, apart from adults. But, like Kipling, Ransome valued the virtues of craft; in their complex games the Swallows and Amazons and their friends do labour. Prospecting and mining and panning gold in *Pigeon Post* (1936) involve drudgery; smoothing the dinghy's mast in *Swallowdale* takes days of careful, repetitive work. Ransome relates these apprentice efforts to those who work on the land around the children, and makes some important points about the middle classes and the workers. In *The Picts and the Martyrs* (1943), two middle-class children play at living alone in the woods, and it is the local farmer's boy, Jacky, who shows them how actually to survive. For him, childhood is work:

'I' mun be getting along [said Jacky]. Summer and back end's our busy time.'

'Whose busy time?' asked Dick.

'Farmers,' said Jacky, as if he owned a thousand acres. 'Aye busiest time when other folks are having holidays. I'se going wi' dad to market to-day. We've young pigs to sell.'[41]

Work has to be taken seriously. When Nancy Blackett in *Swallows and Amazons* suggests having 'a last blaze on the camp fire' by burning the hay from the haybags on which they have been sleeping, Mr Jackson, the farmer, will have none of it: ' "Nay," said Mr Jackson, "It's good hay that." So it was spared to be eaten by cows.'[42] The people highest in the hierarchy of respect for Ransome's children are the skilled workers, and the children, although treated with respect, are not indulged. Thus when, in *The Big Six*, the boatbuilders' sons are accused of the cardinal sin for the Norfolk Broads—casting off boats—one of the mothers says, 'Casting off boats and that is no good in a place like this, and [the boatbuilding company] would have sacked your Dad if he weren't too good a boatbuilder to lose.'[43] The structure of Ransome's books, as we have seen, is generally the folk-tale pattern of serious preparation followed by the exercise of acquired skills: your life may well depend, directly, upon the quality of your work.

Alan Garner's *The Stone Book Quartet* charts the relationship between craft and craftsman and children over four generations and the gradual decline of tradition. The book is full of images of work. In *Granny Reardun* Joseph, who is to become a master smith, contemplates his grandfather's work:

That great steeple, that great work. It was a pattern left on sand and air. The glint of the sun from the weathercock shimmered his gaze, and the gleam about the stone right to the earth. He saw golden brushes, the track of combing chisels, every mark. The stone was only the finish of the blow. The church was the print of chisels in the sky.[44]

Obviously, the old crafts make more entertaining reading than, say, chartered accountancy, and so some of the power of these books must come from nostalgia. But they show that childhood does not need to be isolated from the adult world, nor does work need to be seen as a negative counterpoint.

5. *Journeys and Places*

The relationship of child to adult is a theme that also recurs in terms of the child's literal place in the world: very many books originate in a sense of place. This, combined with the frequent journey motif—often itself allegorical—and the desire in the child to comprehend the shape of the world, literally and metaphorically, has led to a singular use of landscape, and the map. There are also certain advantages for the authors, as Stevenson observed:

The author should know his countryside, whether real or imaginary, like his hand . . . It is my contention . . . that he who is faithful to his map, and consults it, and draws from it his inspiration, daily and hourly, gains positive support, and not mere negative immunity from accident. The tale has a root there; it grows in that soil; it has a spine of its own behind the words.[45]

For younger children, the journey is generally a metaphor for exploration and education; readers go, like Tolkien's Hobbit, 'there and back again' in a circle that enables them to gain knowledge—to be stabbed by experience—and to return to home and security, and to a satisfying psychological 'closure'. As the readers grow, so the journeys become longer, and the circles are broken: the text becomes a *Bildungsroman*, accounts of rites of passage are metaphorized as quests.

But fantasy only works with reference to an understandable norm; as Irwin says, the reader 'is persuaded to play the new system of "facts", which he has wilfully and speculatively accepted, against the established facts, which he only pretends to reject'.[46] Because of the closeness of both reality and fantasy in the child's world—as well as the possibility, the permitting of, fantasy—children's books are based in narrative. Indeed, they are often about narrative—about the business of getting on with the story; two of the basic themes of the fairy-tale, quest and flight/pursuit, have been taken over. Linked to this is the sequential 'chaining' of primitive narrative, to which children may respond because it is close to their natural idiom; the elemental thrust of story-telling in an oral culture (to which children belong, at least residually) lends itself to the journey—just as the early novel used the picaresque.[47]

In British children's books writers have frequently appealed, as it were, to the third dimension of landscape. Because of its history, places in Britain carry resonances—a fact exploited most explicitly by Kipling in the 'Puck' books: British places *mean*—whereas American children's fantasy tends to be set in secondary worlds. This use of tradition and history, which is a rich source of plotting, can be related to adults' nostalgia and romanticism, as well as to the wish to pass on national-istic traditions and codes of conduct. The dialectic of past and present is seen very strongly in Alan Garner: Neil Philip notes, a little picturesquely, of *The Weirdstone of Brisingamen*, that it 'was not conjured from some airy inspiration, but drawn from the rock, soil, and sky of Cheshire'.[48] Certainly *The Owl Service*, *Red Shift*, and—more positively—*The Stone Book Quartet* are motivated by just such continuity. As the last of the four stories, *Tom Fobble's Day*, ends, 'The line did hold. Through hand and eye, block, forge and loom to the hill and all he owned, he sledged sledged sledged for the black and glittering night and the sky flying on fire and the expectation of snow.'[49]

English fantasy, then, tends to explore a national psyche, with the 'objective correlative' of place being projected on to the fundamental patterns of growth. Also, at various levels, the maps used 'cage the landscape' and are both reductive and suggestive—as well as symbolizing the tension between the real landscape and the adult- and child-fantasies that inhabit it.

For example, Michael Wood observes that Tolkien has 'a fascination with the . . . journey . . . it becomes a figure or type of death, the happy release', and also that his 'old times are . . . simply historical, a picture of pre-industrial England, a place of unspoiled greenery, fields and forests'.[50] Thus, although 'Middle Earth' is a secondary world, it obviously borrows heavily from a real England. As Tolkien said, of the picture of England that he portrays so idyllically at the beginning of *The Lord of the Rings*, and which is so damaged at the end:

The country in which I lived in childhood was being shabbily destroyed before I was ten, in days when motor-cars were rare objects . . . Recently I saw in a paper a picture of the last decrepitude of the once thriving corn-mill beside its pool that long ago seemed to me so important.[51]

Just as most of the place-names in his book can be found on real maps, so the Shire is a very potent image of an unspoiled, idyllic, rural Arcadia-England, such as every generation seems to feel the need to create—the world of Sir Roger de Coverley in the eighteenth century, of Surtees and Jefferies in the nineteenth, and of H. E. Bates, John Moore, Flora Thompson (for adults) and 'BB', Mary Norton, Beatrix Potter, Kipling, Grahame, and Ransome (for children) in the twentieth. (These authors are themselves becoming part of the 'nostalgia industry'.[52]) The Hobbits 'love peace and quiet and good tilled earth: a well-ordered and well-farmed countryside was their favourite haunt.'[53]

Its distance from the pastoral world of much English fantasy may account for the comparative lack of success in this sense of C. S. Lewis's Narnia, and why it seems so weak as fantasy but strong as allegory. Unlike Tolkien's or Garner's worlds, Lewis's huge cast has nowhere to live; the journeys (despite the symbolic gestures at maps in the books) are spiritual, notional, abstract, as in *The Faerie Queene* or, to take a more recent example, Jan Mark's *Divide and Rule* (1979).

The relationship between journey and landscape, and its multiple layers of metaphor and symbol, can be seen in domestic fantasy as well. *The Wind in the Willows* was, as we have seen, part of the 'artistic' anti-urban movement of the turn of the century, and, as Carpenter points out: 'Of all the Victorians and Edwardians who tried to create Arcadia in print, only Grahame really managed it. His opening chapter gives us a full, rich portrait of the earthly paradise, expressed in a symbol that is likely to strike a chord with all readers . . . the River.'[54]

But the point is that it is not just any river, or The river, in some metaphysical/metaphorical sense. It is very clearly the River Thames, Old Father Thames, the most English of rivers as far as literature is concerned. It is also the Thames at its most English, as it were, around the very middle-class Cookham—the same Thames explored in another classic that attempts to tap the same levels of folk-memory of 'golden ages', and which has now become reading for children: Jerome K. Jerome's *Three Men in a Boat*. (An extract from this book is published in Helen Cresswell's *The Puffin Book of Funny Stories* (1992).) The over-lush descriptions of the river, with the half-hidden river-gods, contrasts (poignantly enough, as they are less read) with Toad's adventures among the un-hobbit-like machines, cars, and trains which are full of the corruption of modern life. What is beyond the dim hills on the horizon is to be avoided. In a sense this is a highly regressive book: the English landscape asserts itself over the exotic; the comfortable over the confrontation—and this may be moving the book out of the sphere of the modern child.

Restlessly the Rat wandered off once more, climbed the slope that rose gently from the north bank of the river, and lay looking out towards the great ring of Downs that barred his vision further southwards—his simple horizon hitherto, his Mountains of the Moon, his limit behind which lay nothing he had cared to see or to know.[55]

The journeys in this book, then, represent a conflict between the nostalgic/repressed adult and the growing child. This may well be the reason why the endpaper maps of the places in *The Wind in the Willows* drawn by Shepard seem irrelevant. The landscape is notional as well as actual.

There is also some nationalistic difference within Britain, if we regard the River Bank as being quintessentially English. Wales is frequently seen as resisting Englishness; similarly, the Scottish highlands are spiritually unconquered, and even Stevenson, for all his insistence on the map, uses the country both as symbol and fact in *Kidnapped* and *Catriona*.

This complex 'recruiting' of the landscape to the cultural armoury begins at a very early age—consider Milne's 'Pooh' books, books about small, safe journeys from small homes. The Shepard map shows the Hundred Acre Wood as something within the child's grasp: there is nothing outside it (except the North Pole). If this is compared to the real map, then the wood becomes 500 acres and Owl's house is half a mile from the six pine trees.[56] To comprehend the real-sized landscape, as Ransome found, it must be shifted around, just as Alan Garner's Cheshire is carefully edited:

The whale-backed Pennines, in their southern reaches, crumble into separate hills which join up with the Staffordshire moors, and from the Cheshire plain two hills stand out above all the rest. One is Bosley Cloud, its north face sheer, and southwards a graceful sweep to the feet of the Old Man of Mow, but for all that, a brooding, sinister mountain, forever changing shape when seen from meandering Cheshire lanes.[57]

This is, of course, the same romantic, dramatizing, and simplifying impulse that leads New York to become Gotham City. In some cases, such as Ransome's 1930s Lake District, the romanticizing has been done by time passing: Ransome's maps very precisely cage the landscape. It is not insignificant that the most dangerous of the books, *We Didn't Mean to Go to Sea*, has an adult chart of the North Sea as its guide, whereas the sequel, the very safe and domesticated *Secret Water*, is a book about map *making*.

The writers, therefore, in using real landscape and maps in various degrees of veracity are using both the landscape and the culture, and creating a new myth. Thus Ransome edits out a lot of houses—and people; Cheshire shifts back to a more golden age; and, perhaps most spectacularly, virtually the whole of 'civilization' disappears from the rabbit's-eye view of the world in *Watership Down*. In a sense, the journey through the British landscape becomes four-rather than three-dimensional, and the ambiguity of the defining yet simplifying overviews of the maps suggests the tensions felt by the authors.

8

Conclusion: Stalking the Perfect Children's Book

We live in our own world,
A world that is too small
For you to enter
Even on hands and knees,
The adult subterfuge.
And though you probe and pry
With analytic eye . . .
You cannot find the centre
Where we dance, where we play . . .

(R. S. Thomas, 'Children's Song')

The ideas surrounding children's literature are as rich and complex as the books themselves—but is there a central, Platonic ideal of the children's book around which the ideas circle, or through which they intersect? The historical survey might give some clues: some of the most obvious recurrent features that we have seen include strong nostalgic/nature images; a sense of place or territory; egocentricity; testing and initiation; outsider/insider relationships; mutual respect between adults and children; closure; warmth/security—and food; and, perhaps most important, the relationship between reality and fantasy. Are any of these, or any combination, of the essence?

In many ways, the use of fantasy is at the heart of the adult–child relationship in literature. Paradoxically, fantasy embodies radical revelations of the human psyche and thus, apparently, is suitable for children: reality and realism, presenting the probable or actual actions of recognizable beings in recognizable circumstances, is treated, as we have seen, most circumspectly. Nevertheless, as Sheila Egoff has written,

'Modern fantasy in its totality, is the richest and most varied of all the genres.'[1]

Certainly, the types of fantasy offer children different modes of experience. 'Domestic' fantasy is rooted in a world recognizable to the child; like *Winnie-the-Pooh* it offers power and comfort simultaneously. 'High' fantasy, on the other hand, set in a secondary world (such as *The Hobbit*), offers wider scope for the imagination paralleled with a simpler set of moral solutions. Between these two are two other types: first, books in which the secondary world is 'framed' by the primary one: characters from 'our' world enter or leave the other worlds, thus keeping them in perspective (*Alice's Adventures in Wonderland, The Wizard of Oz*); and second, a much more sinister genre in which the secondary world impinges upon the real—as in Garner's *The Weirdstone of Brisingamen* or Cooper's 'The Dark is Rising' sequence. That children's literature is centred upon such books is, as Sullivan has pointed out, a function of comparatively recent adult thinking: early works that are now thought of as fantasy, from *Beowulf* to *The Tempest*, were not regarded by their contemporaries as such.[2]

A good deal of time has been spent on theorizing about fantasy; it is seen variously as a retreat from 'reality', using metaphor or allegory to simplify and characterize human traits, to simplify concepts of good and evil, and to gratify the simple wish to overcome them, rectify the world, and satisfy both good and evil impulses. Not unnaturally, many of these traits have been seen as negative and intellectually unsatisfying, belonging to a cruder phase of human development. Consequently, they have either been prescribed for children or have found a place in the popular arts. In folk literature and legend, such traits have emerged in the need for the weak to inherit the earth, and who weaker than that excluded group, children? In a fine paradox, the very savage and crude impulses (now seen most graphically in contemporary cinema) are embodied in the fairy-tale, now marketed for children.

Henry James's validation of the novel as a serious art form ('The Art of Fiction') laid down the dictum that 'you will not write a good novel unless you possess the sense of reality'.[3] Ursula Le Guin, as we have seen, felt that 'this fear of dragons' was symbolic of the adult refusal to face basic impulses and fundamental problems.[4] Other critics have suggested that authors use fantasy to sublimate their dubious impulses: the books they produce are the last things that should be given to children, if childhood is to be protected.

On the other hand, the polarization of good and evil and, in a sense, the comprehensibility of the created worlds have led some critics to downgrade the texts to the status of low-level reading experiences (which are, of course, conterminous with writing for children). Paradoxically, the psychological truth of fantasy may be exactly the thing that makes it suitable for the more resilient state of childhood.

Or is this discussion simply a reflection of adult preferences—either direct preferences or preferences expressed on behalf of children (which means, in effect, on behalf of an idea of childhood)? Is, for example, this statement by Frank Flanagan a description of actuality or an expression of hope?

Children's books embody a world view which we need reminding of from time to time, a 'benign world hypothesis', the assertion that the world is, after all, despite the cruelty, greed, materialism, suffering and injustice, a good place to be: that there is a moral order, a moral pattern, which we transgress at our cost.[5]

Children's literature is an ideological minefield; it is easy to be simplistic, and to overlook obvious difficulties.

Jim Trelease, an ardent advocate of books for children, quotes C. S. Lewis's dictum: 'I am almost inclined to set it up as a canon that a children's story which is enjoyed only by children is a bad children's story' and goes on: 'In much the same way, a book which is not worth reading at age 50 is not worth reading at age 10, either.'[6] One of the themes of this book has been that these conclusions are neither identical, nor on the side of the child and the book.

Barbara Wall has addressed this problem at several points: 'the first test of a children's book should be that it is genuinely for children and not that it is comfortable for and extends adults.' Her argument is with the critical theory which partly denies the existence of a genre 'writing for children' by insisting that a good children's book is a good book 'in its own right', and partly demands that good writing for children, such as it is, should not too obviously appear to be for children. For many adult readers 'the real value in children's books is likely to be found only in stories in which the narrator addresses child narratees so circumspectly that adult readers are not forced to acknowledge their existence'. In fact the only acceptable children's books are those that either do not look like children's books at all (*The Stone Book Quartet*) or address a dual audience (the 'Pooh' books) rather than a double audience.[7]

Thus arguments about what books should contain, whether they are for education or for 'literary' responses (or both, or neither), are ideological. It would seem that British experts who extol the virtues of 'literature' in schools are not theorists. The likes of Aidan Chambers and Margaret Meek, Geoff Fox and Liz Waterland, Elaine Moss and Jim Trelease (a very formidable band) are to a person immensely involved, dedicated, experienced. They are liberal, literate people, orientated to both books and children; Aidan Chambers was only tired of being told that Garner's *The Stone Book Quartet* was inaccessible to children because he and his colleagues had worked with children who found it 'one of the most stimulating books available'.[8] And yet ... They all share the assumption that children's books lead on to adult books, that good books and/or good habits of reading—that is literary readings *of literary texts*—will lead to a literary, literate life. And, of course, the further assumption that that is a good thing of itself. I share that view: but it is an article of faith, not a fact.

One answer to this merry-go-round of ideas is that the less a book appeals to those literary values, or artistic values—the less it appeals to adults, in fact—the more it is a children's book. The terrifying and unmanageable idea is that the books that are positively bad from the adult point of view may be the good children's books: but we can only accept this if we get rid of the idea that books are merely a stepping stone to higher things. The adult may well enjoy a children's book in which the focus is very clearly on child behaviour (*Stanley and Rhoda*) or may enjoy the aura of books which have already charmed by devices that are essentially whimsical (such as Sandra Boynton's *But not the Hippopotamus* (1984)).

Just as rap music and Mozart both deal in sound, but cannot reasonably be compared otherwise, so the same reasoning extends to children's books: our aesthetic training may, for example, prefer Shepard's rendition of Pooh, or Doré's *Beauty and the Beast* to Disney's version, but it seems confusing at best and unwise at worst to disguise this cultural preference behind terms such as 'deep' or 'resonant'.[9] And this is complicated by, for example, the status of the cliché in texts read by inexperienced readers. A great deal of intellectual *Angst* would be saved if we could free the study of children's literature from these inappropriate and outdated modes of thought.

In short, children's literature gives of its best—and, looking back over its history, it cannot be denied that it is a hugely varied best—if it is approached with an open mind. Recently, Peter Hollindale reported on a new course in children's literature at the University of York:

Having begun my course at York with some fear that it might merely academicize the property of children, I ended it in sheer delight at what students had achieved. Conscious in some cases that their reading had been professionalised by lit crit far too early in their school careers, they seized the chance to compensate for this by re-learning to read. Spontaneously they developed a reading strategy which combined the 'common' and 'uncommon reader', the enjoyment of story and the multiple skills of the professional critic.[10]

Adult readers of children's literature, by developing this dual skill, can not only pass on whatever they find good to the next generation of children, but they can also expand their literary horizons, and perhaps revitalize the whole of their reading experience.

A Chronology of Children's Literature

This chronology sets out key books and events in the history of children's literature to 1992. I have listed historically significant works, and works that delimit the productive periods of key writers. Works are generally listed under the date of their first publication in book form, with short titles.

1391   Geoffrey Chaucer, *Tretis of the Astrolabie*

1580   Jost Amman, *Book of Art and Instruction for Young People*

1658   Comenius, *Orbis sensualium pictus*

1686   John Bunyan, *A Book for Boys and Girls; or, Country Rhymes for Children*

1692   James Janeway, *A Token for Children*

1697   Charles Perrault, *Histoires ou contes du temps passé*

1707   Countess d'Aulnoy, *Diverting Works*

1715   Isaac Watts, *Divine Songs*

1729   Charles Perrault, *Histories, or Tales of Past Times, Told by Mother Goose* [1697]

1744   [Mary Cooper], *Tommy Thumb's Song Book*; [John Newbery], *A Little Pretty Pocket Book*

1749   Sarah Fielding, *The Governess; or, The Little Female Academy*

1756   [Samuel Richardson], *The Paths of Virtue Delineated*

1757[?]   *Young Misses' Magazine*

1778   Anna Laetitia Barbauld, *Lessons for Children* (and 1794, 1803)

1786   Mrs Trimmer, *Fabulous Histories* [*The History of the Robins*]

1788   Mary Wollstonecraft, *Original Stories from Real Life*

1801   Maria Edgeworth, *Early Lessons*

1802   Mrs Trimmer, *The Guardian of Education* (–1806)

1804　Jane and Ann Taylor, *Original Poems for Infant Minds*

1806　[dated 1807] Charles and Mary Lamb, *Tales from Shakespeare*; William Roscoe, *The Butterfly's Ball*

1814　Johann Wyss [trans. Godwin], *The Family Robinson Crusoe* [*Der Schweizerische Robinson*; 1812–13]

1818　Mary Martha Sherwood, *The History of the Fairchild Family* (part 2, 1842; part 3, 1847)

1823　Clement Clarke Moore, 'A Visit from St. Nicholas'; The Brothers Grimm, *German Popular Stories*

1827　'Peter Parley', *Tales of Peter Parley about America*

1839　Catherine Sinclair, *Holiday House*

1841　Harriet Martineau, *The Crofton Boys*; Captain Marryat, *Masterman Ready*

1843　'Felix Summerley', *The Home Treasury*

1844　Francis Paget, *The Hope of the Kotzekopfs*

1846　Hans Andersen, *A Danish Story Book*, *Danish Fairy Legends and Tales*; Edward Lear, *A Book of Nonsense*

1848　Heinrich Hoffmann, *The English Struwwelpeter*

1850　'Elizabeth Wetherell', *The Wide, Wide, World*

1851　W. H. G. Kingston, *Peter the Whaler*; John Ruskin, *The King of the Golden River*

1855　Charles Kingsley, *Westward Ho!*; Mrs Molesworth, *The Carved Lions*; W. M. Thackeray, *The Rose and the Ring*

1856　R. M. Ballantyne, *The Young Fur Traders*; Charlotte Yonge, *The Daisy Chain*

1857　Thomas Hughes, *Tom Brown's Schooldays*

1858　Frederick Farrar, *Eric; or, Little by Little*

1860　*Good Words* (–1906)

1862　Christina Rossetti, *Goblin Market*

1863　Charles Kingsley, *The Water Babies*

1865　'Lewis Carroll', *Alice's Adventures in Wonderland*

1866　*Boys of England* (–1906), *Chatterbox* (–1946)

1868　Louisa May Alcott, *Little Women*; Horatio Alger, Jr., *Ragged Dick*; Charles Dickens, *A Holiday Romance*

1869   Jean Ingelow, *Mopsa the Fairy*

1870   Juliana Horatia Ewing, *The Brownies and Other Tales*

1871   'Lewis Carroll', *Through the Looking Glass*; 'Susan Coolidge', *What Katy Did*; G. A. Henty, *Out on the Pampas; or, The Young Settlers*; George Macdonald, *At the Back of the North Wind*

1872   George Macdonald, *The Princess and the Goblin*

1873   Mary Mapes Dodge (ed.), *St. Nicholas*

1875   'Brenda', *Froggy's Little Brother*

1876   'Mark Twain', *The Adventures of Tom Sawyer*

1877   Mrs Molesworth, *The Cuckoo Clock*; Anna Sewell, *Black Beauty*

1879   *Boy's Own Paper* (–1967); Kate Greenaway, *Under the Window*

1880   *Girl's Own Paper* (–1908); Joel Chandler Harris, *Uncle Remus*; Johanna Spyri, *Heidi*

1882   Richard Jefferies, *Bevis*; 'Hesba Stretton', *Jessica's First Prayer*

1883   Robert Louis Stevenson, *Treasure Island*

1885   Robert Louis Stevenson, *A Child's Garden of Verses*

1886   Frances Hodgson Burnett, *Little Lord Fauntleroy*; H. Rider Haggard, *King Solomon's Mines*

1887   Talbot Baines Reed, *The Fifth Form at St. Dominic's*

1888   Oscar Wilde, *The Happy Prince*

1889   Andrew Lang (ed.), *The Blue Fairy Book*

1890   [Alfred Harmsworth], *Comic Cuts*; Joseph Jacobs, *English Fairy Tales*

1894   Rudyard Kipling, *The Jungle Book*; Ethel Turner, *Seven Little Australians*

1895   Kenneth Grahame, *The Golden Age*; Bertha and Florence Upton, *The Adventures of Two Dutch Dolls—and a Golliwogg*

1898   J. Meade Falkner, *Moonfleet*

1899   Helen Bannerman, *The Story of Little Black Sambo*; Kenneth Grahame, *Dream Days*; Rudyard Kipling, *Stalky and Co.*; E. Nesbit, *The Story of the Treasure Seekers*

1900   L. Frank Baum, *The Wizard of Oz*

1902   Walter de la Mare, *Songs of Childhood*; Rudyard Kipling, *Just So Stories*; E. Nesbit, *Five Children and It*; Beatrix Potter, *The Tale of Peter Rabbit*

1903   L. Leslie Brooke, *Johnny Crow's Garden*; Kate Douglas Wiggin, *Rebecca of Sunnybrook Farm*

1904   J. M. Barrie, *Peter Pan* (first performance); Laura Lee Hope, *The Bobbsey Twins; or, Merry Days Indoors and Out*

1905   Frances Hodgson Burnett, *A Little Princess*

1906   Angela Brazil, *The Fortunes of Philippa*; Rudyard Kipling, *Puck of Pook's Hill*; Arthur Ransome, *A Child's Book of the Garden*

1907   Selma Lagerlöf, *The Wonderful Adventures of Nils*; *Gem* (–1939)

1908   Kenneth Grahame, *The Wind in the Willows*; L. M. Montgomery, *Anne of Green Gables*; *Magnet* (–1940)

1909   Gene Stratton-Porter, *A Girl of the Limberlost*

1910   Rudyard Kipling, *Rewards and Fairies*; Mary Grant Bruce, *A Little Bush Maid*

1911   Frances Hodgson Burnett, *The Secret Garden*; John Masefield, *Jim Davis*

1912   Howard Garis, *Uncle Wiggly's Adventures*; Jean Webster, *Daddy-Long-Legs*

1913   Eleanor H. Porter, *Pollyanna*; Arthur Rackham, *Mother Goose*

1914   Edgar Rice Burroughs, *Tarzan of the Apes*

1916   Dorothy Canfield, *Understood Betsy*; Edmund Dulac, *Fairy-Book*; Eleanor Farjeon, *Nursery Rhymes of London Town*; Arthur Ransome, *Old Peter's Russian Tales*

1918   Norman Lindsay, *The Magic Pudding*

1919   Daisy Ashford, *The Young Visiters*; *School Friend* (–1929)

1920   Constance Howard, *Ameliaranne and the Green Umbrella*; Hugh Lofting, *The Story of Dr Dolittle*; Elsie J. Oxenham, *The Abbey Girls*; 'Rupert Bear' appears in the *Daily Express*

1922   Margery Williams Bianco, *The Velveteen Rabbit*; Richmal Crompton, *Just—William*; Carl Sandberg, *The Rootabaga Stories*

1923   Enid Blyton, *Child Whispers*; Felix Salten, *Bambi*; American Library Association Newbery Medal established

1924   A. A. Milne, *When We Were Very Young*

1925   Elinor M. Brent-Dyer, *The School at the Chalet*

1926   Will James, *Smoky, the Cow-Horse*; A. A. Milne, *Winnie-the-Pooh*

1927   'Franklin W. Dixon', *The Tower Treasure* (the Hardy Boys); John Masefield, *The Midnight Folk*; A. A. Milne, *Now We Are Six*

1928   Wanda Gág, *Millions of Cats*; S. G. Hulme Beaman, *Tales of Toytown*; A. A. Milne, *The House at Pooh Corner*; William Nicholson, *Clever Bill*

1929   Alison Uttley, *The Squirrel, the Hare, and the Little Grey Rabbit*; Eric Kästner, *Emil and the Detectives* [UK, 1931]

1930   'Carolyn Keene', *The Hidden Staircase* (Nancy Drew); André Maurois, *Patpoufs et Filifers* [as *Fattypuffs and Thinifers* UK 1941]; Arthur Ransome, *Swallows and Amazons*

1931   Jean de Brunhoff, *The Story of Babar*

1932   W. E. Johns, 'The White Fokker' (first appearance of Biggles) in *Popular Flying*; John Buchan, *The Magic Walking Stick*; Laura Ingalls Wilder, *Little House in the Big Woods*

1933   Marjorie Flack, *The Story about Ping*

1934   P. L. Travers, *Mary Poppins*; Geoffrey Trease, *Bows against the Barons*

1935   Enid Bagnold, *National Velvet*; Carol Rylie Brink, *Caddie Woodlawn*; John Masefield, *The Box of Delights*

1936   Edward Ardizzone, *Little Tim and the Brave Sea Captain*; Munro Leaf, *The Story of Ferdinand*; Noel Stretfeild, *Ballet Shoes*, Carnegie Medal established

1937   Enid Blyton, *Adventures of the Wishing Chair*; Eve Garnett, *The Family from One-End Street*; J. B. S. Haldane, *My Friend Mr Leakey*; Dr Seuss, *And to Think that I Saw it on Mulberry Street*; J. R. R. Tolkien, *The Hobbit; or, There and Back Again*

1938   Elizabeth Enright, *Thimble Summer*; [Walt Disney], *Snow White and the Seven Dwarfs*; Marjorie Kinnan Rawlings, *The*

Yearling; Ursula Moray Williams, *The Adventures of the Little Wooden Horse*; Caldecott Medal established

1939   Kitty Barne, *Visitors from London*; Ludwig Bemelman, *Madeline*; T. S. Eliot, *Old Possum's Book of Practical Cats*; Hardy Gramatky, *Little Toot*; Robert L. May, *Rudolph the Red-Nosed Reindeer*

1940   Maud Hart Lovelace, *Betsy-Tacy*; Eric Knight, *Lassie Come-Home*

1941   Eleanor Estes, *The Moffats*; Robert McCloskey, *Make Way for Ducklings*; H. A. Rey, *Curious George*; Mary Treadgold, *We Couldn't Leave Dinah*

1942   'BB', *The Little Grey Men*; Enid Blyton, *Five on a Treasure Island*; Virginia Lee Burton, *The Little House*; Diana Ross, *The Little Red Engine Gets a Name*

1943   Esther Forbes, *Johnny Tremain*; Eric Linklater, *The Wind on the Moon*; Malcolm Saville, *Mystery at Witchend*

1945   Revd W. Awdrey, *The Three Railway Engines*

1946   Graham Greene, *The Little Train*

1947   William Pene Du Bois, *Twenty-one Balloons*

1950   'Andy Pandy' on BBC-TV *Watch with Mother*; Anthony Buckeridge, *Jennings Goes to School*; Roger Duvoisin, *Petunia*; C. S. Lewis, *The Lion, the Witch, and the Wardrobe*; James Thurber, *The Thirteen Clocks*; *Eagle* (–1969)

1952   Ben Lucien Burman, *High Water at Catfish Bend*; Catherine Storr, *Clever Polly*; Mary Norton, *The Borrowers*; E. B. White, *Charlotte's Web*

1953   William Mayne, *Follow the Footprints*

1954   L. M. Boston, *The Children of Green Knowe*; Louise Fation/ Roger Duvoisin, *The Happy Lion*; Rosemary Sutcliff, *The Eagle of the Ninth*; J. R. R. Tolkien, *The Fellowship of the Ring*

1956   Beverley Cleary, *Fifteen*; Ian Serraillier, *The Silver Sword*; Eve Titus (ill. Paul Galdone), *Anatole*; Kate Greenaway Medal established

1957   Edward Ardizzone, *Tim All Alone*; Dr Seuss, *The Cat in the Hat*

1958   Philippa Pearce, *Tom's Midnight Garden*

1960   Shirley Hughes, *Lucy and Tom's Day*; Alan Garner, *The Weirdstone of Brisingamen*

1963   Anne Holm, *I Am David*; Peggy Parrish, *Amelia-Bedelia*; Maurice Sendak, *Where the Wild Things Are*

1964   Louise Fitzhugh, *Harriet the Spy*; Lloyd Alexander, *The Book of Three*; Roald Dahl, *Charlie and the Chocolate Factory*

1965   Susan Cooper, *Over Sea, Under Stone*

1966   Raymond Briggs, *The Mother Goose Treasury*

1967   Helen Cresswell, *The Piemakers*; Alan Garner, *The Owl Service*; Russell Hoban, *The Mouse and his Child*; E. L. Konigsberg, *From the Mixed-Up Files of Mrs Basil E. Frankweiler*; K. M. Peyton, *Flambards*; S. A. Wakefield, *Bottersnikes and Gumbles*

1968   Peter Dickinson, *The Weathermonger*; Ted Hughes, *The Iron Man*; Ursula Le Guin, *A Wizard of Earthsea*; Patricia Wrightson, *I Own the Racecourse!*

1969   Penelope Farmer, *Charlotte Sometimes*; Paul Zindel, *My Darling, my Hamburger*

1970   Judy Blume, *Are You there, God? It's Me, Margaret*; Barbara Willard, *The Lark and the Laurel*

1972   Richard Adams, *Watership Down*; Norma Klein, *Mom, the Wolfman, and Me*

1973   Nina Bawden, *Carrie's War*

1974   Robert Cormier, *The Chocolate War*; Russell Hoban and Quentin Blake, *How Tom Beat Captain Najork and his Hired Sportsmen*; Alan Garner, *The Stone Book*

1975   Judy Blume, *Forever*

1977   Anthony Browne, *A Walk in the Park*; John Burningham, *Come away from the Water, Shirley*; Gene Kemp, *The Turbulent Term of Tyke Tyler*; Kathleen Paterson, *Bridge to Terabithia*; Jan Mark, *Thunder and Lightnings*; Jenny Wagner (illustrated by Ron Brooks) *John Brown, Rose and the Midnight Cat*

1978   Janet and Allan Ahlberg, *Each Peach Pear Plum*; Aidan Chambers, *Breaktime*; Rosemary Wells, *Stanley and Rhoda*

1979   Chris Van Allsburg, *The Garden of Abdul Gasazi*

1980   Quentin Blake, *Mister Magnolia*; Robert M. Munsch, *The Paper Bag Princess*

1981   Michelle Magorian, *Goodnight Mr. Tom*; Maurice Sendak, *Outside Over There*; Jean Ure, *See You Thursday*

1982   Virginia Hamilton, *Sweet Whispers, Brother Rush*; David McKee, *I Hate my Teddy Bear*; Gabrielle Vincent, *Ernest and Celestine*

1983   Anthony Browne, *Gorilla*; Lynley Dodd, *Hairy Maclary from Donaldson's Dairy*; Mem Fox (illustrated by Julie Vivas), *Possum Magic*; Jan Mark, *Handles*; Cynthia Voight, *Homecoming*

1984   James Aldridge, *The True Story of Lilli Stubeck*; John Burningham, *Granpa*; Janni Howker, *Badger on the Barge*

1985   Patricia MacLachlan, *Sarah, Plain and Tall*

1986   Janet and Allan Ahlberg, *The Jolly Postman*; Robert Leeson, *Time Rope*

1987   Margaret Mahy, *Memory*; Geraldine McCaughrean, *A Little Lower than the Angels*

1988   Ted Hughes, *Moon Whales*; Felix Pirani (illustrated by Christine Roche), *Abigail at the Beach*

1989   Ann Fine, *Goggle-Eyes*; Iona Opie (ed.), *Tail Feathers from Mother Goose*; Michael Rosen (illustrated by Helen Oxenbury), *We're Going on a Bear Hunt*

1990   Gillian Cross, *Wolf*; Libby Gleeson, *Dodger*

1991   Berlie Doherty, *Dear Nobody*

1992   William Mayne, *Low Tide*

Notes

Chapter 1

1. A. A. Milne, 'Introduction' to *Books for Children* (National Book League, 1948), repr. in Ann Thwaite, *The Brilliant Career of Winnie-the-Pooh* (London: Methuen, 1992), 147.

2. Ursula Le Guin, 'This Fear of Dragons', in Edward Blishen (ed.), *The Thorny Paradise* (Harmondsworth: Kestrel, 1975), 87–92.

3. J. M. S. Tompkins, *The Art of Rudyard Kipling* (London: Methuen, 1959), 55.

4. C. S. Lewis, 'On Three Ways of Writing for Children', in Virginia Haviland (ed.), *Children and Literature: Views and Reviews* (London: Bodley Head, 1973), 234.

5. Perry Nodelman, 'Cott im Himmel', *Children's Literature*, 13 (New Haven, Conn.: Yale University Press, 1985), 206.

6. See Jacqueline Rose, *The Case of Peter Pan; or, The Impossibility of Children's Literature* (London: Macmillan, 1984).

7. Fred Inglis, *The Promise of Happiness* (Cambridge: Cambridge University Press, 1981), 76, and see 70–85; see also Nicholas Tucker, *What is a Child?* (London: Open Books/Fontana, 1977).

8. E. M. Forster, *Aspects of the Novel* (Harmondsworth: Penguin, 1976), 26.

9. See Peter Hunt, *Criticism, Theory, and Children's Literature* (Oxford: Blackwell, 1991), 23–36.

10. Chris Powling, 'Farewell to the Big Friendly Giant', *Books for Keeps*, 66 (1991), 10, 11.

11. Quoted by Betsy Hearne, 'Research in Children's Literature in the US and Canada: Problems and Possibilities', in International Youth Library (ed.), *Children's Literature Research* (Munich: K. G. Saur, 1991), 111.

12. Barbara Wall, *The Narrator's Voice: The Dilemma of Children's Fiction* (London: Macmillan Academic, 1991), 233.

13. Lewis, 'On Three Ways of Writing for Children', 234.

14. Brian Morse, *Poetry Books for Children* (South Woodchester: Thimble Press, 1992), 1, 17.

15. See Jane Doonan, *Looking at Pictures in Picture Books* (South Woodchester: Thimble Press, 1993); Perry Nodelman, *Words about Pictures* (Athens, Ga.: University of Georgia Press, 1988).

16. See Gillian Klein, *Reading into Racism* (London: Routledge, 1985), 36–7.

17. J. R. R. Tolkien, *Tree and Leaf* (London: Allen & Unwin, 1970), 34.

18. Sarah Trimmer, *The Guardian of Education*, ii (1803), quoted in Nicholas Tucker (ed.), *Suitable for Children?* (London: Sussex University Press, 1976), 38.

19. Alison Lurie, *Don't Tell the Grown-Ups: Subversive Children's Literature* (London: Bloomsbury, 1990), 19.

20. See Myles McDowell, 'Fiction for Children and Adults: Some Essential Differences', in Geoff Fox *et al.* (eds.), *Writers, Critics and Children* (London: Heinemann, 1976), 140–56.

21. 'The Reader in the Book', in Aidan Chambers, *Booktalk: Occasional Writing on Literature and Children* (London: Bodley Head, 1985), 34–58.

22. Wall, *The Narrator's Voice*, 35.

23. John Stephens, *Language and Ideology in Children's Fiction* (Harlow: Longman, 1992), 158.

24. Quoted by Thwaite, *The Brilliant Career of Winnie-the-Pooh*, 105.

25. A. A. Milne, *Now We Are Six* (1927; London: Methuen, 1965), 85.

26. Robert N. Munsch, *The Paper Bag Princess* (London: Scholastic, 1982), n.p.

27. Frank Eyre, *British Children's Books in the Twentieth Century* (London: Longman, 1971), 156.

28. See Nicholas Tucker, *The Child and the Book: A Psychological and Literary Exploration* (Cambridge: Cambridge University Press, 1981), 197.

29. Nicholas Tucker, 'Edward Ardizzone', *Children's Literature in Education*, 1/3 (1970), 23; Edward Ardizzone, 'Creation of a

Picture Book', in Sheila Egoff *et al.* (eds.), *Only Connect* (Toronto: Oxford University Press, 1969), 293.

30. Don Aitkin, 'Taking Some Flak over Biggles', in Peter Berresford Ellis and Piers Williams, *By Jove, Biggles!* (London: W. H. Allen, 1965), 243.

31. John Rowe Townsend, 'Standards of Criticism for Children's Literature', in Peter Hunt (ed.), *Children's Literature: The Development of Criticism* (London: Routledge, 1990), 63.

32. Steve Bowles, 'New Horizons', *Books for Keeps*, 42 (1987), 17.

33. Hunt, *Criticism, Theory, and Children's Literature*, 144–5.

34. Hugh Walpole, 'Introduction to the Tenth Printing' of *The Story of Dr Dolittle* (1920; New York, Stokes, 1922), pp. vii, viii, x.

35. Geoffrey Williams, 'Letter to the Editor', *Reading Time*, 101 (1986), 11.

36. Peter Hunt (ed.), *Literature for Children: Contemporary Criticism* (London: Routledge, 1992), 2–14.

37. Wallace Hildick, *Children and Fiction* (London: Evans Brothers, 1970), 142.

38. Tessa Rose Chester, *Sources of Information about Children's Books* (South Woodchester: Thimble Press, 1989), 73–4.

39. Elaine Moss, *Part of the Pattern* (London: Bodley Head, 1986), 115.

40. Elizabeth Hammill, *Waterstone's Guide to Children's Books, 1989–90* (London: Waterstone, 1989), 52.

41. Roald Dahl, *Charlie and the Chocolate Factory* (Harmondsworth: Penguin, 1973), 121, 90.

42. Michele Landsberg, *The World of Children's Books* (London: Simon & Schuster, 1988), 90.

43. Cited by Powling, 'Farewell to the Big Friendly Giant', 11.

44. Justin Wintle and Emma Fisher, *The Pied Pipers* (London: Paddington Press, 1974), 111.

45. Eric Hadley, 'Roald Dahl', in Tracy Chevalier (ed.), *Twentieth Century Children's Writers* (Chicago: St James Press, 3rd edn., 1989), 256. See also Charles Sarland, 'The Secret Seven vs The Twits: Cultural Clash or Cosy Combination?', *Signal*, 42 (1983), 155–71.

46. Powling, 'Farewell to the Big Friendly Giant', 11.

47. Inglis, *The Promise of Happiness*, 236.

48. Quoted by Brian Alderson, 'Pirouetting on Pierrot', *Times Educational Supplement* (9 Nov. 1990).

49. Frederick C. Crews, *The Pooh Perplex* (London: Arthur Barker, 1964).

Chapter 2

1. F. J. Harvey Darton, *Children's Books in England: Five Centuries of Social Life* (1932), 3rd edn., rev. Brian Alderson (Cambridge: Cambridge University Press, 1982); John Rowe Townsend, *Written for Children* (Garnett Miller, 1965; anniversary edition, London: Penguin, 1990).

2. Darton, *Children's Books in England*, p. vii.

3. David Bennet, 'Alan Garner', *Books for Keeps*, 77 (1992), 21.

4. Barbara Wall, *The Narrator's Voice: The Dilemma of Children's Fiction* (London: Macmillan Academic, 1991), 41.

5. Percy Muir, *English Children's Books* (London: Batsford, 1954), 28, 29.

6. Margery Fisher, *The Bright Face of Danger* (Sevenoaks: Hodder & Stoughton, 1986), 16.

7. See e.g. Humphrey Carpenter, *Secret Gardens* (London: George Allen & Unwin, 1985).

8. Rudyard Kipling, *Something of Myself* (1937; Harmondsworth: Penguin, 1977), 142.

9. Robert Louis Stevenson, 'My First Book', in Lance Salway (ed.), *A Peculiar Gift* (Harmondsworth: Kestrel, 1976), 415.

10. Robert Leeson, *Reading and Righting* (London: Collins, 1985), 110; Marcus Crouch, *The Nesbit Tradition* (London: Benn, 1937), 17.

11. Sarah Fielding, *The Governess; or, The Little Female Academy*, ed. Jill E. Grey (London: Oxford University Press, 1968); introd. by Mary Cadogan (London: Pandora Press (Routledge), 1987).

12. Robert Liddell, *A Treatise on the Novel* (1947; London: Cape, 1965), 24.

13. See Fred Inglis, *The Promise of Happiness* (Cambridge: Cambridge University Press, 1981), 3; Perry Nodelman (ed.), *Touchstones: Reflections on the Best in Children's Literature* (West Lafayette, Ind.: Children's Literature Association, 1985), 7.

Chapter 3

1. F. J. Harvey Darton, *Children's Books in England* (Cambridge: Cambridge University Press, 1982), pp. x, 1.

2. Meradith Tilbury McMunn and William Robert McMunn, 'Children's Literature in the Middle Ages', *Children's Literature*, 1 (1972), 24.

3. Eric Quayle, *Early Children's Books: A Collector's Guide* (Newton Abbot: David & Charles, 1983), 13.

4. Joyce Irene Whalley and Tessa Rose Chester, *A History of Children's Book Illustration* (London: John Murray/Victoria and Albert Museum, 1988), 98–9.

5. Bettina Hürlimann, *Three Centuries of Children's Books in Europe*, trans. and ed. Brian Alderson (Oxford: Oxford University Press, 1967), p. xii.

6. Whalley and Chester, *A History of Children's Book Illustration*, 14.

7. Patricia Demers and Gordon Moyles (eds.), *From Instruction to Delight: An Anthology of Children's Literature to 1850* (Toronto: Oxford University Press, 1982), 44.

8. Darton, *Children's Books in England*, 111.

9. Tony Ross, *The Three Pigs* (London: Andersen Press, 1983), n.p.

10. Jack Zipes, *The Trials and Tribulations of Little Red Riding Hood: Versions of the Tale in Sociocultural Context* (South Hadley Mass.: Bergin & Garvey, 1983); Jack Zipes, *Don't Bet on the Prince* (New York: Methuen, 1986); and see also Betsy Hearne, *Beauty and the Beast: Visions and Revisions of an Old Tale* (Chicago: University of Chicago Press, 1989).

11. See Iona and Peter Opie (eds.), *The Oxford Dictionary of Nursery Rhymes* (1951; Oxford: Clarendon Press, 1973), facing p. 154.

12. Geoffrey Summerfield, *Fantasy and Reason: Children's Literature in the Eighteenth Century* (London: Methuen, 1984), 86.

13. Janet and Allan Ahlberg, *The Jolly Christmas Postman* (London: Heinemann, 1991).

14. Sarah Fielding, *The Governess; or, The Little Female Academy*, ed. Jill E. Grey (London: Oxford University Press, 1968), 79.

15. Fielding, *The Governess* (Oxford University Press), 87–8.

16. Mary Cadogan, 'Introduction' to Sarah Fielding, *The Governess* (London: Pandora (Routledge), 1987), p. vii.

17. Fielding, *The Governess* (Oxford University Press), 165–6.

18. M. Nancy Cutt, *Mrs Sherwood and her Books for Children* (London: Oxford University Press, 1974), 39.

19. Mary F. Thwaite, *From Primer to Pleasure in Reading* (London: Library Association, 1963), 55.

20. Whalley and Chester, *A History of Children's Book Illustration*, 36.

21. Thwaite, *From Primer to Pleasure*, 59.

22. Mary V. Jackson, *Engines of Instruction, Mischief, and Magic* (London: Scolar Press, 1989), 215.

23. Darton, *Children's Books in England*, 190.

24. Charles Lamb, *Collected Letters*, ed. E. V. Lucas (London: Methuen, 1935), i. 326.

25. Darton, *Children's Books in England*, 183.

26. Quoted ibid. 170.

27. Cutt, *Mrs Sherwood and her Books for Children*, 6–7, 99–100.

28. Barbara Wall, *The Narrator's Voice* (London: Macmillan Academic, 1991), 45.

29. Hürlimann, *Three Centuries of Children's Books*, 26–8, 38–9.

30. Jack Zipes, *The Brothers Grimm* (New York: Routledge, 1988), 12, 14.

31. Charles Dickens, 'Frauds on the Fairies', *Household Words*, 8/184 (Oct. 1853), repr. in Peter Hunt (ed.), *Children's Literature: The Development of Criticism* (London: Routledge, 1990), 25.

32. Quoted by Demers and Moyles, *From Instruction to Delight*, 179.

33. Heinrich Hoffmann, introd. to *The English Struwwelpeter*, 40th English edn., n.d. (Frankfurt: Rutten & Loening for the Ger-

man Literary Society, n.d.); reproduced by Hürlimann, *Three Centuries of Children's Books*, 57.

34. Quoted by J. S. Bratton, *The Impact of Victorian Children's Fiction* (London: Croom Helm, 1981), 159.

35. Ibid. 99–100, 101.

36. 'Hesba Stretton' [Sarah Smith], *Jessica's First Prayer* (London: Religious Tract Society, n.d. [1882]), 64–5.

37. See Gillian Avery, 'Introduction' to Charlotte Yonge, *Village Children* (London: Gollancz, 1967), 8–9.

38. Quayle, *Early Children's Books*, 150.

39. Whalley and Chester, *A History of Children's Book Illustration*, 53.

40. Joseph Bristow, *Empire Boys: Adventures in a Man's World* (London: HarperCollins Academic (Reading Popular Fiction), 1991), 54.

41. Darton, *Children's Books in England*, 286.

42. Quayle, *Early Children's Books*, 157.

43. Rudyard Kipling, *Stalky and Co.* (London: Macmillan, 1908), 64, 66.

44. Martin Green, *Dreams of Adventure, Deeds of Empire* (London: Routledge & Kegan Paul, 1980), 36–7.

45. J. S. Bratton, 'Introduction' to R. M. Ballantyne, *The Coral Island* (Oxford: Oxford University Press, 1990), p. x.

46. Green, *Dreams of Adventure*, 43.

47. Wall, *The Narrator's Voice*, 46, 48.

48. Captain Marryat, *The Children of the New Forest* (1847; Harmondsworth: Penguin, 1948), 5.

49. Quoted by Oliver Warner, 'Introduction' to Captain Marryat, *Mr Midshipman Easy* (1836; London: Pan Books, 1967), pp. xvi–xvii.

50. Stuart Hannabus, 'Ballantyne's Message of Empire', in Jeffrey Richards (ed.), *Imperialism and Juvenile Literature* (Manchester: Manchester University Press, 1989), 56; and see Bratton, 'Introduction' to Ballantyne, *The Coral Island*, p. xxi.

51. Richards (ed.), *Imperialism and Juvenile Literature*, 2, 3.

52. Quoted by Quayle, *Early Children's Books*, 236.

Chapter 4

1. F. J. Harvey Darton, *Children's Books in England* (Cambridge: Cambridge University Press, 1982), 320.

2. Joyce Irene Whalley and Tessa Rose Chester, *A History of Children's Book Illustration* (London: John Murray/Victoria and Albert Museum, 1988), 84. See also Richard Dalby, *The Golden Age of Children's Book Illustration* (London: Michael O'Mara Books, 1991), 18.

3. Patrick A. Dunae, 'New Grub Street for Boys', in Jeffrey Richards (ed.), *Imperialism and Juvenile Literature* (Manchester: Manchester University Press, 1989), 16–17.

4. Arthur Ransome, 'A Hundred Years of Children's Books', *Spectator*, 4 Dec. 1953.

5. Kimberley Reynolds, *Girls Only? Gender and Popular Fiction in Britain, 1880–1910* (London: Harvester Wheatsheaf, 1990), 15.

6. George Perry and Alan Aldridge, *The Penguin Book of Comics* (Harmondsworth: Allen Lane The Penguin Press, rev. edn., 1971), 16.

7. Quoted by E. S. Turner, *Boys Will Be Boys* (Harmondsworth: Penguin, 1976), 12, 297.

8. Kevin Carpenter, *Penny Dreadfuls and Comics: English Periodicals for Children from Victorian Times to the Present Day* (London: Victoria and Albert Museum, 1983), 6.

9. Darton, *Children's Books in England*, 269.

10. Carpenter, *Penny Dreadfuls and Comics*, 23.

11. Quoted in P. W. Musgrave, *From Brown to Bunter: The Life and Death of the School Story* (London: Routledge, 1985), 114.

12. See Edward Salmon, 'What Girls Read', *Nineteenth Century*, 20 (Oct. 1886).

13. Reynolds, *Girls Only?*, pp. xv, 24.

14. Jane Bingham and Grayce Scholt, *Fifteen Centuries of Children's Literature* (Westport, Conn.: Greenwood Press, 1980), 388–92.

15. Quoted in Carpenter, *Penny Dreadfuls and Comics*, 6.

16. Joseph Bristow, *Empire Boys: Adventures in a Man's World* (London: HarperCollins Academic, 1991), 16–17, 32.

17. Perry and Aldridge, *The Penguin Book of Comics*, 14.

18. Quoted by Carpenter, *Penny Dreadfuls and Comics*, 53.

19. Perry and Aldridge, *The Penguin Book of Comics*, 52.

20. Darton, *Children's Books in England*, 275.

21. Quoted by Eleanor Grahame in Robert Louis Stevenson, *A Child's Garden of Verses* (Harmondsworth: Penguin, 1952), 14.

22. Brian Morse, *Poetry Books for Children* (South Woodchester: Thimble Press, 1992), 18.

23. Quoted by Richards, *Imperialism and Juvenile Literature*, 73.

24. Quoted by Guy Arnold, *Held Fast for England* (London: Hamish Hamilton, 1980), 89.

25. Ibid. 39.

26. Margaret Blount, *Animal Land* (London: Hutchinson, 1974), 250.

27. Anna Sewell, *Black Beauty, his Grooms and Companions* (London: Gollancz, 1990), 78.

28. Humphrey Carpenter and Mari Pritchard, *The Oxford Companion to Children's Literature* (Oxford: Oxford University Press, 1984), 357.

29. J. R. R. Tolkien, 'On Fairy-Stories', in *Tree and Leaf* (London: George Allen & Unwin, 1964), 41.

30. Oscar Wilde, 'The Nightingale and the Rose', in *The Happy Prince and Other Stories* (1888; Harmondsworth: Penguin, 1971), 74, 9.

31. Brian Alderson, 'Introduction' to J. Meade Falkner, *Moonfleet* (Oxford: Oxford University Press, 1993), pp. xvi–xvii.

32. See Gillian Klein, *Reading into Racism* (London: Routledge, 1985), 40–3.

33. Sheila Ray, *The Blyton Phenomenon* (London: André Deutsch, 1982), 68.

34. Eric Quayle, *Early Children's Books* (Newton Abbot: David & Charles, 1983), 177, 178.

35. John Goldthwaite, 'Sis Beatrix', *Signal*, 53 (1987), 117–37; *Signal*, 54 (1987), 161–9.

36. See Opal Moore and Donnarae MacCann, 'The Uncle Remus Travesty', *Children's Literature Association Quarterly*, 11/2

(1986), 96–9 (quoted 97). Cf. John Goldthwaite, 'The Black Rabbit', *Signal*, 47 (1985), 86–111; *Signal*, 48 (1985), 148–67.

37. Perry Nodelman, 'On Words and Pictures, Neglected Noteworthies, and Touchstones in Training', in Perry Nodelman (ed.), *Touchstones: Reflections on the Best in Children's Literature*, iii (West Lafayette, Ind.: Children's Literature Association, 1989), 10, 12.

38. Barbara Wall, *The Narrator's Voice* (London: Macmillan Academic, 1991), 79.

39. Gillian Avery, *Childhood's Pattern* (London: Hodder & Stoughton, 1975), 147.

40. Mrs Molesworth, *The Cuckoo Clock* (London: Puffin, 1988), 41–2.

41. Ann Thwaite, *The Brilliant Career of Winnie-the-Pooh* (London: Methuen, 1992), 24–6.

42. Ruth K. MacDonald, 'Louisa May Alcott', in Jane M. Bingham (ed.), *Writers for Children* (New York: Charles Scribner's Sons, 1988), 3.

43. Brenda Niall, *Seven Little Billabongs* (Ringwood: Penguin, 1982), 65.

44. Ibid.

45. J. S. Bratton, 'L. T. Meade', in Tracy Chevalier (ed.), *Twentieth-Century Children's Writers* (Chicago: St James Press, 3rd edn., 1989), 1108.

46. Jack Zipes, *Fairy Tales and the Art of Subversion* (New York: Wildman Press, 1983), 101.

47. George Macdonald, *A Dish of Orts*, quoted by Roderick McGillis, 'Introduction' to George Macdonald, *The Princess and the Goblin* and *The Princess and Curdie* (Oxford: Oxford University Press, 1990), p. xv.

48. Roger Lancelyn Green, 'Introduction' to *The Light Princess and Other Tales* (London: Gollancz, 1973), 8.

49. Humphrey Carpenter, *Secret Gardens* (London: Unwin Hyman, 1987), pp. ix, 70.

50. Wall, *The Narrator's Voice*, 59.

51. Carpenter, *Secret Gardens*, 39.

52. Darton, *Children's Books in England*, 265.

53. Ibid. 260.

54. Margery Fisher, *Classics for Children and Young People* (South Woodchester: Thimble Press, 1986), 60–1.

55. Derek Hudson, *Lewis Carroll: An Illustrated Biography* (London: Constable, 1976), 114.

56. Lewis Carroll, *Through the Looking Glass*, in Martin Gardner (ed.), *The Annotated Alice* (Harmondsworth: Penguin, 1970), 306–7.

57. Lewis Carroll, *Alice's Adventures in Wonderland*, in Gardner, *The Annotated Alice*, 82–3.

58. Edmund Wilson, 'C. L. Dodgson: The Poet Logician', in Robert Phillips (ed.), *Aspects of Alice* (Harmondsworth: Penguin, 1974), 247.

59. Lewis Carroll, *The Annotated Snark*, ed. Martin Gardner (Harmondsworth: Penguin, 1973), 22.

60. Lewis Carroll, *Sylvie and Bruno*, in *The Complete Works of Lewis Carroll* (London: Nonesuch Press, n.d. [1950?]), 295.

61. Lewis Carroll, *Sylvie and Bruno Concluded*, in *The Complete Works of Lewis Carroll*, 624–5. See also Wall, *The Narrator's Voice*, 107; and cf. Richard Jefferies, *Bevis* (Oxford: Oxford University Press, 1989), 77.

62. Darton, *Children's Books in England*, 295.

63. Robert Louis Stevenson, 'My First Book', in Lance Salway (ed.), *A Peculiar Gift* (Harmondsworth: Kestrel, 1976), 415.

64. See Margery Fisher, *The Bright Face of Danger* (London: Hodder & Stoughton, 1986), 390–8.

65. Julia MacRae, 'Blind Spot', *Books for Keeps*, 71 (1991), 27.

66. Arthur Ransome, *The Autobiography of Arthur Ransome* (London: Cape, 1976), 36.

67. Robert Louis Stevenson, 'A Humble Remonstrance' (1884), in Miriam Allott, *Novelists on the Novel* (London: Routledge & Kegan Paul, 1965), 83.

68. Quoted by Michael Patrick Hearne, 'Mark Twain, 1835–1910', in Bingham, *Writers for Children*, 573.

69. Bingham, *Writers for Children*, 575.

70. Carpenter, *Secret Gardens*, 112.

71. Quoted by Leslie Linder, *A History of the Writings of Beatrix Potter* (London: Frederick Warne, 1971), 211.

72. Quoted ibid., p. xxv.

73. Anne Stevenson Hobbes, 'The Little Books', in Judy Taylor *et al.*, *Beatrix Potter, 1866–1943: The Artist and her World* (London: Frederick Warne/National Trust), 107.

74. See Peter Hunt, *Criticism, Theory, and Children's Literature* (Oxford: Basil Blackwell, 1991), 26–32.

75. Graham Greene, 'Beatrix Potter', in Sheila Egoff *et al.* (eds.), *Only Connect: Readings on Children's Literature* (Toronto: Oxford University Press, 1980), 258, 265.

76. Jacqueline Rose, *The Case of Peter Pan* (London: Macmillan, 1984), 67.

77. J. M. Barrie, *Peter Pan in Kensington Gardens and Peter and Wendy* (Oxford: Oxford University Press, 1991), 226.

78. Peter Hollindale, 'Introduction' to Barrie, *Peter Pan in Kensington Gardens and Peter and Wendy*, pp. xxiv–xxv.

79. Julia Briggs, *A Woman of Passion: The Life of E. Nesbit, 1858–1924* (London: Penguin, 1987), p. xi.

80. Marcus Crouch, *The Nesbit Tradition* (London: Benn, 1972), 16.

81. Quoted in Doris Langley Moore, *E. Nesbit* (London: Benn, 1967), 277.

82. E. Nesbit, *The Wouldbegoods* (1912; London: Fisher Unwin, 1926), 2–3.

83. E. Nesbit, *The Railway Children*, ed. Dennis Butts (Oxford: Oxford University Press, 1991), 182.

84. Ibid. 183–4.

85. Ann Thwaite, *Waiting for the Party* (London: Secker & Warburg, 1974), 95.

86. See Dennis Butts, 'Introduction' to Frances Hodgson Burnett, *The Secret Garden* (Oxford: Oxford University Press, 1987), pp. xxiii–xxiv.

87. Patrick R. Chalmers, *Kenneth Grahame: Life, Letters and Unpublished Work* (London: Methuen, 1933), 51.

88. Quoted in Peter Green, *Kenneth Grahame* (London: John Murray, 1959), 160.

89. Lois Kuznets, *Kenneth Grahame* (Boston: Twayne, 1987), p. viii.

90. Kenneth Grahame, *The Golden Age* (London: John Lane, Bodley Head, 1922), 29–30.

91. See Elspeth Grahame (ed.), *First Whispers of 'The Wind in the Willows'* (London: Methuen, 1944).

92. Wall, *The Narrator's Voice*, 140.

93. Kenneth Grahame, *The Wind in the Willows* (London: Methuen, 1978), 194.

94. Darton, *Children's Books in England*, 306.

95. John Rowe Townsend, *A Sounding of Storytellers* (Harmondsworth: Kestrel, 1979), 9–10.

96. Rudyard Kipling, *The Jungle Book* (Oxford: Oxford University Press, 1987), 44.

97. John Rowe Townsend, *Written for Children* (Harmondsworth: Penguin, 1983), 118.

98. Darton, *Children's Books in England*, 301.

99. Rudyard Kipling, *Stalky and Co.* (London: Macmillan, 1908), 151.

100. Quoted by Gillian Avery, 'The Children's Writer', in John Gross (ed.), *Rudyard Kipling: The Man, his Work and his World* (London: Weidenfeld & Nicolson, 1972), 118.

101. Rudyard Kipling, *Just So Stories* (London: Pan, 1975), 119.

102. Rudyard Kipling, *Something of Myself* (Harmondsworth: Penguin, 1977), 139.

103. Rudyard Kipling, *Puck of Pook's Hill* (Oxford: Oxford University Press, 1993), 13.

104. Kipling, *Something of Myself*, 142.

105. Arthur N. Applebee, *The Child's Concept of Story: Ages Two to Seventeen* (Chicago: University of Chicago Press, 1978).

106. Marcus Crouch, *Treasure Seekers and Borrowers* (London: Library Association, 1962), 37.

107. Walter de la Mare, *Peacock Pie* (London: Faber & Faber, 1980), 118.

108. A. A. Milne, *It's Too Late Now* (London: Methuen, 1939). Quoted by Thwaite, *The Brilliant Career of Winnie-the-Pooh*, 32.

109. Mary Cadogan and Patricia Craig, *Women and Children First: The Fiction of Two World Wars* (London: Gollancz, 1978), 67.

Chapter 5

1. Victor Watson, 'Poetry and Pirates: Swallows and Amazons at Sea', *Signal*, 66 (1991), 167.

2. Quoted in Robert Leeson, *Reading and Righting* (London: Collins, 1985), 110.

3. Geoffrey Trease, 'The Revolution in Children's Literature', in Edward Blishen (ed.), *The Thorny Paradise* (Harmondsworth: Kestrel, 1975), 14, 6.

4. Eleanor Graham, 'The Bumpus Years', *Signal*, 9 (1972), 105.

5. 'Frank Richards', *The Autobiography of Frank Richards* (London: Skilton, 1952), quoted by E. S. Turner, *Boys Will Be Boys* (Harmondsworth: Penguin, 1976), 233. See also George Orwell, 'Boys' Weeklies', *Horizon*, 1/3 (1939), 174–200.

6. Kevin Carpenter, *Penny Dreadfuls and Comics: English Periodicals for Children from Victorian Times to the Present Day* (London: Victoria and Albert Museum, 1983), 58.

7. Mary Cadogan and Patricia Craig, *You're a Brick, Angela!* (London: Gollancz, 1986), 170.

8. Patricia Craig and Mary Cadogan, *The Lady Investigates* (Oxford: Oxford University Press, 1986), 150.

9. Joyce Irene Whalley and Tessa Rose Chester, *A History of Children's Book Illustration* (London: John Murray/Victoria and Albert Museum, 1988), 194.

10. A. A. Milne, *It's Too Late Now* (London: Methuen, 1939), 238.

11. Ibid. 241.

12. Ibid. 239.

13. J. B. Morton, *The Best of Beachcomber* (Harmondsworth: Penguin, 1966), 74.

14. See Dorothy Parker, *The Penguin Dorothy Parker* (Harmondsworth: Penguin, 1973), 437.

15. A. A. Milne, *When We Were Very Young* (London: Methuen, 1979), 99–100.

16. A. A. Milne, *Winnie-the-Pooh* (London, Methuen, 1965), 16, 2, 22–3.

17. A. A. Milne, *The House at Pooh Corner* (London: Methuen, 1965), 128.

18. See Peter Hunt, 'Winnie-the-Pooh and Domestic Fantasy', in Dennis Butts (ed.), *Stories and Society: Children's Literature in its Social Context* (London: Macmillan, 1992), 114.

19. Christopher Milne, *The Enchanted Places* (London: Eyre Methuen, 1974), 164.

20. *Unesco Statistical Yearbook 1978–9*, 1099, quoted by Sheila Ray, *The Blyton Phenomenon* (London: André Deutsch, 1982), 7.

21. Sheila Ray, 'Enid Blyton', in Tracy Chevalier (ed.), *Twentieth-Century Children's Writers* (Chicago: St James Press, 3rd edn., 1989), 109.

22. Bob Dixon, *Catching them Young* (London: Pluto Press, 1977), 99.

23. Quoted by Nicholas Tucker, *The Child and the Book* (Cambridge: Cambridge University Press, 1981), 97.

24. Quoted by Marcus Crouch, *Treasure Seekers and Borrowers* (London: Library Association, 1962), 98.

25. Barbara Wall, *The Narrator's Voice* (London: Macmillan, 1991), 191.

26. Geoffrey Trease, 'Old Writers and Young Readers', in John Lawlor (ed.), *Essays and Studies 1973* (London: John Murray, 1973), 99–100.

27. Margery Fisher, *Classics for Children and Young People* (South Woodchester: Thimble Press, 1986), 26.

28. Perry Nodelman (ed.), *Touchstones: Reflections on the Best in Children's Literature*, iii (West Lafayette, Ind.: Children's Literature Association, 1989), 9.

29. Geoffrey Trease, *Bows against the Barons*, rev. edn. (London: Hodder & Stoughton, 1966), 28, 149.

30. Noel Streatfeild, *The Circus is Coming* (1938; Harmondsworth: Penguin (rev. edn.), 1956), 9.

31. Nina Bawden, *Humbug* (London: Gollancz, 1992), 8.

32. Laura Ingalls Wilder, *By the Shores of Silver Lake* (1939 (UK 1961); Harmondsworth: Penguin, 1967), 48.

33. Quoted by Hugh Brogan, *The Life of Arthur Ransome* (London: Cape, 1984), 35.

34. Watson, 'Poetry and Pirates: Swallows and Amazons at Sea', 167.

35. Brogan, *The Life of Arthur Ransome*, 379.

36. Arthur Ransome, *Swallowdale* (1931; London: Cape, 1961), 227.

37. See Valerie Mcleod, 'The Amazons in Secret Water: Thoughts of Impending War', *Mixed Moss* (The Journal of the Arthur Ransome Society), 1/3 (1992), 31–2; Peter Hunt, *Approaching Arthur Ransome* (London: Cape, 1991), 132–3.

38. See John Barr, *Illustrated Children's Books* (London: British Library, 1986), 77.

39. Whalley and Chester, *A History of Children's Book Illustration*, 189.

40. William Feaver, *When We Were Young: Two Centuries of Children's Book Illustration* (London: Thames & Hudson, 1977), 9.

41. Robert Graves and Alan Hodge, *The Long Weekend* (1940; London: Four Square, 1961), 428.

42. Crouch, *Treasure Seekers and Borrowers*, 87.

43. Peter Berresford Ellis and Piers Williams, *By Jove, Biggles!* (London: W. H. Allen, 1981), 131.

Chapter 6

1. Wallace Hildick, *Children and Fiction* (London: Evans Brothers, 1970), 141.

2. Mary Cadogan and Patricia Craig, *Women and Children First* (London: Gollancz, 1978), 238.

3. Margery Fisher, *Classics for Children and Young People* (South Woodchester: Thimble Press, 1986), 28.

4. Quoted in Sheila Ray, *The Blyton Phenomenon* (London: André Deutsch, 1982), 24.

5. W. E. Johns, *Biggles: The Rescue Flight* (London: Collins, 1974), 28, 7.

6. Margery Fisher, *The Bright Face of Danger* (London: Hodder & Stoughton, 1986), 363.

7. Quoted in John Rowe Townsend, *A Sounding of Storytellers* (Harmondsworth: Kestrel, 1979), 165.

8. Nina Bawden, *Carrie's War* (London: Gollancz, 1992), 135.

9. See e.g. Robert Westall, 'The Hunt for Evil', *Signal*, 34 (1981), 3–13.

10. Robert Westall, 'How Real do you Want your Realism?', *Signal*, 28 (1979), 37–8.

11. Marcus Crouch, *Treasure Seekers and Borrowers* (London: Library Association, 1962), 101–2.

12. Raymond Tallis, *In Defence of Realism* (London: Edward Arnold, 1988), 132, 134.

13. David Holbrook, 'The Problem of C. S. Lewis', in Geoff Fox *et al.* (eds.), *Writers, Critics, and Children* (New York: Agathon Press, 1976), 124.

14. Margaret and Michael Rustin, *Narratives of Love and Loss* (London: Verso (New Left Books), 1987), 58.

15. Aidan Chambers, *Booktalk* (London: Bodley Head, 1985), 49–50, 58.

16. Margery Fisher, *Intent upon Reading*, 2nd edn. (Leicester: Brockhampton Press, 1974), 123.

17. Barbara Wall, *The Narrator's Voice* (London: Macmillan Academic, 1991), 197.

18. Mary Norton, *The Borrowers Afield* (London: Dent, 1955), 2.

19. See Perry Nodelman, 'Text as Teacher: The Beginning of *Charlotte's Web*', *Children's Literature*, 13 (New Haven, Conn.: Yale University Press, 1985), 109–27; Lucy Rollin, 'The Reproduction and Mothering in *Charlotte's Web*', *Children's Literature*, 18 (New Haven, Conn.: Yale University Press, 1990), 42–52.

20. *Times Literary Supplement*, quoted in Neil Philip, *A Fine Anger* (London: Collins, 1981), 87.

21. John Rowe Townsend, *Written for Children* (Harmondsworth: Penguin, 1983), 250.

22. Ann Swinfen, *In Defence of Fantasy* (London: Routledge, 1984), 186.

23. Quoted by Jay Williams, 'Very Iffy Books: An Interview with Peter Dickinson', *Signal*, 13 (1974), 26.

24. Ursula Le Guin, *Earthsea Revisioned* (Cambridge: Children's Literature New England in association with Green Bay Publications, 1993), 7.

25. See C. W. Sullivan III, *Welsh Celtic Myth in Modern Fantasy* (New York: Greenwood Press, 1989).

26. Susan Cooper, *The Dark is Rising* (Harmondsworth: Penguin, 1976), 16, 26.

27. Louisa Smith, 'Layers of Language in Lively's *The Ghost of Thomas Kempe*', *Children's Literature Association Quarterly*, 10/3 (1985), 115, 116.

28. Elaine Moss, 'The Seventies in British Children's Books', in Nancy Chambers (ed.), *The Signal Approach to Children's Books* (Harmondsworth: Kestrel, 1980), 58.

29. Townsend, *Written for Children*, 229.

30. See Juliet Dusinberre, *Alice to the Lighthouse* (London: Macmillan, 1987), 243–5.

31. Wall, *The Narrator's Voice*, 206.

32. Quoted by Stephanie Nettell, 'Authorgraph No. 63', *Books for Keeps*, 63 (1990), 15.

33. Peter Hollindale, *Choosing Books for Children* (London: Elek Books, 1974), 157.

34. Wall, *The Narrator's Voice*, 207; Charles Sarland, 'The Chorister Quartet', *Signal*, 18 (1975), 107–13.

35. William Mayne, *Barnabus Walks* (London: Walker, 1986), n.p.

36. William Mayne, *The Twelve Dancers* (Harmondsworth: Penguin, 1964), 7.

37. Wall, *The Narrator's Voice*, 212, 214.

38. Grace Kempster, 'The Carnegie Medal [1992]', *Books for Keeps*, 75 (1992), 32.

39. See Charles Sarland, *Young People Reading: Culture and Response* (Milton Keynes: Open University Press, 1991).

40. Moss, 'The Seventies in British Children's Books', 60.

41. Alan Garner, *Granny Reardun* (London: Collins, 1979), 30–1.

42. Michele Landsberg, *The World of Children's Books* (London: Simon & Schuster, 1988), 195.

43. Ibid. 189.

44. Townsend, *Written for Children*, 279.

45. Ann Scott Macleod, 'Robert Cormier', in Tracy Chevalier (ed.), *Twentieth Century Children's Writers* (Chicago: St James Press, 3rd edn., 1989), 237.

46. Judith Elkin *et al.*, 'Cormier Talking', *Books for Keeps*, 54 (1989), 12–13; Robert Cormier, 'Creating *Fade*', *Horn Book*, 65 (1989), 166–73; Perry Nodelman, 'Robert Cormier's *The Chocolate War*: Paranoia and Paradox', in Dennis Butts (ed.), *Stories and Society: Children's Literature in its Social Context* (London: Macmillan, 1992), 22–36.

47. See Tessa Krailing, *How to Write for Children* (London: Allison & Busby, 1988), 79–87.

48. 'Arlene Hale', *The Impossible Love* (New York: Scholastic Book Services (Wildfire series), 1982), 127.

49. Aidan Chambers, *Breaktime* (London: Bodley Head (New Adults series), 1978), 122–6.

50. Agnes Nieuwenhuizen, *No Kidding: Top Writers for Young People Talk about their Work* (Chippendale: Pan Macmillan, 1991), p. xix.

51. Betty Gilderdale, *A Sea Change: 145 Years of New Zealand Junior Fiction* (Auckland: Longman Paul, 1982), 237.

52. See e.g. Elliott Gose, 'Fairy Tale and Myth in Mahy's *The Changeover* and *The Tricksters*', *Children's Literature Association Quarterly*, 16/1 (1991), 6–11.

53. Crouch, *Treasure Seekers and Borrowers*, 58.

54. Joyce Irene Whalley and Tessa Rose Chester, *A History of Children's Book Illustration* (London: John Murray/Victoria and Albert Museum, 1988), 216.

55. Douglas Martin, *The Telling Line* (London: Julia MacRae, 1989), 243.

56. See Jane Doonan, '*Outside Over There*: A Journey in Style', part 1, *Signal*, 50 (1986), 92–103; part 2, *Signal*, 51 (1986), 172–88.

57. Rosemary Wells, *Timothy Goes to School* (New York: Dial, 1981), n.p.

58. Brian Morse, *Poetry Books for Children* (South Woodchester: Thimble Press, 1992), 3.

59. Michael Benton, 'Poetry for Children: A Neglected Art', quoted in Peter Hunt (ed.), *Literature for Children: Contemporary Criticism* (London: Routledge, 1992), 127.

60. Allan Ahlberg, *Please Mrs. Butler* (London: Penguin, 1983), 13.

Chapter 7

1. See Hugh Crago, 'Children's Literature: On the Cultural Periphery', *Children's Book Review*, 4/4 (1974), 157–8.

2. Alan Garner, quoted in Aidan Chambers, 'An Interview with Alan Garner', in Nancy Chambers (ed.), *The Signal Approach to Children's Books* (Harmondsworth: Kestrel, 1980), 327.

3. See Peter Hunt, *Criticism, Theory, and Children's Literature* (Oxford: Blackwell, 1991), 138–62.

4. Treld Pelkey Bicknell and Felicity Trotman (eds.), *How to Write and Illustrate Children's Books and Get them Published!* (London: Macdonald, 1989), 47. See also Edward B. Jenkinson, *Censors in the Classroom* (New York: Avon, 1982).

5. Gillian Klein, *Reading into Racism* (London: Routledge, 1985), 28, 1.

6. Rudine Sims, 'What Happened to the "All-White" World of Children's Books?', in Barbara Harrison and Gregory Maguire (eds.), *Innocence and Experience: Essays and Conversations on Children's Literature* (New York: Lothrop, Lee & Shepard, 1987), 478; and see Mark West, *Children, Culture and Controversy* (Hamden, Conn.: Archon Press, 1988), and *Trust your Children: Voices against Censorship in Children's Literature* (New York: Neal-Schuman, 1988); and Jean Ure, 'Who Censors?', *Books for Keeps*, 58 (1989), 19.

7. Tessa Wilkinson, *The Death of a Child* (London: Julia MacRae, 1991).

8. Mary Cadogan and Patricia Craig, *You're a Brick, Angela!* (London: Gollancz, 1986), 373.

9. Klein, *Reading into Racism*, 146.

10. A. A. Mendilow, *Time and the Novel*, quoted by Damien Grant, *Realism* (London: Methuen, 1970), 69.

11. Quoted in Neil Barron (ed.), *Fantasy Literature: A Reader's Guide* (New York: Garland, 1990), 371.

12. J. R. R. Tolkien, *Tree and Leaf* (London: Allen & Unwin, 1964), 35.

13. John Rowe Townsend, *Written for Children* (Harmondsworth: Penguin, 1983), 261.

14. Michele Landsberg, *The World of Children's Books* (London: Simon & Schuster, 1988), 192.

15. Ibid.

16. Raymond Tallis, *In Defence of Realism* (London: Arnold, 1988), 21 ff.; Barbara Hardy, 'Towards a Poetics of Fiction: An Approach through Narrative', in Margaret Meek *et al.* (eds.), *The Cool Web* (London: Bodley Head, 1977), 12.

17. Tallis, *In Defence of Realism*, 215.

18. John Peck and Martin Coyle, *Literary Terms and Criticism* (London: Macmillan, 1984), 115, 116.

19. Robert Westall, 'How Real do you Want your Realism?', *Signal*, 28 (1979), 42.

20. Julie Vivas, *The Nativity* (Cambridge: Cambridge University Press, 1988); Sarah Moon, *Little Red Riding Hood* (Minneapolis: Creative Education, 1984).

21. Betsy Hearne, 'Whammo, You Lose', *Booklist* (1974), 1199; Norma Bagnall, 'Realism: How Realistic is it? A Look at *The Chocolate War*', *Top of the News*, 36 (1980), 214, quoted by Perry Nodelman, 'Robert Cormier's *The Chocolate War*: Paranoia and Paradox', in Dennis Butts (ed.), *Stories and Society* (London: Macmillan, 1992), 35.

22. Chana Byers Abells, *The Children We Remember* (London: Julia MacRae, 1986); Margaret Wild and Julie Vivas, *Let the Celebrations Begin* (London: Bodley Head, 1991); Roberto Innocenti and Christophe Gallaz, *Rose Blanche* (Mankato, Minn.: Creative Education, 1985).

23. Hamida Bosmajian, 'Narrative Voice in Young Readers' Fictions about Nazism, the Holocaust, and Nuclear War', in Charlotte F. Otten and Gary A. Schmidt (eds.), *The Voice of the*

Narrator in Children's Literature (Westport, Conn.: Greenwood Press, 1989), 313. See also Eric Kimmell, 'Confronting the Ovens: The Holocaust in Juvenile Fiction', *Horn Book Magazine*, 53 (1977), 84–91.

24. Toshi Maruki, *Hiroshima no Pika* (New York: Lothrop, Lee & Shepard, 1982); Junko Morimoto, *My Hiroshima* (Sydney: Collins, 1987).

25. Barbara Harrison, 'Howl Like the Wolves', *Children's Literature*, 15 (New Haven, Conn.: Yale University Press, 1987), 81.

26. Robert Whitehead, *Children's Literature: Strategies of Teaching* (Englewood Cliffs, NJ: Prentice-Hall, 1968), 1.

27. Charlotte S. Huck, Susan Hepler, and Janet Hickman, *Children's Literature in the Elementary School* (New York: Holt, Rinehart & Winston, 4th edn., 1987); Mary Lou White, *Instructor's Manual to Accompany Children's Literature in the Elementary School* (New York: Holt, Rinehart & Winston, 1987).

28. Jan Nicholas, 'The Case for Reading Schemes', *Books for your Children*, 23/3 (1988), 16.

29. Jill Bennett, 'Introduction to the Third Edition', *Learning to Read with Picture Books* (South Woodchester: Thimble Press, 1989), 3.

30. Liz Waterland, 'Ranging Freely: The Why and What of Real Books', in Morag Styles *et al.*, *After Alice: Exploring Children's Literature* (London: Cassell, 1992), 161–2.

31. C. S. Lewis, 'On Three Ways of Writing for Children', in Virginia Haviland, *Children and Literature: Views and Reviews* (London: Bodley Head, 1973), 240.

32. Alan C. Purves and Dianne L. Monson, *Experiencing Children's Literature* (Glenview, Ill.: Scott, Foresman, 1984), 186.

33. Robert Protherough, *Developing Response to Fiction* (Milton Keynes: Open University Press, 1983), 172.

34. See Huck, Hepler, and Hickman, *Children's Literature in the Elementary School*, 10–12; see also Jim Trelease, *The Read-Aloud Handbook* (Harmondsworth: Penguin, 1984), 30; Joan E. Cass, *Literature and the Young Child*, 2nd edn. (London: Longman, 1984), 2; Frank Smith, *Reading*, 2nd edn. (Cambridge: Cambridge University Press, 1985), 48; Aidan Cham-

bers, *The Reading Environment* (South Woodchester: Thimble Press, 1991), 42.

35. Ursula Le Guin, 'This Fear of Dragons', in Edward Blishen (ed.), *The Thorny Paradise: Writers on Writing for Children* (Harmondsworth: Kestrel, 1975), 87–92.

36. J. S. Bratton, *The Impact of Victorian Children's Fiction* (London: Croom Helm, 1981), 51.

37. Sarah Wintle, introd. to Rudyard Kipling, *Puck of Pook's Hill* (London: Penguin, 1987), 10.

38. Kipling, *Puck of Pook's Hill*, 146.

39. Rudyard Kipling, *Rewards and Fairies* (London: Penguin, 1987), 96.

40. *Puck of Pook's Hill*, 56.

41. Arthur Ransome, *The Picts and the Martyrs* (London: Cape, 1943), 131.

42. Arthur Ransome, *Swallows and Amazons* (London: Cape, 1931), 366.

43. Arthur Ransome, *The Big Six* (London: Cape, 1941), 273.

44. Alan Garner, *The Stone Book Quartet* (London: Collins, 1983), 72.

45. Robert Louis Stevenson, 'My First Book', in Lance Salway (ed.), *A Peculiar Gift* (London: Kestrel, 1978), 418–19.

46. W. R. Irwin, *The Game of the Impossible: A Rhetoric of Fantasy* (Urbana, Ill.: University of Illinois Press, 1976), 67.

47. See Walter Ong, *Orality and Literacy* (London: Methuen, 1982), 139 ff.

48. Neil Philip, *A Fine Anger* (London: Collins, 1981), 12.

49. Garner, *The Stone Book Quartet*, 224.

50. Michael Wood, 'Tolkien's Fictions', in Nicholas Tucker (ed.), *Suitable for Children?* (London: Sussex University Press, 1976), 168, 169.

51. J. R. R. Tolkien, 'Foreword' to *The Lord of the Rings* (London: Unwin Paperbacks, 1978), 10.

52. See Tony Watkins, 'Making a Break for the Real England: The River-Bankers Revisited', *Children's Literature Association Quarterly*, 9/1 (1984), 34–5.

53. Tolkien, *The Lord of the Rings*, 13.

54. Humphrey Carpenter, *Secret Gardens* (London: Allen & Unwin, 1985), 155.

55. Kenneth Grahame, *The Wind in the Willows* (London: Methuen, 1978), 170.

56. See Christopher Milne, *The Enchanted Places* (London: Methuen, 1974).

57. Alan Garner, *The Weirdstone of Brisingamen* (Harmondsworth: Penguin, 1963), 166.

Chapter 8

1. Sheila Egoff, *Thursday's Child: Trends and Patterns in Contemporary Children's Literature* (Chicago: American Library Association, 1988), 82.

2. C. W. Sullivan III, 'Fantasy', in Dennis Butts (ed.), *Stories and Society: Children's Literature in its Social Context* (London: Macmillan, 1992), 97.

3. Quoted by Felicity A. Hughes, 'Children's Literature: Theory and Practice', in Peter Hunt (ed.), *Children's Literature: The Development of Criticism* (London: Routledge, 1990), 73.

4. Ursula Le Guin, 'This Fear of Dragons', in Edward Blishen (ed.), *The Thorny Paradise* (Harmondsworth: Kestrel, 1975), 90.

5. Frank Flanagan, 'Bequeathing the Moral Vision', *Children's Books in Ireland*, 7 (1992), 7.

6. Jim Trelease, *The Read-Aloud Handbook* (Harmondsworth: Penguin, 1984), 78.

7. Barbara Wall, *The Narrator's Voice* (London: Macmillan Academic, 1991), 233, 198.

8. Aidan Chambers, *Booktalk* (London: Bodley Head, 1985), 15, 14, 19. See also Elaine Moss, 'The Adult-eration of Children's Books', in *Part of the Pattern* (London: Bodley Head, 1986), 116.

9. Charles Sarland, *Young People Reading* (Milton Keynes: Open University Press, 1991), 142.

10. Peter Hollindale, 'Child Readers and Adult Critics', *Times Educational Supplement* (15 May 1992), Supplement, 5.

Short Bibliography

The twenty-five most useful books on children's literature

AVERY, GILLIAN, and BRIGGS, JULIA, *Children and their Books* (Oxford: Oxford University Press, 1989). [Literary essays]

BATOR, ROBERT (ed.), *Signposts to Criticism of Children's Literature* (Chicago: American Library Association, 1983). [Critical essays]

BRATTON, J. S., *The Impact of Victorian Children's Fiction* (Brighton: Croom Helm, 1981).

BUTTS, DENNIS (ed.), *Stories and Society: Children's Literature in its Social Context* (London: Macmillan, 1992). [Theoretical and critical essays]

CADOGAN, MARY, and CRAIG, PATRICIA, *You're a Brick, Angela! The Girls' Story, 1839–1985* (London: Gollancz, 1986). [Very readable standard work]

CARPENTER, HUMPHREY, and PRICHARD, MARI, *The Oxford Companion to Children's Literature* (Oxford: Oxford University Press, 1984). [Standard reference work]

CHAMBERS, AIDAN, *Booktalk: Occasional Writing on Literature and Children* (London: Bodley Head, 1985). [Standard work for literature and education]

CHAMBERS, NANCY (ed.), *The Signal Approach to Children's Books* (Harmondsworth: Kestrel, 1980). [Critical essays]

CHEVALIER, TRACY (ed.), *Twentieth-Century Children's Writers*, 3rd edn. (Chicago: St James Press, 1989). [Standard bibliographic/critical reference]

DARTON, F. J. HARVEY, *Children's Books in England*, 3rd edn., rev. Brian Alderson (Cambridge: Cambridge University Press, 1982). [Standard history, best on pre-1900]

DEMERS, PATRICIA (ed.), *A Garland from the Golden Age* (Toronto: Oxford University Press, 1984). [Sample texts 1850–1900]

—— and MOYLES, GORDON (eds.), *From Instruction to Delight* (Toronto: Oxford University Press, 1980). [Sample texts pre-1850]

EGOFF, SHEILA, et al. (eds.), *Only Connect: Readings on Children's Literature*, 2nd edn. (Toronto: Oxford University Press, 1980). [Critical essays and extracts]

FISHER, MARGERY, *The Bright Face of Danger* (London: Hodder, 1986). [Generic survey]

HUNT, PETER (ed.), *Children's Literature: The Development of Criticism* (London: Routledge, 1990).

—— *Criticism, Theory, and Children's Literature* (Oxford: Blackwell, 1991).

INGLIS, FRED, *The Promise of Happiness: Value and Meaning in Children's Fiction* (Cambridge: Cambridge University Press, 1981). [Political and social implications of children's literature]

MEEK, MARGARET, *et al.* (eds.), *The Cool Web: The Pattern of Children's Reading* (London: Bodley Head, 1977). [Mixed critical/ education essays]

SALWAY, LANCE (ed.), *A Peculiar Gift: 19th Century Writing on Books for Children* (Harmondsworth: Kestrel, 1976). [Reprinted essays]

SAXBY, MAURICE, and WINCH, GORDON (eds.), *Give them Wings: The Experience of Children's Literature* (South Melbourne: Macmillan, 1987). [Australian critical essays]

STYLES, MORAG, *et al.* (eds.), *After Alice: Exploring Children's Literature* (London: Cassell, 1992). [Child-oriented essays]

TOWNSEND, JOHN ROWE, *Written for Children* (Penguin, 1974; rev. edn. London: Kestrel/Penguin, 1988, 1991). [Standard history; readable]

TUCKER, NICHOLAS, *The Child and the Book: A Psychological and Literary Exploration* (Cambridge: Cambridge University Press, 1981). [Psychological/educational survey]

WALL, BARBARA, *The Narrator's Voice: The Dilemma of Children's Fiction* (London: Macmillan, 1991). [History from a theoretical standpoint]

ZIPES, JACK, *Fairy Tales and the Art of Subversion: The Classical Genre for Children and the Process of Civilization* (New York: Wildman, 1983). [Sociological and historical criticism]

Index

MORE OXFORD PAPERBACKS

This book is just one of nearly 1000 Oxford Paperbacks currently in print. If you would like details of other Oxford Paperbacks, including titles in the World's Classics, Oxford Reference, Oxford Books, OPUS, Past Masters, Oxford Authors, and Oxford Shakespeare series, please write to:

UK and Europe: Oxford Paperbacks Publicity Manager, Arts and Reference Publicity Department, Oxford University Press, Walton Street, Oxford OX2 6DP.

Customers in UK and Europe will find Oxford Paperbacks available in all good bookshops. But in case of difficulty please send orders to the Cash-with-Order Department, Oxford University Press Distribution Services, Saxon Way West, Corby, Northants NN18 9ES. Tel: 01536 741519; Fax: 01536 746337. Please send a cheque for the total cost of the books, plus £1.75 postage and packing for orders under £20; £2.75 for orders over £20. Customers outside the UK should add 10% of the cost of the books for postage and packing.

USA: Oxford Paperbacks Marketing Manager, Oxford University Press, Inc., 200 Madison Avenue, New York, N.Y. 10016.

Canada: Trade Department, Oxford University Press, 70 Wynford Drive, Don Mills, Ontario M3C 1J9.

Australia: Trade Marketing Manager, Oxford University Press, G.P.O. Box 2784Y, Melbourne 3001, Victoria.

South Africa: Oxford University Press, P.O. Box 1141, Cape Town 8000.

OXFORD BOOKS

THE OXFORD BOOK OF ENGLISH
GHOST STORIES

Chosen by Michael Cox and R. A. Gilbert

This anthology includes some of the best and most frightening ghost stories ever written, including M. R. James's 'Oh Whistle, and I'll Come to You, My Lad', 'The Monkey's Paw' by W. W. Jacobs, and H. G. Wells's 'The Red Room'. The important contribution of women writers to the genre is represented by stories such as Amelia Edwards's 'The Phantom Coach', Edith Wharton's 'Mr Jones', and Elizabeth Bowen's 'Hand in Glove'.

As the editors stress in their informative introduction, a good ghost story, though it may raise many profound questions about life and death, entertains as much as it unsettles us, and the best writers are careful to satisfy what Virginia Woolf called 'the strange human craving for the pleasure of feeling afraid'. This anthology, the first to present the full range of classic English ghost fiction, similarly combines a serious literary purpose with the plain intention of arousing pleasing fear at the doings of the dead.

'an excellent cross-section of familiar and unfamiliar stories and guaranteed to delight' *New Statesman*

THE WORLD'S CLASSICS
THE WIND IN THE WILLOWS
Kenneth Grahame

The Wind in the Willows (1908) is a book for those 'who keep the spirit of youth alive in them; of life, sunshine, running water, woodlands, dusty roads, winter firesides'. So wrote Kenneth Grahame of his timeless tale of Toad, Mole, Badger, and Rat in their beautiful and benevolently ordered world. But it is also a world under siege, threatened by dark and unnamed forces—'the Terror of the Wild Wood' with its 'wicked little faces' and 'glances of malice and hatred'—and defended by the mysterious Piper at the Gates of Dawn. *The Wind in the Willows* has achieved an enduring place in our literature: it succeeds at once in arousing our anxieties and in calming them by giving perfect shape to our desire for peace and escape.

The World's Classics edition has been prepared by Peter Green, author of the standard biography of Kenneth Grahame.

'It is a Household Book; a book which everybody in the household loves, and quotes continually; a book which is read aloud to every new guest and is regarded as the touchstone of his worth.' A. A. Milne

Oxford
Paperback
Reference

THE CONCISE OXFORD COMPANION
TO ENGLISH LITERATURE

Edited by Margaret Drabble and
Jenny Stringer

Derived from the acclaimed *Oxford Companion to English Literature*, the concise maintains the wide coverage of its parent volume. It is an indispensable, compact guide to all aspects of English literature. For this revised edition, existing entries have been fully updated and revised with 60 new entries added on contemporary writers.

* **Over 5,000 entries on the lives and works of authors, poets and playwrights**

* **The most comprehensive and authoritative paperback guide to English literature**

* **New entries include Peter Ackroyd, Martin Amis, Toni Morrison, and Jeanette Winterson**

* **New appendices list major literary prize-winners**

From the reviews of its parent volume:

'It earns its place at the head of the best sellers: every home should have one'
Sunday Times